# Rail Transit Station Area Development

Small Area Modeling in Washington, D.C.

# Rail Transit Station Area Development

## Small Area Modeling in Washington, D.C.

Rodney D. Green and David M. James

*M.E. Sharpe*

Armonk, New York
London, England

**Library of Congress Cataloging-in-Publication Data**

Green, Rodney D.
Rail transit station area development: small area modeling in
Washington, DC / by Rodney D. Green and David M. James.
p. cm.
Includes bibliographical references (p.  ) and index.
ISBN 0-87332-696-2
1. Subways—Stations—Economic aspects—Washington Metropolitan
Area—Econometric models. 2. Subways—Washington Metropolitan Area—
Stations—Planning—Econometric models.  I. James, David M.
II. Title
HE4491.W43G74  1991
388.4′2′09753—dc20
91-12343
CIP

Printed in the United States of America

The paper used in this publication meets the minimum requirements
of American National Standard for Information Sciences—
Permanence of Paper for Printed Library Materials,
ANSI Z39.48-1984.
∞
MV 10  9  8  7  6  5  4  3  2  1

# Contents

# Tables

**Appendix 3.2**

x

# Figures

# Preface and Acknowledgments

Wherever you may locate, in the outskirts of a capital, a railroad depot,
it is the death of a suburb and the birth of a city.
Victor Hugo, *Les Miserables*

The influence of transportation requirements on the pattern of urban settlement and activity has been important at least since the days of neolithic Catal Huyuk (about 8,000 years ago in what is today known as Turkey). Archaeologists assure us that outlying small villages formed around Catal Huyuk as subcenters of specialized economic activity (usually agricultural), even as the center itself diversified into an ancient forerunner of a central business district. Such subcentering was needed to provide loci for the networked relationships among dwellers tied to Catal Huyuk, although the centers were connected only by paths. While times have changed, transportation and communication requirements still shape settlement and production location patterns. The strong relationship between transportation networks and economic activity becomes apparent when one observes modern U.S. cities. The question swiftly arises, what could dramatically alter urban patterns? Could they perhaps be rearranged by a rapid transit system with fixed stations, which in effect shrinks a large region, but only between small discrete places within it?

In recent years, several U.S. cities have acquired new rail transit systems, none more extensive than the Metrorail system in Washington, D.C. The opportunity for careful investigation of the effects of Metrorail on the patterns of economic activity in the Washington region has been recognized before (in particular, the Urban Mass Transportation Administration funded the extensive Before and After Metrorail study conducted by the Metropolitan Washington Council of Governments), but there has been no previous attempt to use statistical and modeling techniques to assess these effects. The present study was supported by the Office of University Research in the Office of the

Secretary of Transportation under contract DTRS5683-C-00035 to pursue this and related goals. Additional support from Howard University's University-Sponsored Faculty Research Program in the Social Sciences, Humanities, and Education made possible the revision of that earlier work, and is gratefully acknowledged. Final preparation of the manuscript was supported by the Collaborative Core Unit in Labor, Race, and Political Economy of the Graduate School of Arts and Sciences at Howard University.

Because of the magnitude and length of this project, the list of people who helped along the way is long. The steady stream of creative comment and constructive criticism by Edward Weiner, of the Office of the Secretary of Transportation, and Frederick Ducca, now of the Urban Land Institute, has been vital to this work. The assistance provided in all aspects of the project by Stephen Putman, who primarily served as subcontractor in the improvement, calibration, and forecasting work with the regional model Integrated Transportation and Land-Use Package (ITLUP), was also invaluable. Responsibility for the contents of this monograph, of course, remains ours alone. In gathering data throughout the Washington region, we received generous assistance in terms of time and resources from many individuals and organizations. We are especially grateful to Nat Levy (Washington, D.C., Office of Planning), Bob Hnat (Montgomery County Office of Planning), Ruth Prendable (Prince George's County Office of Planning), Ralph Bean (Prince George's County Real Estate Assessment Office), Lucy Koltisko (Arlington County Real Estate Assessment Office), Susie Dorman (Fairfax County Real Estate Assessment Office), Gary Molyneaux (Office of Comprehensive Planning in Fairfax County), and Teckla Cox (Loudoun County Office of Planning).

Vital information also came from the Metropolitan Washington Council of Governments. Bob Dunphy (now at the Urban Land Institute) got us off to a good start, George Wickstrom and David Cardwell provided major assistance with our data needs, and Paul Desjardin and Ken Flick helped extensively.

Howard University played an important role in providing cost-sharing resources and general support for this project, particularly through the good offices of the Dean of the Graduate School of Arts and Sciences, William Sadler, his predecessor, the late Edward Hawthorne, and their associates Wilbert Nixon, Esther Ottley, Johnetta Davis, and George Littleton. The chairmen of the Economics Department (Cleveland Chandler, Vincent McDonald, and Ducarmel Bocage) in which this project was housed also provided important resources throughout the six years of activity. Emily Blank was helpful in sorting out some statistical problems. Excellent and timely secretarial support was provided by Thelma Paige, Claudette McClain, and Odette Davis in their usual outstanding fashion.

The computer center personnel were, as always, quick to offer support for our computing needs. Thanks go especially to systems analyst Curtis Butler and to Ron Crockett, Director of Computing Services, as well as to the ever-cooperative operators. Administrative support in this large a project was vital to its success. Here thanks go especially to Estela Aspinwall, Vivian Myrick, and Deloris Prioleau of the Restricted Accounts Office.

The work of over twenty students on this project is gratefully acknowledged. Among them, Arlease Salley stands out as a dedicated right arm in organizing and executing the data gathering, refinement, and entry activities. Gail Grass also played a central role in all aspects of the project throughout its life. Jean-Claude Assad worked diligently and creatively on many research tasks, Kim Coleman displayed an enormous amount of enthusiasm and creativity during the early years of the project, and Corman Franklin, Abbass Entessari, Okorie Uchendu, Kingsley Ajoku, Bernice Scott, Sipho Moyo, Mohamed Hassan, Modibo Coulibaly, Chris Fugar, and Mike Ogbu also made outstanding contributions.

We also wish to express our gratitude to our wives, Pauline and Becky, for their patience and support throughout the many years of this work.

Rodney Green
David James

# Rail Transit Station Area Development

## Small Area Modeling in Washington, D.C.

# One

# The Study of Transit Station Impacts in the Washington, D.C., Region

This study presents several complementary evaluations of the role, impact, and possible future of the rapid-transit stations of the Metrorail system in the economic development of the Washington, D.C., region. The research plan is described in this chapter, followed by a general overview of the structure, transit history, and transit-related issues of the region.

The literature on local development analysis is reviewed in Chapter 2. Chapter 3 presents a series of statistical analyses of development in rapid-transit station areas and corridors in the region. After a review of the literature on regional modeling in Chapter 4, two versions of the Local Development (LOCDEV) model are presented and discussed. The structural version of LOCDEV is developed and used to compare station area development cross-sectionally in the region in Chapter 5, and the forecasting version is calibrated in Chapter 6 and used in Chapter 7 for an indicative forecasting experiment for currently open station areas in the region. A user's guide is included to assist in transferring the modeling approach to other urban areas (Chapter 8). Conclusions about advances in modeling as well as substantive conclusions about the Washington region complete the study (Chapter 9).

## The Research Plan

Do new rapid-transit station sites play a significant role in inducing commercial development in their vicinities? Can the development process in small areas around such sites be modeled? These are the two questions around which this research project has been organized. One intuitively expects the answer to the first question to be "yes" (surely the access advantages conferred on areas around new stations must attract development), but objective confirmation of this has been lacking, in part because of the difficulties represented by the second question. Strong development effects of stations are small-area phenomena—after all, a station offers significant access advantages only to areas within easy walking distance—and small areas have been considered inherently unmodelable because the many factors peculiar to each locale cannot readily be included in either behavioral or statistical models.

Modeling studies from economics, business, and planning literatures reveal that regional models have made considerable progress in their accuracy, reliability, and transferability between cities. The Integrated Transportation and Land-Use Package (ITLUP) is especially noteworthy in this regard, and plays an important role in this research project (see Putman, 1983, 1991). ITLUP makes projections of employment and residence locations in a region, disaggregated by subareas called zones, and of trips between all pairs of zones in the region, using historical zonal data and forecasted regional control totals for many of these variables. The zones tend to be rather large; in this project, for instance, ITLUP is calibrated on a 182-zone partition of the Washington, D.C., region. This partitioning is quite disaggregated in comparison to previous applications of such regional models, but it nevertheless leaves a great deal of room for variations (and averaging out) within each zone; it is scarcely a small-area model. Forecasts and analyses at the level of such zones do not provide the degree of detail needed for studying the local development impact of subway station sites. ITLUP does, however, provide important contextual data for such studies. A local area modeling project must generally be linked to such a model for sound results.

The literature on the impact of transportation projects on land use and development reveals that while the general issue has been studied in many ways, few attempts at modeling have been made and most of these have been inconclusive. A very few specific modeling experiments (e.g., the effect of transportation improvements on residential property values) have been conclusive but narrow. The present research is both conclusive and broad, despite the small variable set used in the modeling experiments here.

Despite the widespread perception that new stations cause development to "pop up" around them, more careful studies suggest that development around stations is not universal and may require government intervention to occur. The BART study conducted by the U.S. Department of Transportation, for example, revealed very mixed development effects around stations built in the San Francisco Bay Area, while a look at Toronto shows that the concentrated development around its subway stations has been accomplished through direct government intervention which effectively limits private business locations to those sites. The first order of business of the present project, then, is to determine if rapid-transit station areas in the study area (Washington, D.C., and its suburbs) do in fact have a pronounced development effect on their vicinities. Station areas and rail corridors are compared to nonstation areas and areas outside of rail corridors in a variety of ways. These comparisons, contained in three studies, show that in the Washington region, Metrorail stations do tend to be associated with commercial development; this is the first statistically rigorous demonstration of such a phenomenon. The comparisons also show, however, that this association is not due solely to rail impact: joint public and private development planning and coordination is usually crucial to the development process.

A model to describe the causes of development around station areas cross-sectionally is then developed. This three-equation model is called the Local Development model (LOCDEV). Three development indicators (employment, commercial floor space, and retail employment) are modeled as being determined by a combination of the relative accessibilities of the station areas to the rest of the region and of the economic factors at work in specific station areas. A study of the residual patterns arising from the estimation of the model provides useful insights into the model's capacity to provide information about the differential development tendencies around stations throughout the region.

A second version of LOCDEV, the forecasting model, is then developed to provide some indicative forecasting of development around station areas. Used in tandem with the regional model ITLUP, LOCDEV provides credible forecasts for fifty-two station areas in the Washington region. The reader should be cautioned from the beginning that only a limited number of variables are used in the model; many other, unmodeled, factors affect development, so these forecasts indicate only the likely impact of certain economic factors on the individual station areas and should not be taken as point forecasts of what will (or should) be there. However, the forecasts are a good starting point for understanding where economic forces are exerting (or not exerting) significant pressure for development in the universe of station areas. A further caution is that development in the region as a whole is not concentrated in the station areas, but continues to spread in the standard post–World War II pattern of suburbanization. All indications are that the attractiveness of station areas can no more than slow this trend—if that.

Finally, a summary description of the forecasting version of the model and how to use it is included for anyone who wishes to use this modeling structure in other cities.

## An Overview of Transit and the Washington, D.C., Region

The six major jurisdictions of the Washington, D.C., region are the District of Columbia and the City of Alexandria, Virginia, both of which are urban in character, and Montgomery and Prince George's Counties in Maryland and Arlington and Fairfax Counties in Virginia, all of which are suburban in character. The two cities and Arlington County, which is between them, contain the economic core of the region. Alexandria, in spite of its urban character, and the four counties are collectively referred to as the inner suburbs; each adjoins the District of Columbia and is served by Metrorail (see Figure 1.1.). The remaining jurisdictions of the region, collectively called the outer suburbs, have neither of these attributes. About two-thirds of a million people live in each of the Maryland counties, Fairfax County, and the District, while Arlington County and Alexandria have populations of somewhat over one hundred thousand. The total population of over three million is about equal to that of the Boston area. What is perhaps more relevant is that among cities with new rail systems, the total population of the Washington area is somewhat smaller than that of the San Francisco Bay Area and considerably larger than those of the Atlanta, San Diego, Miami, and Baltimore areas.

The residential distribution of the Washington region has followed common American patterns. For many years the great bulk of residential growth has been in Fairfax, Montgomery, and Prince George's Counties (their aggregate population has increased from less than a quarter of a million in 1950 to over two million today), and Arlington County and Alexandria have experienced modest growth. Meanwhile, the District's population declined by about 25 percent from the 1950s

Figure 1.1.

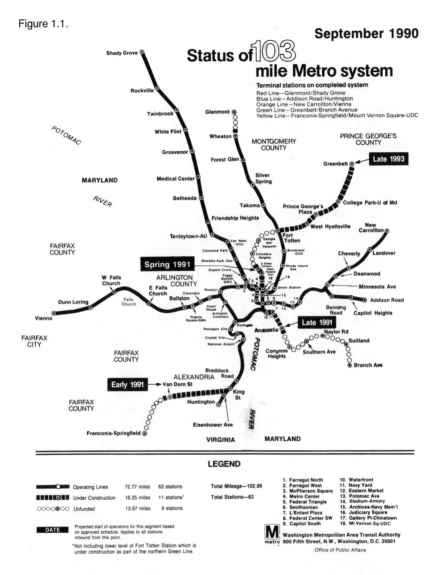

**September 1990**

**Status of 103 mile Metro system**

Terminal stations on completed system
Red Line—Glenmont/Shady Grove
Blue Line—Addison Road/Huntington
Orange Line—New Carrollton/Vienna
Green Line—Greenbelt/Branch Avenue
Yellow Line—Franconia-Springfield/Mount Vernon Square-UDC

**LEGEND**

| | | | | |
|---|---|---|---|---|
| Operating Lines | 72.77 miles | 63 stations | Total Mileage—102.99 | |
| Under Construction | 16.25 miles | 11 stations* | Total Stations—83 | |
| Unfunded | 13.97 miles | 9 stations | | |

DATE Projected start of operations for this segment based on approved schedule. Applies to all stations inbound from this point.

*Not including lower level of Fort Totten Station which is under construction as part of the northern Green Line.

1. Farragut North
2. Farragut West
3. McPherson Square
4. Metro Center
5. Federal Triangle
6. Smithsonian
7. L'Enfant Plaza
8. Federal Center SW
9. Capitol South
10. Waterfront
11. Navy Yard
12. Eastern Market
13. Potomac Ave
14. Stadium-Armory
15. Archives-Navy Mem'l
16. Judiciary Square
17. Gallery Pl-Chinatown
18. Mt Vernon Sq-UDC

**M** metro **Washington Metropolitan Area Transit Authority**
600 Fifth Street, N.W., Washington, D.C. 20001

Office of Public Affairs

through the 1970s before essentially stabilizing in the last decade.

Employment in the Washington metropolitan region is overwhelmingly service-sector. The dominant economic force, the federal government, itself employs over 400,000 people and is responsible through its presence and activities for another 400,000 private service-sector jobs in trade associations, consulting firms, law offices, and the like. A large and vigorous trade sector (both wholesale and retail) employs some 350,000 people and nonfederal governments another 150,000; all other employment categories, including transportation, utilities, construction, and a small amount of manufacturing, account for approximately 300,000 jobs (see, e.g., Cater, 1984).

Federal employment plays the economic role in this region that basic employment plays in most other cities; nonfederal government employment here effectively corresponds to the total "government" category elsewhere. The "basic" category as well can be misleading here. For example, printing, the only manufacturing activity of any significance in the region, makes up a large part of the small basic sector, but much private printing is actually done under federal contracts and therefore behaves more as part of the service sector than as footloose manufacturing; meanwhile, a significant amount of local printing employment is with the federal government itself (which prints many of its documents, including tax forms and paper currency, in its own facilities in the region) and thus is tallied as "government," not as "basic." Nevertheless the most important feature of this type of employment in the region is its insignificance—barely 10 percent of total employment. Office employment (of whatever provenance) dominates to a degree unparalleled among large American urban regions (see Figure 1.2.).

Federal employment in the region has grown at least since shortly after the Second World War, quite rapidly for several decades but more slowly since the mid-1970s. The federally generated private service sector (such as the trade associations) has grown somewhat more steadily and now exceeds direct federal employment in absolute number of jobs in the region. Employment in the other categories is largely dependent on these two and has grown in tandem with them to present levels.

The jurisdictional distribution of the region's employment has generally followed that of its population, with one significant exception: the District of Columbia has gained, not lost, employment, almost keeping pace with the suburbs in absolute numbers of jobs, even though its share of regional employment has of course declined.

This phenomenon warrants some discussion. It is partly due to conditions peculiar to a seat of government. While some federal employment is restricted by tradition or statute to the national capital, the significant thing here is probably not these activities themselves so

Figure 1.2.

## NON-AGRICULTURAL EMPLOYMENT
## DISTRIBUTION, PERCENTS, 1988

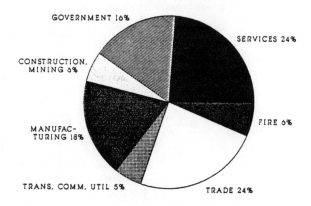

U.S. WORK FORCE

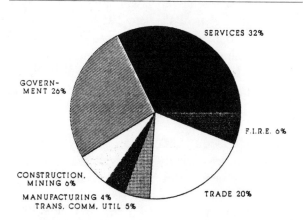

WASHINGTON AREA WORK FORCE

much as their drawing power: private work (notably lobbying and report-ing) as well as public will inevitably cluster in the immediate vicinity of the Capitol and the headquarters of the cabinet departments. This drawing power even extends outside the District; there are notable concentrations of private employment in the parts of Montgomery and

Arlington Counties closest to the District.

At least two other factors may contribute significantly to the amount of private and unconstrained-location federal employment in the District. The first is the unusual mix of a large amount of office work (public and private) with a very small amount of factory work, which may have a dampening effect on "greenfield" tendencies because the theoretical advantages of locating or relocating factories in wide open spaces generally do not apply to office buildings. The other is the existence for more than a decade of a rail transit system, Metrorail, with its main focus in the District's central business district.

This system serves the six major jurisdictions and is operated by the Washington Metropolitan Area Transit Authority (WMATA), a regional compact. It was planned as a complete entity in the middle 1960s (there have been no significant divergences from or changes to the 1968 final plan), construction started in 1969, and the first segment was opened in 1976. Currently (1990), 64 stations in 70 route-miles of track are operating out of a planned total of 87 stations and 103 route-miles; more than 500,000 rides are sold on a typical weekday.

Metrorail grew out of a relatively small part of a freeway-dominated regional transportation plan of the late 1950s. A modest rail transit system, apparently proposed as an attempt to defuse the intense and broadly based opposition among District residents to the planned urban freeways, ended up largely displacing those freeways inside the District (in more senses than the literal one—the District eventually reprogrammed most of its interstate highway subsidies to Metrorail construction). A 25-mile system serving only the District of Columbia and the Pentagon (located in Arlington County) was approved by Congress in 1965. It was widely perceived that a regional system would make far more sense than one limited to the District, and in 1967 WMATA was formed and given responsibility for planning, constructing, and operating a regional rail transit system. The District-based plan was essentially extended into the suburbs, with the precise locations of the extension lines largely determined by the suburban jurisdictions themselves.

The primary purpose of the Metrorail system was to connect employment in and near the Washington central business district (CBD) with residential outlying areas (Richards, 1979), and it was expected to reduce or eliminate automobile traffic congestion in the areas it served, particularly in the regional core. Several of the jurisdictions were content to leave it at that (Fairfax County even rejected a proposed minor realignment of one of its lines to serve the immense commercial and retail concentration at Tyson's Corner), but at least three of them saw generating development as an important secondary purpose of the system. In particular, the District hoped the rail system would reverse the long-term decline of its CBD, while Montgomery and Arlington Counties deliberately routed their rail lines so as to work in concert with such other factors as existing concentrations and zoning incentives to attract or generate new economic activity. In addition, the hope was expressed (generally as a pious afterthought) that improved transit resulting from the rail system would give low-income people, particularly District residents, better access to jobs, particularly in the suburbs.

How well have these purposes been served? The bottom line of over half a million daily rides indicates that the system is definitely serving its primary purpose of moving commuters. A 1988 survey by the Metropolitan Washington Council of Governments showed that 40 percent of all commuters used mass transit for their morning work trip, a record made possible only by the growing popularity of Metrorail. The system has been far less successful as a means of reducing road congestion. In fact, it did this in only one significant way, namely by replacing some bus routes and thereby reducing downtown bus traffic in particular by about two-thirds; this was eventually canceled by increased automobile use, and overall traffic downtown returned to its old levels. Moreover, due to short-sighted, or simply bad, design and planning, many stations are effectively not accessible to pedestrians, and there is a substantial lack of coordination of local bus service with the rail system (even though most bus service in the region is operated by the same agency, WMATA, as Metrorail); one result of this situation has been serious automobile traffic congestion problems outside stations. It seems likely that the goals of moving large numbers of people and of reducing traffic congestion are simply not compatible.

While the decline of downtown retail activity in the District has only been halted, not reversed, the District's CBD is nevertheless flying high on the strength of an office boom; whether Metrorail caused this in any specific sense, it is clear from physical space considerations alone (i.e., the roads—including freeways, the need for which Metrorail obviated—and parking which would otherwise have been necessary in a limited amount of downtown land) that the boom could not have happened without the subway. The results of part of this project (see Chapter 7) show that Montgomery's and Arlington's development focus efforts seem to be working. As with the District's CBD, it is difficult to isolate Metrorail's contribution to the process, but there are definite statistical reasons for believing that it is strictly positive. This result contrasts greatly with such other work as the BART study, which found no such economic effects, but is consistent with various recommendations for "joint development" (i.e., public and private joint ventures) insofar as the two counties' actions constituted this. (It is worth noting here that several stations in the District, all in high-income residential areas, became extremely attractive to developers without any encouragement from the District government; many of the station neighborhoods in Arlington and, especially, Montgomery Counties have the same kind of perceived upscale demographics as these attractive District locations.)

As for giving low-income people better access to jobs, Metrorail gives many people of all income levels one way of getting to many jobs, and this certainly benefits many low-income people in particular. They may even benefit proportionately more than members of higher-income groups, since they have fewer alternatives. However, there are reasons to believe that Metrorail's direct contributions will not go much beyond this basic provision of service, at least in the short run. Some of these are local peculiarities, such as the problems with local bus service and with pedestrian access to stations discussed above, but some are national phenomena. American suburbia is characterized by low-density sprawl, and when employment sites are widely and randomly scattered, no rail system can serve more than a handful of them. This observation does suggest one way that Metrorail may, albeit over time and rather indirectly, nevertheless greatly benefit low-income people in the region: by its potential focusing effect. Insofar as the existence of Metrorail induces employment to cluster near stations instead of scattering across the landscape, low-income people specifically have that much more access to jobs.

*Two*

# The Study of Transportation Project Impacts on Local Land Use and Development

The economic effects of such immense public investments as new rail transit systems are naturally of great general interest. There has correspondingly been a great deal of academic and statistical work on this topic, ranging in scope from assessments of specific developments at particular stations, through studies on the neighborhood, CBD, and jurisdiction level, to comprehensive regional (or at least systemwide) analyses.

Many of the local studies, commissioned for purely local purposes and conducted with little thought of comparative or regional analysis, have correspondingly limited relevance to broad regional development issues; we will nevertheless touch upon several from the Washington region. General implications can be extracted from CBD impact studies for Portland, Oregon, and Los Angeles. However, the regional analyses are the most useful for our purposes. These include the 1979 BART Impact Program (BIP) studies, which considered a wide range of factors in most local areas of the San Francisco Bay region affected by the Bay Area Rapid Transit System (BART), and similar but smaller studies that were later made for Buffalo, San Diego, and Washington. The methods and findings of these precedents lead us to the more general issue of business location determinants, and then to a consideration of joint development processes that can, in principle, shape and facilitate local economic development.

Some academically oriented studies have used statistical techniques to assess changes, generally in property values, associated with transportation improvements in local areas. These studies provide some guidelines for assessing the statistical quality of the employment impact studies and the modeling effort of the present work.

Finally, the Metro Before and After study and other local planning studies for station areas in the Washington region will be reviewed to evaluate the variety of approaches to development supported by the planning and development agencies of the different local jurisdictions.

## Impact Studies

Reducing automobile traffic congestion was a major goal of the designers of transit systems like BART in the 1950s, and their preliminary studies ignored most other impacts. Unfortunately, these analyses tended not only to be limited, but flawed as well, and resulted in many transit stations being placed where they could not even have much effect on highway congestion (such as near main arteries between suburban communities and the CBD).

### The BART Impact Program and Subsequent Studies

The BIP, a pathbreaking step in evaluating transit systems, sought to determine, among other things, if BART had produced land-use patterns that increased regional economic growth overall (Grefe and McDonald, 1979) and if it had influenced location decisions of economic actors in ways that reduced sprawl or revitalized CBDs (Graebner et al., 1979). These approaches marked a departure from the earlier unexamined assumption of planners in the 1950s and 1960s that new transit systems would automatically induce local economic development.

The BART system had been expected from the start to serve as a stimulus to the Bay Area economy, to counteract trends of decline in the city centers of Oakland and San Francisco, to open up new land for development throughout the Bay Area, to increase the mobility and job potential of workers, to greatly expand access to shopping, entertainment, and cultural activities, to meet the needs of the elderly, and otherwise to improve transportation for those without automobiles. All of these things were supposed to happen by themselves; nothing specific was done to further them in the planning phase or later, and the system (as mentioned above) was designed on faulty traffic-impact-only principles. Hence, BART emerged as a commuter train rather than as a rapid-transit system capable of influencing land use toward set goals. It did not even achieve major improvements in moving people within the cities of Oakland and San Francisco (Graebner et al., 1979).

The BIP studies sought to review and analyze the original BART plans to determine specifically what local direct and induced objectives it was designed to meet, and to determine whether the local stations accomplished these goals, and why or why not. They also sought to determine what institutional problems prevented desired impacts from occurring and to evaluate which public policies could be used to guarantee that the objectives would be achieved, so as to create a general rapid-transit development "road map" for local officials.

Using systematic but not especially rigorous methods, Graebner et al. (1979) studied the development experience of various stations in simple quantitative terms, along with associated historical, institutional, and political information about each station area. They concluded that downtown stations could greatly aid revitalization efforts if and only if they were part of a combined planning process of government and private agencies. Stations in urban residential areas induced little development and in fact often seemed to generate community preservation or down-zoning movements that prevented substantial redevelopment or land-use change. Suburban stations remained a bit of a mystery. Those with large parking lots or other barriers between the station and nearby developed (or developable) areas seemed to induce little development, and tended to remain no more than commuter stations. Graebner et al. also found these processes at work in locales outside the Bay Area. The experience of Toronto showed how stations could be the core of concentrated urban development, but only if strong government policy were used to guide development decisions. In sum, this study found that a rail transit system would not by itself induce economic development on the local level around transit station sites in suburban communities and residential neighborhoods. Indeed, there was no evidence that BART had influenced either centralization or decentralization of business districts, and public transportation and BART in particular were found to be minor factors in most employers' location decisions.

This study concluded that the local objectives had not been accomplished, except for some small reductions in traffic congestion; that institutional factors such as zoning should have been coordinated and integrated into the original plan; and that access would continue to be a severe problem in the Bay Area.

Graebner et al. also made recommendations for realizing the development potential of new rail transit systems. These included: (1) transit stations should be located in areas conducive to development; (2) expectations should be based on a careful analysis of demand and the availability and cost of developable land; and (3) planners and decision makers should not expect any transit-oriented development until after construction has begun. In addition, public-private partnerships (joint development) would often be necessary even when all three conditions are met.

The broader studies of Knight (1980) and Knight and Trygg (1977a, 1977b) similarly concluded that high-density development requires, in addition to the transit stations themselves, such other favorable factors as appropriate zoning, a strong demand for such development, and cooperation and coordination among local governments, developers, financial institutions, and citizens' organizations during the land-use planning and transit design stages. Unfortunately, this kind of coordination of activity at each step of the planning process has been difficult to obtain because of the historical separation of land use and transportation planning offices.

The results of an impact study (Eplan, 1980) of two stations of Atlanta's MARTA system parallel and reinforce the BART findings. MARTA was designed to increase transit patronage, relieve peak-hour congestion, and expand the market for public transit beyond the traditional "capture riders." It was an extension of an existing, well-developed bus service. The study, like those of Washington and San Francisco, concluded that the system had not reduced highway congestion; that it had created congestion and parking problems at the two stations, which were located in predominantly residential areas; and that it had induced virtually no new economic activity in either station area (Donnelly et al., 1982).

### Washington Metro Planning Studies

Washington's Metrorail system was constructed during the period of the BART study but did not profit greatly from its recommendations. Metrorail was designed to be both a commuter rail line and a downtown circulation system. Promoting downtown renewal was one of the new rail system's expected benefits (as it had been for BART), but in their planning studies, Metrorail authorities largely ignored the system's possible development impacts. Route selection and property acquisition often reflected this nondevelopment perspective, so that many of the stations were located on undevelopable land, in railroad rights-of-way, or in freeway medians. Development around downtown stations, while often impressive and certainly influenced by the access advantages of the station areas, has nevertheless occurred on a parcel-by-parcel basis, with lot assembly a purely private activity, similar to the patterns in downtown San Francisco (Lovely, 1979). The involvement of Metrorail officials in development activity has generally been limited to negotiating terms for direct access connectors between major department stores and stations near them (WMATA, 1982). Some more concrete planning initiatives around a few downtown stations have come from the publicly supported Pennsylvania Avenue Development Corporation (PADC). PADC projects, however, seem designed to stimulate not bustling mixed-use activity but rather a sense of granite grandeur deemed appropriate for the nation's capital, and PADC's involvement in joint development near stations is therefore particularistic, not generalizable, and not especially helpful in understanding how government partnerships with private developers might meet more conventional urban commercial development and revitalization goals.

An early impact study done by the Montgomery County Planning Board (MCPB, 1977c) of the Silver Spring station indicates that many of the BART findings are transferable between cities. In the absence of joint development initiatives, transit stations do little to induce augmented economic activity in largely residential suburban communities. Automobile traffic not only did not decrease in Silver Spring, it actually increased as a result of Metrorail (Silver Spring was the terminus of the Red Line until 1990). At the time of the study, the station had done little to create any new economic activity in the area and existing businesses had not benefited from the system since most riders who passed Silver Spring were going from the suburbs to the core. The station was constructed on an existing railroad right-of-way that made the station area undevelopable without aggressive public investments (Dunphy and Griffiths, 1981). Since the time of this study, public (i.e., Montgomery County government) commitments to improvements of roads, parking, street lights, and open spaces have helped spur large-scale private redevelopment plans. Some of these plans are so ambitious that citizen reaction to such feared disamenities as increased traffic congestion has somewhat slowed the pace of redevelopment, although it has not stopped it (as often happened in BART station areas). Given the continued strong support of elected public officials and local planners for substantial redevelopment in Silver Spring, it is likely to happen. Note, however, that such an outcome will have required strong public support of private developers' efforts.

Wessel's 1982 study of the sites of the six Metrorail stations to be located in Fairfax County was an attempt to implement stage three (construction with close attention to land-use impacts) of the BART policy plan mentioned above (Graebner et al., 1979). It differed from the BART study in that it was a preconstruction analysis, asking the question, "What will it take for the public sector to guarantee development around sites?" rather than a post hoc, critical study. It analyzed the stations' ability to become focal points for residential and nonresidential development, to enhance the existing character of nearby areas, and to encourage Metrorail ridership. The Fairfax County stations are located in areas that are mostly residential but also have significant tracts of vacant land where the character of development could be strongly influenced by the existence of Metrorail. Unfortunately, these stations are classic examples of the types of station design (e.g., poor pedestrian access) that the BART study found to be incompatible with transit-related development.

Wessel assessed station area developability using such variables as the amount of vacant and redevelopable acreage within 1,500 feet of each station, the character of each station area (i.e., existing land uses), and access and circulation characteristics.

This study broke ground in advancing the idea of joint development for stations prior to construction and in attempting to identify crucial area characteristics for development, but did not go beyond this taxonomic methodology in testing its views about development. It attempted to determine neither the locational patterns and preferences of industry in choosing site locations nor the kinds of businesses that would be successful in the station area, and it did not recommend any specific public policy to encourage development. Furthermore, it selected variables on an ad hoc basis rather than choosing variables that had historically and cross-sectionally proven to be significant in rail station development. No forecasting model was used, so no predictions could be made of development in the station areas that might occur either spontaneously or as a result of public-private ventures.

The analysts projected a second phase of the project in which they would, for each of the six areas, identify opportunities and fiscal, transportation, public facility, and environmental impacts associated with two development scenarios. The options were to reflect the development guidelines established for each station, but would vary as to intensity/density of use and land-use mix. Inputs from the two development options were to be compared to each other as well as to those of recommended land uses in the currently adopted Comprehensive Plan. Thereafter, land-use and transportation recommendations were to be made and proposed as amendments to the Comprehensive Plan. Had this second phase been carried out as planned, it would have taken important variables into account in a way consistent with the idea of joint development. In fact, the only work done was a detailed plan for the development of the West Falls Church station which attempted no statistical modeling or forecasting, and this promising Fairfax approach ended as a purely local, indeed one-station, study. Such studies are, of course, necessary for local planning, but they do little to advance understanding of the general impact of transit on local land use.

## Prospective Studies of Transit Impacts

Because they are prepared after the stations are in place, most local transit studies cannot usefully address the question, "How can we plan transit to maximize its land-use impact potential?" However, this question could be—and was—asked when some cities, including Buffalo, Los Angeles, and Portland, decided to invest in light rail transit (LRT) systems that were designed specifically to revitalize the downtowns by using joint development techniques (Paaswell and Berechman, 1981).

Light rail transit differs from rail rapid transit (RRT) such as Metrorail and BART in cost, speed, station spacing, and usually area covered. LRT systems tend to have from 6 to 20 route-miles while RRT systems usually have (at least in the planning stage) 50 or more route-miles. While LRTs tend not to affect regional land-use patterns, they can have powerful local effects; this may account for the greater pre-implementation interest in local land-use effects. In any event, LRTs have been successful parts of joint development activities aimed at inducing economic growth in declining central business districts.

Los Angeles has both LRT and RRT projects, and is also constructing a $175 million downtown people mover (DPM) lying almost entirely within two redevelopment projects and adjacent to a third. The Community Redevelopment Agency, which oversees land use and transportation development in the relevant urban renewal areas, has used its staff and its powers of land assembly, design and construction review, and contract negotiation to foster the successful integration of the DPM and some downtown development activity. Many Los Angeles businessmen and developers have contributed to the DPM program and the Chamber of Commerce has recommended the creation of a benefit assessment district for the purpose of collecting $1.3 million annually in private sector funding to offset the DPM's operating deficit (Lovely, 1979). These activities seem to fit in very closely with the staging proposal of Graebner et al. (1979), although the project has a lower level of potential impact than BART. Unfortunately, no recent published studies have analyzed whether Los Angeles' auspicious beginnings of ten years ago have realized their promise, or whether there is appropriate coordination between the DPM and the LRT and RRT projects there.

Portland's LRT, the Tri-Met, was planned not only to reduce core area auto congestion and to improve environmental quality, but also as an essential component of a project to create a downtown retail environment that would be competitive with suburban shopping centers (Knight and Trygg, 1977). This project was modeled after Nicollet Mall in Minneapolis, a pedestrian mall with exclusive bus lanes that gained national attention for its success in controlling traffic, improving transit ridership, and substantially increasing the number of downtown shoppers. Portland's transit mall has indeed supported rapid growth in downtown office space, mostly between the transit mall and another major city project (Lovely, 1979).

Denver originally planned to follow a course similar to that of Portland in light of its rapid downtown office development, and made plans for a mall-transit connection that would have helped make the downtown an energetic center of mixed land uses (Lovely, 1979). These plans were not fulfilled, and Denver was left with only a DPM system instead of a full transit mall. The development of future rail lines is doubtful.

Transit system planning in Portland, Los Angeles, and to a lesser extent Denver incorporated the principle of selecting transit station locations specifically to create economic activity in tandem with other public and private investments. However, these systems are somewhat limited (sometimes to the downtown area) and have little if any power to affect land-use patterns outside the core area. Their purpose is to centralize economic activity with patterns similar to those generated by the Montreal transit system, but they rely heavily on automobile connections instead of rail extensions for trips to the core area. In general, these transitways are not conducive for regional planning of economic growth through transit site selections outside the core area.

Paaswell and Berechman's 1981 study was an attempt to investigate the ability of light rail to affect economic growth in Buffalo's central business district, which, unlike the CBDs of Los Angeles, Portland, and Denver, is not "attractive" enough to compete with suburban malls. The study sought to determine the economic impact of Buffalo's new LRT system by addressing the following questions: Is there regional support? What are the associated land-use and activity changes? What is the timetable for these changes and are they affected by the transit investment? Will long-term (postconstruction) changes in the labor force be created or influenced by the transit decision? And will the transit system affect the intraregional mobility of labor?

The study concluded that there would be a decline in residential use of the CBD and an increase in service employment there, but that the LRT system would not reverse current trends of population decline and retail and service activity reductions in zones adjacent to its route. Moreover, Paaswell and Berechman concluded that the system is not sufficient to catalyze new economic development unless it is linked to areas with demonstrated independent growth potential, thus indicating that the LRT encountered the same station site selection problems as RRT systems. However, the study contains only general guidelines for possible joint development activities.

The San Diego LRT system, constructed without federal aid, was unconstrained by federal guidelines. Unlike the BIP, which tried to measure transportation effects on everything from the regional economy to changes in life-styles, San Diego LRT impact studies concentrated on changes in travel characteristics, land-use development, and socioeconomic characteristics resulting from the system's first line (San Diego Association of Governments [SDAG], 1982; and Donnelly et al., 1982). The study found that while the system had robust ridership and was fiscally sound (with fares paying 90 percent of its operating costs), no economic development activity had resulted from its existence. Since the system was intended mostly to serve commuters and the line studied was constructed primarily on a railroad right-of-way, such a finding is not surprising and is consistent with the BIP results (SDAG, 1982). Two subsequent lines of this system seem to have more potential as generators of development, but no reports on their effects have yet appeared.

## *Summary*

Traditional transportation variables such as travel cost and total trips are part of the variable set that reflects the effectiveness of all transit systems in meeting simple travel demand. The additional variables of land-use impacts or "generated development," not always appropriate for all modes of transit, are important for rail transit systems which, because of their high capital cost, must generate broader returns to the public than simple ridership-level changes. The promotion of new or intensified development at station sites is often suggested as an important benefit of rail transit (AMRA, 1976).

The impact studies reviewed above, however, showed that development generally does not occur rapidly or spontaneously at station sites. These areas do not seem to be as attractive to businesses as many had expected, and a closer look at the factors influencing business location decisions is warranted.

## The Business Location Decision and Transit

Business location decisions are complex. The planners' conventional wisdom that access from transit would be decisive in such decisions has not generally been supported by experience (AMRA, 1976; Baltimore Planning Commission [BPC], 1970; Graebner et al., 1979; Dingemans, 1975; Knight, 1980; and Richmond, 1980). This inconsistency stems partly from planners' and economists' ambiguous understanding of the location behavior of business firms (Harrison and Kanter, 1978).

By the late 1970s urban theorists were beginning to move away from the von Thunenesque view that transportation costs are always key determinants of location decisions, and toward the concept of a multifaceted decision matrix facing businessmen in search of a site. Trade journals and industry economists have frequently suggested this

(Herr, 1979; Knight and Trygg, 1977; Lund, 1979; Lund and Winter, 1979; Lynch, 1973; Schmenner, 1975; Struyk, 1972; and Struyk and James, 1975). Rarely, in these views, was access the primary issue in location decisions (see also Callies, 1980; Clay, 1981; and Myers, 1980). For example, a study summarizing the location activity of manufacturing industries in metropolitan regions in 1972 found that while many businesses are attracted to the central business district, the bulk of locational activity has been a steady outward movement of relocating establishments favoring the suburbs regardless of transit innovations (Struyk, 1972). Lynch (1973) found that availability of labor and quality of site took priority over transportation, and Hanushek and Song (1978) found that while highway access is an important determinant of employment locations, the advantage of locations closer to expressways has lessened as expressways have become ubiquitous. Vaughan (1977) noted that transportation per se is only one of many factors influencing business location. These studies indicate that as automobile commuting and shipping by truck became the overwhelming norms, the specific relevance of transportation facilities to location decisions decreased in relative importance. Woodward (1977) listed key factors determining office site location; again, accessibility was only one among many points.

As the new generation of rapid-transit systems has been implemented, it has become clear that basic industry will not locate near a station without additional inducements. Other categories of economic activity may respond sluggishly as well. Joint development activity between public and private concerns has consequently emerged as the most promising path to business development around rail stations (AMRA, 1976; Johnson, 1981; Myers, 1980; and Priest, 1980). The general idea is not new. Cities, counties, and even countries have often offered inducements to draw firms to their locales in order to generate jobs, tax base, and local economic linkages. However, the idea that joint development activity was appropriate specifically for urban and/or transportation planning agencies in conjunction with the development of rapid-transit systems has been a bit novel. Traditionally, transit planners have taken the approach of minimizing construction costs (by, for example, constructing lines and stations along existing railroad rights-of-way), rather than the approach of stimulating regional development with the stations, while land-use planners have taken the transit system and its presumed effects as givens without considering the interaction effects over time of transit and land-use planning. Given the web of factors affecting location decisions of firms, the consensus in the literature is that a helping hand is needed to stimulate the invisible one.

## The Statistical Quality of Transit-related Impact Studies

Most studies related to transit influence on real estate values, levels of employment, business location decisions, and the like in small areas are not statistically robust. This may well be due to the relatively great importance of idiosyncrasies in small areas. For instance, a particular characteristic of a few acres of terrain that makes development difficult would greatly affect a ten-acre zone but not a several-hundred-acre one. More generally, variations in zone definitions can make big differences in otherwise comparable studies, and data problems, rampant in small-area studies, often force researchers to use crude proxy variables instead of the true variables of interest. Small-area studies are nevertheless essential for learning about certain urban processes and impacts, so this section surveys a number of such studies related to transit impacts and attempts to assess what constitutes reasonable findings (in terms of statistical quality) in this context.

Weisbrod and Pollakowski (1984) examined eight revitalized pedestrian/transit malls to see what effect the revitalization process had on nearby business development. A cross-sectional, cross-city multiple regression analysis was performed using 496 "establishment units," each such unit being an aggregation of establishments in five types, two sizes, two ownership types, eight project zones, and for four time intervals. Three dependent variables were specified: rate of employment growth for establishments, mean annual rate of new store entry, and mean annual rate of store exiting. Independent variables included five dummy variables for type of establishment, a before-or-after revitalization variable, the level of local unemployment, and the CBD share of city sales. Instead of the usual $R^2$s, $F$-values for the entire equation were reported; they were significant (assuming that a one-tailed test was justified, since no justification for its use was presented) but not impressive (2.30, 6.13, and 7.86). Only ten of the twenty-four independent variables in the three equations proved to be significant based on their $t$-values, even when the very liberal one-tailed test with a 90 percent confidence interval was used. In only one equation was the crucial before-or-after revitalization variable significant. Although this study provided interesting case studies of the impact of transit malls on revitalization, its statistical findings were anemic.

In a study of anticipated responses of urban real estate values to the Washington Metrorail system, Damm et al. (1980) collected samples, ranging in size from 353 to 771 parcels, of properties near Metrorail station areas. The price of the parcel was taken as dependent upon three groups of variables: transit-system-related variables, demographic variables, and parcel-specific variables. For the single-family and multi-family housing price equations, $R^2$s ranged from 0.59 to 0.79, with several significant explanatory variables. For price of retail establishments, the $R^2$s were lower (around 0.50), again with many significant variables in the equation. The findings of this study support the notion that property close to Metrorail stations includes capitalized transportation savings, but that the impact area is small. The study also concluded that real estate values did tend to rise in anticipation of the opening of a nearby station. The statistical quality of these findings is among the best available for small-area studies.

In work similar to that of Damm et al., Dewees (1973, 1976) examined the effect on real estate values of location near a Toronto subway line. He did a before-and-after study using a standard hedonic equation estimated based on two thousand property sales in five different impact areas. He found some steepening in the rent surface within a third of a mile of the subway line, but did not find any decisive confirmation of his hypothesis that the opening of the line (which replaced a streetcar line) would consistently enhance close-in property values. The statistical quality of his models is hard to evaluate since he reported only $t$-statistics for independent variables (most of which implied significance for the relevant independent variable) but no $R^2$s or $F$-values.

Boyce et al. (1972) found a significant enhancement of close-in real estate values after the opening of the Philadelphia–Lindenwood High-Speed Line. Their regression model yielded strongly significant variables determining real estate values and a reasonably strong $R^2$ of 0.51. Wolf (1979) arrived at similar findings for selected station areas in the Washington region. The statistical quality of her models paralleled that of Boyce et al., with a satisfactory number of significant variables and an overall $R^2$ of 0.54.

Local studies of property value changes due to transit stations or other transit improvements yield results that are statistically reasonable but not generally strong enough for forecasting purposes. Much of this quality is due to the overall precision that is available for hedonic price equations estimated on detailed parcel data. When impacts other than real estate prices were used as dependent variables, the quality of the results declined substantially, as in the case of the transit malls study.

A review of these local empirical studies suggests that models of local impacts of transit developments have generally been conceived of as structural models, not forecasting devices, and that forecasting would be quite inaccurate with such models. Even when the estimated models are moderately strong, the difficulty of forecasting certain categories of independent variables (such as neighborhood characteristics) has apparently ruled out forecasting uses of the models. The relative statistical weakness of some models also stands as an obvious barrier to their use as forecasting tools. Nevertheless, it is possible to estimate structural or explanatory models based on such cross-sectional data sets that may be of use to developers, planners, and analysts, and there may even be some limited forecasting uses for such models.

## The Before-and-After Studies for the Washington Region

The Washington Metrorail system represented an opportunity for a genuine before-and-after study to help assess transit-related impacts. The U.S. Department of Transportation took advantage of this opportunity by contracting with the Washington Metropolitan Area Council of Governments (WASHCOG) to produce a series of studies including a general historical study of Metrorail, a detailed set of case studies of station area development, and reports on trends cross-sectionally and over time in such important land-use and development-related issues as employment, commercial development, residential development, and travel behavior during the 1972–82 period.

While these reports were meticulously detailed, giving absolute levels, absolute changes, and rates of change in many disaggregations of employment and commercial floor space variables, few definitive or rigorous conclusions could be reached because no statistical tests were made of any hypotheses. Indeed, the only effort to go beyond simple tabular reports in these studies was Cater's (1984) attempt to test the hypothesis that economic activity increases in areas around unopened stations in anticipation of Metrorail service by comparing employment changes from 1976 to 1980 in control (i.e., nonstation) areas, unopened station areas, and opened station areas. The numerical results were intriguing—suburban control areas grew faster than either opened or unopened station areas, while central jurisdiction control areas grew faster than opened stations but slower than unopened stations—but the lack of statistical tests of these comparisons precluded any reliable conclusion on this question. Moreover, these findings and others in the Before-and-After series may well have been influenced by WASHCOG's decision to include a zone in the impact area of a Metrorail station if any part of it fell within 0.7 miles of the station; these impact areas consequently contain many locations well over a mile from any station. The literature tends to discredit such an approach; the residential value impact studies mentioned above found impacts generally to be confined to areas within, at most, half of that distance from stations (Wolf, 1979; and Boyce et al., 1972), and planners in most jurisdictions of the region, as described below, consider the major impacts of their stations to occur within similarly short radii (Arlington County uses a 0.25-mile range; Montgomery County planners' impact areas vary in size but none is as large as WASHCOG's). The effect of a too-large impact area is to dilute any effects of the station, potentially quite significantly. For example, if impacts occur only within a quarter-mile of the station, the use of a 0.7-mile radius means that 87 percent of the "impact" area is in reality not affected by the Metrorail station, so that actual Metrorail impacts may be undetectable.

This impact area definition problem may partly account for the striking finding in Flick (1988) that the rate of employment growth in station areas is lower than that of the rest of the region. The present study, as reported in the next chapter, found to the contrary that the growth rates of station areas defined by a quarter-mile radius was much greater than the growth rates of the districts (groups of zones) within which they were located.

## Planning around Station Sites in Suburban Washington

The regional studies conducted by WASHCOG were complemented by local planning efforts by the individual jurisdictions. A review of the documents produced by planning offices in the suburban jurisdictions reveals an uneven pattern in several ways. First, in different jurisdictions different levels of resources are available for planning projects. At the extremes, Prince George's County has published only two rather superficial documents, each discussing plans for a single subway station site (MNCPPC-PG, 1979, 1981), while neighboring Montgomery County has prepared detailed plans for almost all of its station sites (MNCCPC, 1975, 1978a, 1978b, 1978d, 1982; Montgomery County Planning Board [MCPB] 1974a, 1974b, 1974c, 1977a, 1977b, 1977c, 1978, 1980, 1982). Arlington's planning was almost as comprehensive as Montgomery's (Arlington, 1980, 1981, 1983), while Alexandria's was at a much lower level of detail (Alexandria 1983; Artemel et al., 1978, 1980, 1982). Although Fairfax County put significant efforts into trying to assess key development characteristics, and its Office of Comprehensive Planning has worked extensively with developers, very little has been published beyond Wessel's (1982) study and the West Falls Church station plan, noted earlier.

Some of these differences can be attributed to differential progress in building stations. Arlington and Montgomery Counties' stations are almost all open and the last few are nearing completion. None of Prince George's County's Green Line stations will be open for some years (construction has not even begun on many). The majority of Fairfax's stations opened in 1986.

But the reports also indicate differences in perspective. Consider two reports for Arlington (1980, 1981). These station studies emerged from a 1972 general study on the Metrorail corridor in Arlington, later embodied in the goals statement contained in "A Long Range County Improvement Program" approved by the county government in 1975. The General Land Use Plan of 1977 further moved the county toward support for mixed-use development around well-defined station site impact areas. These areas generally extend beyond the immediate quarter-mile station site, sometimes as far as three-quarters of a mile away from the station itself.

In the Courthouse station plan (Arlington, 1981), the county planners envisioned an expanded government office complex, housing most county government operations, surrounded by substantial commercial office space in high-rise buildings. Although significant residential areas near the station (Colonial Village) were to be protected by designation as a Coordinated Preservation and Development District, this appears to be, in the planners' view, an opening for more intense residential and some commercial development within that area. That is, rather than being either kept as is or redeveloped, this neighborhood will be developed through infill and some conversions to include low-density commercial, office, and retail (as well as its present residential) uses. Another nearby neighborhood (Lyon Village) is not likely to be changed substantially because it is a fully developed residential neighborhood, making conversion expensive and controversial, and there are many more development opportunities nearer the station itself (the Central Courthouse subsector). As these developments are completed (and depending upon market forces), the "preserved" neighborhoods may lose their preservation status as other developers move to expand the Courthouse development beyond current plans. In fact, some residents have formed cartels to sell their homes jointly to developers, with county approval. Certainly, the plans for high-rise development within Courthouse will support pressure for redevelopment of residential properties, assuming that office/commercial/retail leasing plans for these projects are successful.

Similarly, the Ballston plan (Arlington, 1980) encouraged development through a multiphase process. According to this plan, intensity of development within the impact area should be tapered in terms of building height, proximity of buildings, and the residential share of development as one moves from the Metrorail station to the previously existing, low-density housing area. The county upgraded the zoning and boldly encouraged high-rise office development in the station site area itself.

The attitude of the Arlington community, as reflected in the development plans that have passed through several years and different levels of public scrutiny, is strongly prodevelopment. Zoning change applications have not met great opposition.

Even here, however, certain key questions remain. Merely wanting development may not produce development, although zoning changes help. There are many other stations competing for business development, as well as many nonstation areas that have good access for large populations (e.g., shopping malls and office complexes off freeway exits). Although there is no indication in the Arlington plan of serious public collaboration with the private sector to facilitate development, actions may speak louder than words. For example, the county subsequently made a major development arrangement with Gulf Land Development at the Courthouse station; as of 1990, several buildings were completed and occupied and the remainder of the development was on schedule.

At the other end of the scale, in Prince George's County, encouraging development around station areas has been a distinctly lower priority for the county than promoting huge, nonstation-area projects like PortAmerica and planning growth around Laurel and Bowie, areas well beyond the reach of Metrorail.

In the plan for College Park station (MNCPPC-PG, 1981), development levels are expected to be rather small. In this official publication the planning agency takes an extremely conservative attitude, arguing that any development initiatives are in the hands of the current owners of undeveloped parcels (ACF and University of Maryland). The report notes that the development of an industrial park, while desirable, would require public support for roadways to connect it to Kenilworth Avenue. The tone of the report is distinctly pessimistic. Perhaps the final statement for the College Park profile report best captures this attitude:

> In order to maximize benefits which Metrorail offers, coordinated development efforts must be employed in concert with the economic and social goals of the area. Access and densities are major issues which must be properly addressed, as well as the buffering of existing neighborhoods from development. Planning priorities, therefore, should be established so that comprehensive and balanced planning will result in the implementation of desired objectives and not in the overburdening of existing facilities or inconveniences to existing residential areas.

If primary concerns are guaranteeing access, "appropriate" densities, and buffered neighborhoods, it is likely that would-be developers of parcels within the quarter-mile radius of the station will be discouraged and seek to locate elsewhere.

In Montgomery County, there is a sophisticated and mixed attitude toward development. The county has enthusiastically supported the wedges and corridors plan for the area, using many tools to channel development to the Rockville Pike/I-270 corridor which abuts the Shady Grove rail line. On the one hand, the planners clearly saw the opportunities for increased commercial and high-density residential development around station areas; on the other hand, some of the stations are sited in relatively well-to-do, established residential areas (e.g., Glenmont and Forest Glen), where the residents prefer less development and wield considerable political influence. Thus, the planners walked a thin line. They carried out a series of public hearings and other public steps to involve local communities as well as prospective developers and current commercial owners. In such station areas as Forest Glen and Glenmont, the planning officials made preservation of the existing residential character of the neighborhood the primary concern (MNCPPC, 1978a, 1978b); at the same time, they designated Silver Spring and Wheaton as areas where development was to be strongly encouraged (MNCPPC, 1975, 1977, 1978d).

Montgomery County's method for judging development possibilities was more developed and a bit more abstract than those of Arlington or Prince George's. A "Development Envelope" was defined and an "Opportunity Analysis" made for a given station area. The envelope was the capacity of an area to accept further development given a set of constraints including federal air pollution requirements and the ability of the current roadways to accommodate projected increases in traffic due to development. This envelope could be expanded by either a relaxation of air quality requirements or an increase in the number of transportation links planned by a developer. The Development Envelope, then, was a passive measure of possibilities. The Opportunity Analysis, an indication of the attractiveness of the area to developers, included an assessment of the amount of buildable but undeveloped land, of the access possibilities for the area, and of the extent of possibly clashing land uses adjacent to each other.

The conclusions of the planners about both the "envelope" and "opportunity" were rather pessimistic for Forest Glen and Glenmont but quite optimistic about the possibilities for Wheaton and Silver Spring. If the planners had been willing to consider supporting the conversion of single-family detached dwellings to commercial areas at the former two station areas, more sanguine commercial development futures might have been forecast for them. Since development pressures are not so strong as to make such a policy a likely outcome in the near future, it is perfectly reasonable for the planners not to consider this approach. For the present, development can occur more easily in areas with large current "opportunities" (like Silver Spring and Wheaton) than in areas where there are significant structural and institutional barriers to development.

## Conclusions

A review of local impact analysis literature demonstrates that the government planning process associated with the development of new rail systems and stations must be far more comprehensive than the narrow engineering studies of the 1950s and early 1960s. The BART Impact Program studies, the surveys by Knight and Trygg, and the extensive literature on business location decision making bring home the fact that development around station areas is not likely to emerge strictly in response to the improved accessibility brought by rapid transit. The web of factors leading to development is complex and hence must be accompanied by complex planning processes. In particular, joint development—the public/private partnership in planning—is needed if the community desires to focus development around station areas.

*Three*

# A Statistical Analysis of Station Areas and Rail Corridors in the Washington, D.C., Region as Centers for Regional Employment and Employment Growth, 1972–80

It is widely believed that subway station areas and the corridors in which they locate eventually must become development centers because their accessibility advantages inevitably draw many firms and government offices to their vicinity. Such location decisions, according to this line of reasoning, in turn create even greater incentives for still other enterprises and activities to come there, in a local multiplier process.

There is merit in this conventional wisdom, since many station areas and rail corridors in Washington, D.C. and other cities have obviously become development centers. There is, however, a distinct countervailing trend. Many station areas and some rail corridors have not developed significantly, nor do they appear to be heading down the development path with any dispatch. There are, after all, important regional forces working against rail-related development effects. The most prominent of these is the steady suburbanization of jobs and residences since the 1960s; the development effects of rail lines tend to be concentrated in areas closest to the downtown area.

For this and other reasons, station area and rail corridor development is neither automatic nor inevitable. Nevertheless, the comparative statistical analyses done in this chapter show that, in the Washington region, areas with rail transit service do generally attract more development than comparable areas without such service.

**Design of the Studies**

Despite much casual discussion of development generated by Washington's Metrorail, there has hitherto been little effort to measure it or to compare the areas affected by the new transit system with other parts of the region. This chapter reports on three studies that grapple with the question of the relative fecundity of areas experiencing the benefits of rapid rail access. The first study compares such impact areas (station areas and rail corridors) with control areas (nonstation areas and areas outside rail corridors, respectively) throughout the region to see whether, and to what extent, the impact areas are development centers relative to the control areas. The second study pairs each rail corridor with a nonrail transportation corridor and compares them in the same fashion. The third study divides the rail corridors into station areas and "in-between" areas without stations to see if, within a transit corridor, the station areas are centers of development relative to the rest of the corridor.

These studies are attempts to answer, in slightly varying ways, the question of whether areas containing rail rapid-transit stations and lines experience higher and faster growing development levels than areas that do not have the benefits of such transportation improvements. The findings of these studies give a strong "yes" answer, although there is considerable unevenness in this effect both across jurisdictions and by type of development. An important aspect of these findings is that in generally conforming to conventional wisdom, they depart somewhat from previous studies (especially from the BART impact study) that found little impact associated with stations.

*Data and Methodology*

To prepare for all three studies, the region is first partitioned into 1,337 traffic zones, each of which is tagged as a station area zone, a rail corridor zone, both, or neither. Any zone within or intersecting a circle with a radius of one quarter-mile around a station is deemed to be a station area zone; if it is crossed by or abuts the rail line, it is considered a rail corridor zone (all station area zones are also rail corridor zones, but not all rail corridor zones are station area zones). Control corridors for the second study are determined in the same way, except that a nonlimited-access highway is used instead of a rail line in determining the zones in the corridor. Corridors of either type are typically two zones in width.

Employment data for 1972, 1976, and 1980 are used to represent development in each zone. In 1972, no rail stations were open; the first few opened in late 1976, and many more were open by 1980. The appropriate data for 1985, by which time most of the lines (except the Green Line) were largely open, were unfortunately not available for this study, so the findings here refer to relatively early effects of the transportation improvements. The 1972–80 comparison is perhaps the best since it conforms most closely to a before-and-after study.

Three variables are used to indicate different ways of looking at development: absolute employment by year, to determine where the greatest amount of development located; absolute change in employment between each of the three pairs of years, to determine where the greatest changes occurred; and percentage change in employment between each of the three pairs of years, to determine where the greatest rate of growth in development occurred. (Methodological issues concerning these variables and the appropriateness of the statistical tests used in the following studies are discussed in Appendix 3.1.)

The tables in Appendix 3.2 and throughout the body of this chapter report the mean value for each group of zones compared in the studies (a variety of jurisdictional disaggregations as well as the region as a whole). It is essential to evaluate the statistical significance of the differences in the means, however, to know if the reported differences can be attributed to the rail impacts or if they are merely chance fluctuations.

The appropriate statistical test is the $t$-test for comparing group means. It takes into account the underlying distribution of the variable (the variance) around the sample's mean, and therefore allows a test of the statistical significance of the differences in the means that appear in the tables in this chapter and in Appendix 3.2. Because of the extreme variability in the values within each group of zones (large variances), these $t$-tests tend to be difficult to pass. Often, the means of an impact/control pair of zone groups appear to be very different but do not test out to be statistically significantly different, and so it is improper to say one mean is greater than the other, despite intuition. When the $t$-tests for differences in means are passed, however, their differences are quite meaningful.

### Expected Results

It is expected that aggregate employment will tend to cluster around station areas and in rail corridors because of their access advantage.

Because of the countereffect of regional suburbanization of employment, such an effect may not be evident for the region as a whole, but for the suburbs, as a whole and taken individually, it is expected to appear in the form of higher levels, larger changes, and larger rates of change in the impact areas in each study.

Not all types of employment are expected to respond equally to the access advantages of the rail improvements. Basic employment, defined here as SIC code 1 (essentially manufacturing activity), is expected to be pulled the least to station areas since such activity needs access to interregional markets that cannot be provided by Metrorail, but that can be provided by the interstate highway system and traditional freight railroad lines. Also, basic industry is not strongly pulled by its interactions with other economic forces in the region; it generally works as the attractor. Government employment (given the preponderant share held by the federal government) should gravitate to station areas because its locations are directly planned with social interests, not private profit, in mind. Thus, minimizing congestion and facilitating worker access to job sites can take on an important role in the location decisions of government facilities (although local government employment location, unlike federal government employment, tends not to be as strongly inclined in this way). Service and wholesale employment is most likely to follow existing centers of activity, and so will tend to follow government facilities. Moreover, service industries require easy access to their clients, which rapid transit can provide; the benefits of agglomeration economies accrue more to such firms than to basic firms. Finally, retail development is likely to follow government and service employment, although it does not benefit quite so much from agglomeration economies (like face-to-face contact with clients and other firms) as does service. Furthermore, retail is pulled ubiquitously, both by residential concentrations and by clusters of firms. Thus, retail employment, like basic employment, may not respond as well as government and service employment to station area and rail corridor location opportunities.

**How to Read This Chapter**

Because of the large number of comparisons carried out here, the reader may wish to proceed to the summaries of the findings that appear at the ends of the reports of each of the three studies, on pages 53, 61, and 69. Conclusions for the entire chapter begin on page 70.

The *t*-tests for the differences between means generated a great many detailed tables. Summary tables and selected detailed tables appear in the text; they are denoted 3.1 to 3.15. The complete set of detailed tables (to which reference is frequently made in the text) appears in Appendix 3.2. Such tables are denoted by the letter A plus a number or number/letter combination. Tables A.1–A.40 are for Study One, Tables A.41A–A.48B are for Study Two, and Tables A.49A–A58B are for Study Three.

Comparisons between means of variables in groups of zones are made throughout the rest of this chapter. In order for the hypothesis that the means are different to be accepted, the very stringent *t*-test described above and in the appendix must be passed. Quite often, the hypothesis that apparently different mean values (say, −20 and 100) actually are different does not pass the test of statistical significance. Unless the test is passed, the mean values must be reported as indistinguishable from each other. At times, this can create apparently inconsistent results. For instance, there may be a statistically significant higher value in the rate of change of aggregate employment in an impact area compared to its control for a particular comparison, but none of the rates of change in the *components* of employment (basic, government, wholesale and services, and retail) turns out to be significantly different from their controls. An inspection of the tables would show in such a case that the changes in the components are in fact consistent with the change in their aggregate, but because of the stringency of the test, only the aggregate ones are "different." The reader is urged to study the referenced tables in Appendix 3.2 whenever such an apparent inconsistency is encountered in the text.

## Study One: Geographical Comparisons

Do areas containing rapid-transit stations and corridors (impact areas) experience high levels and fast growth of development compared to other parts of the region? Impact areas are expected to prove to have more employment than control areas, in part because of the effect of the rail lines but also in part because much of the rail system was planned to serve areas with significant current or expected economic activity. It is also expected that impact areas grow more (and at a more rapid pace) than nonimpact areas largely because of the effect of Metrorail. These expectations are based on the new (and prospective) accessibility advantages offered by the corridors and stations, which should attract businessmen and also interest government planners in maximizing the economic advantages of such a large public investment as Metrorail by locating within easy access of its stations.

To test these hypotheses, station area zones are compared to nonstation area zones, and rail corridor zones are compared to zones outside rail corridors, using the statistical $t$-test noted above. Aggregate employment is studied first, and each of four subcategories of employment (basic, government, service and wholesale, and retail) is then studied separately. This $t$-test procedure is carried out first for all zones in the region, then for all zones in the inner suburbs (all regional jurisdictions excluding Loudon and Prince William Counties and the District of Columbia), and finally for each jurisdiction. Results are given in summary (with selected detail) here, and in full in Tables A.1–A.40 in Appendix 3.2. Note that these comparisons use all zones except some with low base-year employment levels (see Appendix 3.2) in each geographical area under consideration.

The general findings, presented in Tables 3.1–3.6, are that station areas and corridors do tend to have greater levels and rates of growth of employment than other areas in the region. This is especially true for the inner suburbs, taken as a whole, and for government and service employment.

## The Region

In the region as a whole, the average rail corridor zone contained twice as many jobs as the average zone not in a rail corridor in 1972, 1976, and 1980 (see Tables 3.7, 3.8, and A.1–A.5). Similarly, station area zones had roughly two and a half times as many jobs as nonstation area zones. While these ratios (based on significant underlying differences between the two categories of zones) show the importance of rail corridors and station areas in the region's economy, this was already the case in 1972, so the higher employment levels could merely reflect successful planning of the rail lines to serve areas of major economic activity rather than any impact induced by accessibility advantages bestowed by Metrorail.

More indicative of an autonomous Metrorail impact is the 5 : 2 ratio

Table 3.1

**Comparison of Employment, Changes in Employment, and Rates of Change in Employment: Rail Corridor/Noncorridor and Station Areas/Nonstation Areas, Selected Years, Periods, and Geographical Divisions**

| | Total | | Basic | | Government | | Service | | Retail | |
|---|---|---|---|---|---|---|---|---|---|---|
| | Rail | Station | Rail | Station | Rail | Station | Rail | Station | Rail | Station |
| *Region* | | | | | | | | | | |
| Level 1980 | + | + | + | + | | | + | + | | + |
| Change 1972–80 | | + | | | | + | | + | | |
| Rate of change 1972–80 | | | | | | | | | | |
| *Inner suburbs* | | | | | | | | | | |
| Level 1980 | + | + | + | + | + | + | + | + | | + |
| Change 1972–80 | + | + | | | | | + | + | | + |
| Rate of change 1972–80 | | + | | | | | | | | |
| *District of Columbia* | | | | | | | | | | |
| Level 1980 | + | | | + | + | + | | + | | + |
| Change 1972–80 | | | | | | | | + | | |
| Rate of change 1972–80 | | | | | | | | | | |
| *Montgomery County* | | | | | | | | | | |
| Level 1980 | + | + | + | + | | | + | + | + | + |
| Change 1972–80 | + | + | | | | | + | + | + | + |
| Rate of change 1972–80 | + | | | | | | | | | |
| *Prince George's County* | | | | | | | | | | |
| Level 1980 | | | | | | + | | | | |
| Change 1972–80 | | | | | | | | | | |
| Rate of change 1972–80 | | | + | | | | | | | |
| *Arlington County* | | | | | | | | | | |
| Level 1980 | + | + | | + | + | + | | + | + | + |
| Change 1972–80 | | | | | | | | + | | |
| Rate of change 1972–80 | | | | | | | | | | |
| *Alexandria* | | | | | | | | | | |
| Level 1980 | | | | | | | − | | | |
| Change 1972–80 | | | | | | | − | − | − | |
| Rate of change 1972–80 | | | | | | | | | | |
| *Fairfax County* | | | | | | | | | | |
| Level 1980 | | | | | | − | | | − | + |
| Change 1972–80 | | | | | | | | − | − | |
| Rate of change 1972–80 | | | | | | | | | | |

+ = impact area is greater. − = control area is greater. No entry = values are indistinguishable.

Table 3.2

**Region and Inner Suburbs—Comparison of Employment, Changes in Employment, and Rates of Change in Employment: Rail Corridor/Noncorridor and Station Areas/Nonstation Areas, Selected Years and Periods**

| | Total | | Basic | | Government | | Service | | Retail | |
|---|---|---|---|---|---|---|---|---|---|---|
| | Rail | Station | Rail | Station | Rail | Station | Rail | Station | Rail | Station |
| *Region* | | | | | | | | | | |
| Level | | | | | | | | | | |
| 1972 | + | + | + | + | | + | | + | | + |
| 1976 | + | + | + | + | | + | + | + | | + |
| 1980 | + | + | + | + | | | + | + | | + |
| Change | | | | | | | | | | |
| 1972–76 | | + | | + | | | | + | | |
| 1976–80 | | | − | + | | + | | + | | |
| 1972–80 | | | − | − | | | | | | |
| Rate of change | | | | | | | | | | |
| 1972–76 | | + | − | | | + | − | + | − | |
| 1976–80 | | + | | | | + | | | | |
| 1972–80 | | + | | | | | | | | − |
| *Inner suburbs* | | | | | | | | | | |
| Level | | | | | | | | | | |
| 1972 | + | + | + | + | + | + | + | + | | + |
| 1976 | + | + | + | + | + | + | + | + | | + |
| 1980 | + | + | + | + | + | + | + | + | | + |
| Change | | | | | | | | | | |
| 1972–76 | + | + | + | + | | | + | + | | |
| 1976–80 | | | + | + | | | | + | | + |
| 1972–80 | | | − | + | | | | | | |
| Rate of change | | | | | | | | | | |
| 1972–76 | + | + | − | | + | | + | + | | |
| 1976–80 | | + | | − | | | | | | |
| 1972–80 | | + | | | | | | + | − | + |

+ = impact area is larger.
− = control area is larger.
No entry = values are indistinguishable.

Table 3.3

**District of Columbia—Comparison of Employment, Changes in Employment, and Rates of Change in Employment: Rail Corridor/Noncorridor and Station Areas/Nonstation Areas, Selected Years and Periods**

| | | Employment type | | | | | | | | | |
| | | Total | | Basic | | Govern-ment | | Service | | Retail | |
| | | Rail | Station | Rail | Station | Rail | Station | Rail | Station | Rail | Station |
|---|---|---|---|---|---|---|---|---|---|---|---|
| Level | 1972 | | | | + | + | + | | + | | + |
| | 1976 | + | | | + | + | + | | + | | + |
| | 1980 | + | | | + | + | + | | + | | + |
| Change | 1972–76 | | | | | | | | | | |
| | 1976–80 | | | | | | | | + | | |
| | 1972–80 | | | | | | | | + | | |
| Rate of change | 1972–76 | | | | | | | | | + | + |
| | 1976–80 | | | | | | | | | | |
| | 1972–80 | | | | | | | | | | |

+ = impact area is larger.
No entry = values are indistinguishable.

of absolute growth in jobs from 1972–80 in station areas compared to nonstation areas, and a lower but still significant ratio of rail corridor zones to zones outside rail corridors. Impact areas maintained their employment advantage during the early years of Metrorail operation, although they did not grow at a faster pace than the rest of the region (growth was between 17 and 20 percent for the 1972–80 period for all categories). Thus, for the region as a whole, it can be said that the persistent differences in employment levels and changes favoring the impact areas compared to their controls suggest that these areas have been quite important areas of development, but that Metrorail had not, as of 1980, had any further centralizing impact.

Turning to the components of aggregate employment, basic (about 10 percent of aggregate) and service (between 25 percent and 33 percent of aggregate) employment levels proved to be higher in rail corri-

Table 3.4

**Montgomery and Prince George's Counties—Comparison of Employment, Changes in Employment, and Rates of Change in Employment: Rail Corridor/Noncorridor and Station Areas/Nonstation Areas, Selected Years and Periods**

| | | Total | | Basic | | Government | | Service | | Retail | |
|---|---|---|---|---|---|---|---|---|---|---|---|
| | | Rail | Station | Rail | Station | Rail | Station | Rail | Station | Rail | Station |
| **Montgomery County** | | | | | | | | | | | |
| Level | 1972 | + | + | + | + | | | + | + | + | + |
| | 1976 | + | | + | + | + | + | + | + | + | + |
| | 1980 | + | + | + | + | + | + | + | + | + | + |
| Change | 1972–76 | + | + | | + | | | + | + | + | + |
| | 1976–80 | | + | | | + | + | | | | |
| | 1972–80 | + | + | | | | | + | + | + | + |
| Rate of change | 1972–76 | + | + | | | | | | + | | |
| | 1976–80 | | | | | | | | | | |
| | 1972–80 | + | + | | | | | | + | | |
| **Prince George's County** | | | | | | | | | | | |
| Level | 1972 | | | | | | | − | | | |
| | 1976 | | | | | | | | | | |
| | 1980 | | | | | | | | | | |
| Rate of change | 1972–76 | | | − | | | | | | − | |
| | 1976–80 | | | − | − | | − | | | | |
| | 1972–80 | | | | | | | | | | |

+ = impact area is larger.
− = control area is larger.
No entry = values are indistinguishable.
Note: Values are indistinguishable for all comparisons for "Change" for Prince George's County.

dors for all three years studied, but basic employment grew more slowly there than in the zones outside rail corridors during the 1976–80 period. Similarly, retail (between 15 and 25 percent of aggregate) and service employment both grew more slowly in the rail corridors during the earlier period (1972–76), although in the later period (1976–80) and the combined period (1972–80) there were no differences. All four

Table 3.5

**Arlington County and the City of Alexandria—Comparison of Employment, Changes in Employment, and Rates of Change in Employment: Rail Corridor/Noncorridor and Station Areas/Nonstation Areas, Selected Years and Periods**

| | | Total | | Basic | | Government | | Service | | Retail | |
|---|---|---|---|---|---|---|---|---|---|---|---|
| | | Rail | Station | Rail | Station | Rail | Station | Rail | Station | Rail | Station |
| **Arlington County** | | | | | | | | | | | |
| Level | 1972 | + | + | | + | + | + | | + | + | + |
| | 1976 | + | + | + | + | + | + | | + | + | + |
| | 1980 | + | + | + | + | + | + | | + | | + |
| Change | 1972–76 | | | | | | | | | | |
| | 1976–80 | | | | | | | + | + | | |
| | 1972–80 | | | | | | | | + | | |
| Rate of change | 1972–76 | | | | | | | | | | |
| | 1976–80 | | | | | | | | | − | |
| | 1972–80 | | + | | | | | | | | |
| **Alexandria** | | | | | | | | | | | |
| Level | 1972 | | | + | | | | − | | | |
| | 1976 | | | | | | | − | − | − | |
| | 1980 | | | | | | | − | − | | |
| Change | 1972–76 | | | − | | | | − | − | − | |
| | 1976–80 | | | | | | | | | | |
| | 1972–80 | | | | | | | − | − | | |
| Rate of change | 1972–76 | − | − | − | | | | | | | |
| | 1976–80 | | + | | | | | | | | |
| | 1972–80 | | | | | | | | | | |

+ = impact area is larger.
− = control area is larger.
No entry = values are indistinguishable.

categories of employment were larger in the station areas than in non-station areas in the region as a whole; changes in basic (1972–76), government (1972–76 and 1972–80), and service (all periods) employment were also greater in the station areas, while basic employment

Table 3.6

**Fairfax County—Comparison of Employment, Changes in Employment, and Rates of Change in Employment: Rail Corridor/Noncorridor and Station Areas/Nonstation Areas, Selected Years and Periods**

| | | Employment type | | | | | | | | | |
|---|---|---|---|---|---|---|---|---|---|---|---|
| | | Total | | Basic | | Govern-ment | | Service | | Retail | |
| | | Rail | Station | Rail | Station | Rail | Station | Rail | Station | Rail | Station |
| Level | 1972 | | | | | − | | − | − | | |
| | 1976 | | | | | − | | | − | | |
| | 1980 | | | | | − | | | − | | |
| Change | 1972–76 | | | | | | | | − | | |
| | 1976–80 | | | | | | | | | | |
| | 1972–80 | | | | | | | | | − | + |
| Rate of change | 1972–76 | | | | | | | | − | | |
| | 1976–80 | | | | | | | | − | | |
| | 1972–80 | | | | | | | | − | | |

+ = impact area is larger.
− = control area is larger.
No entry = values are indistinguishable.

changes (1976–80) were greater in nonstation areas. Few of these findings translated into differences in rates of change, with the exceptions that government and service employment in station areas outpaced that outside station areas in the early period (1972–76), while basic and retail employment grew faster outside station areas in the later period (1976–80).

## *The Inner Suburbs*

The inner suburbs provide an excellent sample of zones to study for Metrorail impacts. They are much more similar to each other than those in the full region, and there are fewer non-Metrorail factors to distort the comparison. Dropping the District of Columbia's zones from the sample is especially helpful since it greatly reduces the con-

Table 3.7

**Comparison of Employment Levels and Changes:
Rail Corridors versus Areas outside Rail Corridors
and Station Areas versus Nonstation Areas—Regional
Total Employment, Mean Zonal Values**

|  | Rail corridors | Areas outside rail corridors | Station areas | Nonstation areas |
|---|---|---|---|---|
| **Employment levels** | | | | |
| 1972 | 2,119‡ | 1,007 | 2,472‡ | 1,006 |
| 1976 | 2,345‡ | 1,094 | 2,793‡ | 1,073 |
| 1980 | 2,489‡ | 1,206 | 2,968‡ | 1,176 |
| **Employment changes** | | | | |
| 1972–76 | 226† | 87 | 321‡ | 67 |
| 1976–80 | 143 | 112 | 175‡ | 31 |
| 1972–80 | 369‡ | 199 | 496‡ | 171 |
| **Percentage changes in employment** | | | | |
| 1972–76 | 10.7 | 8.6 | 13.0 | 6.7 |
| 1976–80 | 6.1 | 10.2 | 6.3 | 9.6 |
| 1972–80 | 17.3 | 19.7 | 20.1 | 17.0 |

† Difference between means is significant at 0.10 level, two-tailed $t$-test.
‡ Difference between means is significant at 0.05 level, two-tailed $t$-test.

flation of two processes, that is, the District's loss of share of regional jobs due to suburbanization and the impact of Metrorail in fostering job growth. The District's growth rate in jobs, although positive, is far below that of the suburban areas, and District zones tend to grow much less rapidly than suburban zones, whether they are influenced by Metrorail or not. Combining District and suburban zones in a comparison of impact and control zones (as was done in the regional analysis above) consequently reduces the capability of $t$-tests to capture only the influence of Metrorail on development, while testing the suburban zones separately somewhat controls for the trend toward suburbanization of jobs. It is also reasonable to exclude from this sample the zones of Prince William and Loudoun Counties (the outer suburbs) since these jurisdictions have no rail lines and therefore are not greatly affected one way or another by Metrorail, yet are growing rather rapidly

Table 3.8

**Comparison of Employment Levels and Changes:
Rail Corridors versus Areas outside Rail Corridors
and Station Areas versus Nonstation Areas—Regional
Government Employment, Mean Zonal Values**

|  | Rail corridors | Areas outside rail corridors | Station areas | Nonstation areas |
|---|---|---|---|---|
| **Employment levels** | | | | |
| 1972 | 966‡ | 361 | 1,181‡ | 352 |
| 1976 | 1,060‡ | 361 | 1,311‡ | 350 |
| 1980 | 1,061‡ | 362 | 1,312‡ | 350 |
| **Employment changes** | | | | |
| 1972–76 | 95† | 0 | 130‡ | −2 |
| 1976–80 | 0 | 1 | 1 | 1 |
| 1972–80 | 95 | 1 | 131‡ | −1 |
| **Percentage changes in employment** | | | | |
| 1972–76 | 9.8 | −0.1 | 11.0‡ | −0.6 |
| 1976–80 | 0.0 | 0.3 | 0.1 | 0.2 |
| 1972–80 | 9.8 | 0.3 | 11.1† | −0.4 |

† Difference between means is significant at 0.10 level, two-tailed *t*-test.
‡ Difference between means is significant at 0.05 level, two-tailed *t*-test.

(from typically low base levels, adding further to the distortions in the sample) as suburbanization proceeds into this new area.

## *The Findings*

The effects of Metrorail appear pronounced in the inner suburban sample, perhaps due to improved comparability as noted above. The average zone in a rail corridor had more aggregate basic, government, and service employment than the average zone outside such corridors for all three years of the study (see Tables 3.2, 3.9, and A.6–A.10). Similarly, the changes in total employment (1972–76 and 1972–80 periods) and service employment (1972–80) favored rail corridors, as expected. The change in basic employment was larger in the rail corridors in 1972–76 but smaller in the ensuing four-year period, leading to no difference in this variable over the entire period (1972–80). The rates

Table 3.9

**Comparison of Employment Levels and Changes:**
**Rail Corridors versus Areas outside Rail Corridors**
**and Station Areas versus Nonstation Areas—Inner Suburban**
**Total Employment, Mean Zonal Values**

| | Rail corridors | Areas outside rail corridors | Station areas | Nonstation areas |
|---|---|---|---|---|
| Employment levels | | | | |
| 1972 | 1,633‡ | 973 | 1,921‡ | 982 |
| 1976 | 1,901‡ | 1,048 | 2,384‡ | 1,035 |
| 1980 | 2,085‡ | 1,174 | 2,643‡ | 1,152 |
| Employment changes | | | | |
| 1972–76 | 268 | 75 | 463‡ | 54 |
| 1976–80 | 184 | 126 | 259 | 116 |
| 1972–80 | 452† | 202 | 722‡ | 170 |
| Percentage changes in employment | | | | |
| 1972–76 | 16.4 | 7.7 | 24.1† | 5.5 |
| 1976–80 | 9.7 | 12.1 | 10.9 | 11.2 |
| 1972–80 | 27.6 | 20.7 | 37.6† | 17.3 |

† Difference between means is significant at 0.10 level, two-tailed $t$-test.
‡ Difference between means is significant at 0.05 level, two-tailed $t$-test.

of change for employment categories were not different from each other for any of the time periods except for retail and basic in the 1972–76 period, when they both favored areas outside rail corridors in line with the expectations that these two components of employment would not be strongly drawn to rail lines.

If we turn to the station areas versus nonstation areas, an even stronger picture of development in Metrorail impact areas emerges. All employment levels for all five categories of employment for all three years of interest were higher in station areas than in nonstation areas. The change in aggregate employment was higher there as well for the 1972–80 and 1972–76 periods. The station areas experienced greater changes in the level of service employment in all three periods of study, in retail employment (1972–76 and 1972–80) and in the level of basic employment (1972–76). In the crucial overall employment growth rate category, the station areas exceeded their opposite numbers in both the 1972–76 and 1972–80 periods; service employment grew faster as well in the 1972–80 period. Also, as anticipated, the growth rate in basic industry was less in the station areas than in nonstation areas.

## The Individual Jurisdictions

The various suburban jurisdictions differ considerably not only from the District but also from each other. Arlington County, with substantial high-density residential and commercial areas, is very much a part of the core of the region although much of it has more conventional suburban densities. Alexandria, confined by water and rail and very close to the District of Columbia, shares the core status, with a thriving central business district of its own. The other three jurisdictions are more traditional suburbs, each with certain unique features. Growth sprawls unbridled throughout Fairfax County, while Montgomery County, with a strong tradition of planning, channels development into specific corridors; both are rapidly gaining share of regional employment. Prince George's, with a blue-collar reputation (in contrast to Fairfax and Montgomery) and moreover behind in receiving Metrorail service (its two long segments of the Green Line will not open for years, although its operating New Carrollton line has been of great interest because of its close proximity to both highways and interstate rail), is a late bloomer in terms of development. In short, although the inner-suburb sample above comes much closer to capturing differences due only to rail impacts, there still remains a great deal of variation by jurisdiction that justifies separate comparisons of the impact and control zones within each suburban jurisdiction as well as those in the District.

### The District of Columbia

The District of Columbia has experienced a steady erosion of its regional employment share, and its Metrorail stations have often been seen as mechanisms to hold on to employment rather than to foster new development. There have nevertheless been many large redevelopment projects in the downtown areas above station sites. A review of the D.C. results suggests slow growth in both impact and control areas (see Tables 3.3 and A.11–A.15).

Table 3.10

**Comparison of Employment Levels and Changes:**
**Rail Corridors versus Areas outside Rail Corridors and**
**Station Areas versus Nonstation Areas—Montgomery County**
**Total Employment, Mean Zonal Values**

|  | Rail corridors | Areas outside rail corridors | Station areas | Nonstation areas |
|---|---|---|---|---|
| Employment levels |  |  |  |  |
| 1972 | 1,803‡ | 777 | 2,084‡ | 859 |
| 1976 | 2,438‡ | 749 | 3,383‡ | 786 |
| 1980 | 2,767‡ | 863 | 3,722‡ | 927 |
| Employment changes |  |  |  |  |
| 1972–76 | 635‡ | − 28 | 1,299‡ | − 74 |
| 1976–80 | 329‡ | 114 | 338† | 141 |
| 1972–80 | 964‡ | 86 | 1,638‡ | 68 |
| Percentage changes in employment |  |  |  |  |
| 1972–76 | 35.2‡ | −3.7 | 62.4‡ | −8.6 |
| 1976–80 | 13.5 | 15.2 | 10.0 | 18.0 |
| 1972–80 | 53.5‡ | 11.0 | 78.6‡ | 7.9 |

† Difference between means is significant at 0.10 level, two-tailed $t$-test.
‡ Difference between means is significant at 0.05 level, two-tailed $t$-test.

Total employment is higher (more than twice as large) in rail lines (1976, 1980) and station areas (all years) than elsewhere in the District, but both the changes and rates of change in total employment are indistinguishable in the two comparisons. At the disaggregated level, service employment grew more in station areas than outside them (1972–80), but at indistinguishable rates. Retail employment fell less swiftly in both rail corridors and station areas compared to their opposite categories (1976–80). The accessibility advantages of the rail stations may therefore have slowed the departure of retail economic activity from the District.

*Montgomery County*

Montgomery County shows the most extensive impacts from Metrorail of all the jurisdictions (see Tables 3.4, 3.10, 3.11, and A.16–A.20). All

Table 3.11

**Comparison of Employment Levels and Changes:**
**Rail Corridors versus Areas outside Rail Corridors and**
**Station Areas versus Nonstation Areas—Montgomery County**
**Service Employment, Mean Zonal Values**

|  | Rail corridors | Areas outside rail corridors | Station areas | Nonstation areas |
|---|---|---|---|---|
| Employment levels | | | | |
| 1972 | 614‡ | 250 | 633‡ | 296 |
| 1976 | 848‡ | 277 | 1,134‡ | 296 |
| 1980 | 962‡ | 321 | 1,270‡ | 345 |
| Employment changes | | | | |
| 1972–76 | 234† | 26 | 502‡ | 0 |
| 1976–80 | 114 | 44 | 136 | 49 |
| 1972–80 | 348‡ | 71 | 637‡ | 49 |
| Percentage changes in employment | | | | |
| 1972–76 | 38.1 | 10.6 | 79.3‡ | 0.1 |
| 1976–80 | 13.5 | 15.9 | 11.9 | 16.6 |
| 1972–80 | 56.7 | 28.2 | 100.7† | 16.7 |

† Difference between means is significant at 0.10 level, two-tailed $t$-test.
‡ Difference between means is significant at 0.05 level, two-tailed $t$-test.

employment types in all years were larger in zones in rail corridors than in zones outside the corridors (except for government employment in 1972). Similarly, the changes in aggregate (1972–76 and 1972–80), government (all periods), service (1972–80), and retail employment (1972–76 and 1972–80) favored rail corridors. Growth rates in total employment were greater in the rail corridors (1972–76 and 1972–80) than outside them, but apparently similar trends in the components of employment turned out not to be statistically significant.

The station area differences were more pronounced. The comparison of employment levels for all three years duplicated the rail corridor comparison above. The changes in total employment favored the station areas for all three periods of analysis. Employment changes were larger in station areas for basic (1972–76), government (all periods), service (1972–76 and 1972–80), and retail (1972–76 and 1972–80). The growth rates in station areas were larger than in areas outside them for aggregate employment (1972–76 and 1972–80), as in the rail corridor comparison above, and (unlike the corridor comparison) the growth rate in service employment was greater in the 1972–76 and 1972–80 periods as well. Consistent with expectations, basic employment grew more slowly in the station areas than outside them.

*Prince George's County*

Most stations planned in Prince George's County have not opened, and current construction schedules indicate that this will remain the case for some years. The New Carrollton line and the very short Addison Road line are open, but none of the Green Line (Branch Avenue and Greenbelt) stations are. This fact may well explain the infrequency of significant differences in impact and control areas in the county, since zones in station areas and rail corridors as yet unopened were tagged as impact areas. More intense development effects may appear a few years after the opening of the Green Line.

Even with this caveat, there are instances where the station areas and rail corridors seem to have experienced some effect from Metrorail (see Tables 3.4 and A.21–A.25). Station areas grew faster in aggregate employment and more in government employment than their controls during 1972–76, but not thereafter. During the early period both basic and government employment grew more inside the rail corridors than outside them, and the latter grew faster as well. Service employment was at higher levels outside the rail corridor zones in 1972 and 1976, but there was no difference in service employment levels in station area or rail corridor zones by 1980. The station areas did grow more in service employment in 1972–80 than nonstation areas, but this difference did not translate into a faster rate of growth. Retail employment grew at a faster rate in 1972–76 outside the rail corridor than inside, but no differences in rates were confirmed for other periods.

*Arlington County*

Arlington County bears some resemblance to the District of Columbia in that it contains a concentration of government workers and has been losing share of regional employment. This relative stagnation contributes to the infrequency of findings of differences within the county between impact and nonimpact areas (see Tables 3.5 and A.26–A.30).

Total employment was over three times larger in rail corridors and over four times larger in station areas than in their respective control areas for all years of the study. Similarly, basic employment (1980), service employment (all years), and retail employment (1976) are larger in the rail corridors than outside them. Station areas show a more pronounced pattern: all four components of employment for all three years are larger there than in nonstation areas.

Basic employment grew more in rail corridors in 1972–80 than in control areas, while retail grew faster outside the corridor in 1976–80. All these changes were very minor in absolute terms, however. In the largest components, government and service, no differences between rail corridors and their control areas appeared. However, the absolute changes in station areas exceeded those outside station areas by about ten to one in 1972–80; while this large difference did not translate into a significantly larger rate of change in station areas, its effect was quite physically visible.

*Alexandria*

Stations opened later in Alexandria than in some other suburban jurisdictions, and little development near Metrorail stations has occurred so far. Some development has begun near the King Street station and recently major plans for the Eisenhower Avenue station area have been announced. Significant changes may lie ahead for the Alexandria station areas, but few differences in impact and control areas emerged in the time period studied here (see Tables 3.5 and A.31–A.35).

Employment levels were, in the aggregate, quite similar for impact and control areas, although service employment was consistently higher outside the corridors, and government employment was consistently higher inside the corridors. Retail also was larger outside the corridors for 1976.

In the rail corridors, aggregate employment grew faster outside the prospective rail corridors in 1972–76, but no statistical difference could be detected for later periods. In this same period (1972–76), basic employment grew faster outside the corridors (in fact declining inside the corridors) and both service and retail employment grew more outside the corridors. Retail also grew faster outside the corridor during the 1972–80 period.

The station area comparisons revealed similar relations between impact and control areas. In aggregate employment, the nonstation areas grew faster first (1972–76) but the station areas grew faster later (1976–80). Government employment, which was over three times larger in station areas compared to nonstation areas in 1980, grew faster in the station areas from 1976 to 1980 (in fact, government employment fell in the nonstation areas during that period). Service employment did slightly better in the nonstation areas than in the station areas, growing more in 1972–76 and reaching a significantly higher level in 1976.

*Fairfax County*

Development in Fairfax County is booming. It would be difficult indeed for station areas to be growing faster than the rest of this fast-developing county. Also, serious planning for these station areas has been comparatively recent; plans for Vienna and Dunn Loring were announced only in the late 1980s. A sparse Metrorail impact is therefore not surprising (see Tables 3.6 and A.36–A.40).

Indeed, few differences appeared. In the corridors there was faster growth in service employment in 1972–80 and in retail employment in 1972–76. The station areas experienced faster growth in service employment in 1972–80 and in retail employment in 1972–76 and 1972–80 than did nonstation areas.

**Summary of Study One**

Of all the suburban jurisdictions, Montgomery County alone demonstrates a clear, consistent pattern of Metrorail-related focused growth. Data for the other four counties indicate irregular but generally positive effects of Metrorail on their development patterns. In Prince George's, more growth in government and service employment has occurred in station areas than in nonstation areas; in Arlington, there is a remarkable concentration of employment in station areas (with growth in service employment exceeding that outside the station areas); in Alexandria, government employment is growing faster in the station areas than in the rest of the jurisdiction; and in Fairfax, a significantly higher rate of growth of service employment in station areas relative to their controls has emerged in the most recent period. These findings, combined with the general findings for the inner suburbs, suggest that the inner suburbs will continue to sustain major growth and development effects from Metrorail around their station areas.

## Study Two: Rail and Control Line Comparisons

In the first study, zones deemed large enough for analysis were used exhaustively; each and every such zone fell into either an impact or a control group. In effect, the impact zones in each geographical area studied were compared with all the other zones in that area. This approach proved fruitful, but carried costs as well. Many regional variables that might have influenced the results were not reflected in the simple *t*-test procedure, and there were many inconclusive findings where the null hypothesis of no Metrorail-related effect could not be rejected.

The second study took another approach: the control areas consisted of zones selected to correspond as much as possible to those in the impact areas except for the presence of rail service. While such control areas can never be perfect, they can in principle limit the effects of non-Metrorail factors.

It is expected that comparisons of rail corridor/control corridor pairs will show that employment levels and rates of growth are generally larger in the rail corridors than in the control corridors, reinforcing the findings from Study One. The findings generally support this expectation.

### *Methodology*

Control areas were selected in the five inner suburban jurisdictions to match the segments of Metrorail with termini at Shady Grove, Glenmont, Greenbelt, New Carrollton, and Vienna. The control areas were sections of busy, nonlimited-access highways that did not coincide with the rail lines. Rail and control segments were matched by suburban jurisdiction, so that the Vienna rail line and its controls were divided into an Arlington portion and a Fairfax portion. Zones that touch or are crossed by the control highway are considered the set of control zones for that particular rail line, while the zones adjacent to or crossed by the rail line constitute the set of impact zones.

The unbuilt Greenbelt line was included since it will not open before the mid-1990s and therefore should not show any Metrorail-related effect between 1972 and 1980. It functions as a control of the overall experiment.

Two-tailed *t*-tests were performed to test hypotheses of differences in means for the variables representing levels, changes, and rates of change in employment (the same variables as those used in Study One) for (1) all zones in rail lines compared to all zones in control corridors; (2) all zones in rail lines compared to all zones in control corridors excluding rail and control zones in Fairfax County; and (3) zones in each rail line separately compared to those in the corresponding control corridor. The first experiment maximizes the available information while allowing uncontrolled non-Metrorail-related jurisdictional differences to enter the comparison. The second experiment reduces this error by omitting the one rail/control combination that seems most anomalous. The third set of experiments provides the most precise comparisons of rail and control areas that is possible in this method, although each contains a limited number of observations.

Summary findings for all experiments appear in Table 3.12. Detailed results are reported in Tables A.41A to A.48B in Appendix 3.2.

### All Rail and Control Corridors

Aggregate employment in rail corridors significantly exceeded (by 50 percent) that in the controls in 1980. Basic and service employment also were at higher levels there than in the controls in 1980. By contrast, in 1972 (before Metrorail impacts), there were no differences between rail and control areas.

Changes in employment favoring the rail corridors occurred for aggregate and government employment during the 1972–76 and 1972–80 periods, and for retail during the 1976–80 and 1972–80 periods. The rate of change in aggregate employment for rail lines during the 1972–80 period was significantly greater than in the control corridors, in fact almost ten times as great, although there was no statistical significance in the differences between the disaggregated components of employment (see Tables A.41A and A.41B).

### All Corridors except Vienna (Fairfax) and Its Control

Vienna (Fairfax) displays tendencies opposite to those of the rest of the pairs in that the rail line lagged well behind its control (see below). Because of this, the regional study was redone excluding this anoma-

Table 3.12

## Comparison of Employment Levels and Changes:
## Rail Lines and Their Controls, Mean Zonal Values

| | Employment type | | | | |
|---|---|---|---|---|---|
| | Total | Basic | Govern-ment | Service | Retail |
| **All lines** | | | | | |
| Level, 1980 | + | + | | + | |
| Change, 1972–80 | + | | + | | + |
| Rate of change, 1972–80 | + | | | | |
| **All lines except Vienna** | | | | | |
| Level, 1980 | + | + | | + | |
| Change, 1972–80 | + | | + | + | + |
| Rate of change, 1972–80 | + | + | | | + |
| **Shady Grove line** | | | | | |
| Level, 1980 | + | + | + | + | + |
| Change, 1972–80 | + | | + | + | + |
| Rate of change, 1972–80 | + | | | + | + |
| **Glenmont line** | | | | | |
| Level, 1980 | | + | | + | |
| Change, 1972–80 | | | | | + |
| Rate of change, 1972–80 | | | | | |
| **New Carrollton line** | | | | | |
| Level, 1980 | | | – | – | |
| Change, 1972–80 | | | | | + |
| Rate of change, 1972–80 | | | | | |
| **East Falls Church line** | | | | | |
| Level, 1980 | | + | | + | |
| Change, 1972–80 | | | | | |
| Rate of change, 1972–80 | | + | + | | |
| **Vienna line** | | | | | |
| Level, 1980 | | | – | | – |
| Change, 1972–80 | | | | | – |
| Rate of change, 1972–80 | | | | | |
| **Greenbelt line (unopened)** | | | | | |
| Level, 1980 | | + | | | |
| Change, 1972–80 | | | | | |
| Rate of change, 1972–80 | | | | | |

+ = mean of rail line zones is greater than that of control line zones.
– = mean of control line zones is greater than that of rail line zones.
No entry = means are indistinguishable.

Table 3.13

**Employment Levels and Changes: Rail Lines Compared to Control Areas—All Lines except Vienna (Fairfax) and Its Control, Total and Basic Employment, Mean Zonal Values**

| | Total employment | | Basic employment | |
|---|---|---|---|---|
| | Rail corridors | Control corridors | Rail corridors | Control corridors |
| Employment levels | | | | |
| 1972 | 1,405 | 1,164 | 200 | 159 |
| 1976 | 1,747‡ | 1,041 | 223† | 121 |
| 1980 | 1,973‡ | 1,104 | 219† | 111 |
| Employment changes | | | | |
| 1972–76 | 342† | −123 | 23 | −37 |
| 1976–80 | 225 | 63 | − 3 | − 9 |
| 1972–80 | 567‡ | − 60 | 20 | −47 |
| Percentage changes in employment | | | | |
| 1972–76 | 24.4† | −10.6 | 11.7 | −23.8 |
| 1976–80 | 12.9 | 6.0 | − 1.6‡ | − 8.1 |
| 1972–80 | 40.4‡ | − 5.1 | 10.0† | −30.0 |

† Difference between means is significant at 0.10 level, two-tailed $t$-test.
‡ Difference between means is significant at 0.05 level, two-tailed $t$-test.

lous pair. Given the relatively late opening dates of the Fairfax stations, the low level of emphasis on station site development by planners in Fairfax (at least until well into the 1980s, after the periods covered in the present study), and booming land prices (unrelated to a parcel's access to Metrorail) in the county, such an exclusion is reasonable. The results of this experiment are much stronger than those of the previous one (see Table 3.13 and 3.14). Several more comparisons became significant. Aggregate (1976, 1980), basic (1976, 1980), and service (1980) employment were larger in the rail lines compared to their controls, although no employment category was significantly different in the rail and control categories in the 1972 "before" year. The change in aggregate (1972–76 and 1972–80), government (1972–76 and 1972–80), service (1976–80 and 1972–80), and retail (all three periods) was greater in the rail zones than in the controls. These changes translated into rates of increase favoring the rail zones in

Table 3.14

**Employment Levels and Changes: Rail Lines Compared to Control Areas—All Lines except Vienna (Fairfax) and Its Control, Government, Service, and Retail Employment, Mean Zonal Values**

| | Government employment | | Service employment | | Retail employment | |
|---|---|---|---|---|---|---|
| | Rail corridors | Control corridors | Rail corridors | Control corridors | Rail corridors | Control corridors |
| **Employment levels** | | | | | | |
| 1972 | 436 | 401 | 431 | 289 | 337 | 315 |
| 1976 | 545 | 278 | 569 | 352 | 409 | 288 |
| 1980 | 621 | 373 | 683‡ | 351 | 448 | 268 |
| **Employment changes** | | | | | | |
| 1972–76 | 109† | −122 | 138 | 63 | 71† | − 26 |
| 1976–80 | 76 | 94 | 114‡ | −1 | 339† | − 20 |
| 1972–80 | 185† | − 27 | 252† | 62 | 110‡ | − 46 |
| **Percentage changes in employment** | | | | | | |
| 1972–76 | 25.2 | −30.5 | 32.0 | 22.0 | 21.1 | −8.4 |
| 1976–80 | 13.9 | 34.0 | 20.0 | − 0.5 | 9.5 | −7.0 |
| 1972–80 | 42.6 | − 6.8 | 58.4 | 21.4 | 32.6† | −14.9 |

† Difference between means is significant at 0.10 level, two-tailed $t$-test.
‡ Difference between means is significant at 0.05 level, two-tailed $t$-test.

aggregate (1972–76, 1972–80), basic (1976–80, in which the rail zones lost employment at a lower rate than the controls), and retail (1972–80) employment categories. These findings strongly support the notion of a rail impact, especially since the 1972 levels are indistinguishable in all comparisons. While it is possible that other things contributed to the differential development rates, it is hard not to point to Metrorail as the primary cause.

## Montgomery County Corridors

The Montgomery County lines behaved differently from each other. Shady Grove showed decisive development relative to its control while Glenmont was not greatly different from its control.

*The Shady Grove Line*

The Shady Grove line was larger in all employment categories in all years (except for retail, which was indistinguishable from its control in 1972 and 1976). Its changes in employment also were greater than its controls' (see Tables A.43A and A.43B). Growth in aggregate employment (all periods), government employment (1976–80 and 1972–80), service employment (1976–80 and 1972–80), and retail employment (1972–80) all exceeded changes in the control corridors, where employment levels fell steadily in most categories over the relevant time period. The rail corridor rates of growth also exceeded those in the control corridor for aggregate (1972–76 and 1972–80), service (1972–76 and 1972–80), and retail (1972–76 and 1972–80) employment categories. The 50 percent gain in aggregate employment per zone (from 2,000 in 1972 to 3,000 in 1980) is the largest gain per zone on top of the highest level of aggregate employment per zone for any rail or control corridor in this study.

*The Glenmont Line*

There were many fewer differences attributable to Metrorail in the Glenmont line. Basic employment on the rail line was larger than that on its control in 1972 and 1980, but accounted for less than 20 percent of employment on the line and control. Service employment on the Glenmont line was greater than on its control in 1980 by a factor of four as well. Aggregate (1976–80) and retail (1976–80 and 1972–80) employment growth on the line exceeded the control's, which in fact were negative. However, only in basic employment did Glenmont's rate of growth exceed that of its control in a statistically significant way.

**Prince George's County Corridors**

Two lines were studied for Prince George's—New Carrollton and Greenbelt. The latter is not scheduled to open until the 1990s, although it traverses rapidly developing communities. The former is located in a largely industrial area that suffers from the many disamenities associated with industrial activity. Despite these surrounding conditions, the open line did better in development terms than the prospective line.

*The New Carrollton Line*

Although the New Carrollton line's control had roughly four times the level of government and service employment as the rail line over the periods studied, aggregate employment on the line nevertheless increased at a greater rate than in the control area over the eight years of interest (from 48 percent as much aggregate employment as the control to 61 percent as much). It gained significantly more retail employment in 1972–80, and had higher rates of growth in aggregate (1972–80), basic (1972–80, during which time it declined at a less rapid pace than its control), and retail (1972–80). (See Tables A.45A and A.45B.)

*The Greenbelt Line*

The Greenbelt line differed little from its control (see Tables A.46A and A.46B). This result was expected, since the line will not open until the 1990s and it is therefore unlikely that anticipation of Metrorail would have been much of a factor by 1980. There were few differences in employment levels, although the Greenbelt rail zones did exceed their controls in every year for basic employment and in 1972 for government employment, and also lost less retail employment per zone from 1976 to 1980. Their mean rates of growth in the basic (1976–80) and retail (1976–80) employment categories were greater than those of the control, but the reverse was true in retail for 1972–76.

**Arlington County Orange Line Corridors**

The Arlington line (East Falls Church to Rosslyn) began in 1972 at a level of basic employment indistinguishable from that of its control, but exceeded it threefold in 1976 and sevenfold in 1980 (see Tables A.47A and A.47B). Its 9 percent growth rate from 1972 to 1980 far exceeded the 76 percent decline in basic employment in the control area. In government employment, the Arlington line grew faster in 1972–76 and declined slower in 1972–80 than did its control area. Finally, in service employment it grew faster in 1976–80 than its control, reaching a level roughly two and a half times that of the control. Nevertheless, there were no statistically significant differences between the levels, changes, and rates of change in aggregate employment of the line and of its control, limiting the importance of the findings in basic, government, and service employment.

### Fairfax County Orange Line Corridors

The only significant finding for the Fairfax line was that retail employment grew more slowly there than in the control corridor in the 1976–80 period (see Tables A.48A and A.48B). The findings for Fairfax County fit the general trends discussed earlier, that is, a relative neglect of station area development within the county as a whole, at least up to the early 1980s. The control is, in most categories of employment, larger than the line for most years. Also, the control's growth in retail employment was larger than that in the rail line (1972–1976, 1972–1980), while its rate of decline was much less during the 1976–80 period than the rail line's. The rail lines in Fairfax will certainly experience growth in the coming period, however; the aggregate employment in the corridors almost doubled in the 1972–80 period. Given the overall rapid growth rates in Fairfax County (as reflected in the control area), such a sharp rise is not especially notable there.

### Summary of Study Two

The rail lines generally had a higher level and/or a faster pace of development than the control areas, with the exception of the Orange Line in Fairfax, consistent with the expectation that rail lines attract development more than their controls. This was especially evident when all lines were taken together (with or without the Fairfax pair).

The findings with regard to employment sectors are more mixed. The expectation was that basic activity would not respond greatly to rail, but in fact this type of employment turned out to be larger and/or growing faster in rail lines than in controls in the merged experiments, and in all of the individual cases except Fairfax. The zonal average of basic employment in the rail lines rarely went over two hundred employees, and sometimes was very small, allowing only restrained conclusions about the importance of basic employment in the development process in rail corridors despite the statistical significance of these findings.

Government employment did not perform as strongly as expected. In the merged experiments, it grew more in the lines than in the controls, but not at a faster rate. The same result held true for the Shady Grove line. In Arlington it grew faster and declined slower in the line than in the control, but in New Carrollton, the control area actually declined significantly less than the rail line, while in Glenmont, Greenbelt, and Fairfax there were no differences (except for a greater absolute level of government employment in Fairfax's control area). Two reasons for this contratheoretic finding may be that District of Columbia and Alexandria lines were not included in this study, effectively eliminating most federal government workers from consideration, and that government employment stagnated in the 1976–80 period throughout the region, merely maintaining its prior location and size.

Service employment also performed more weakly than originally expected. The absolute zonal increase in service employment in the merged experiment was greater in the rail corridors than in their controls, but the rates of increase were not distinguishable. The same finding occurred for the Arlington line. Only in the Shady Grove line was the rate of growth of service employment significantly greater in the rail line than in the control.

Retail employment grew more in both the 1972–80 and the 1976–80 periods for all rail lines, but at a faster rate only in the New Carrollton and Shady Grove lines. It fell faster in the Fairfax rail line than in the control area. Such performance is consistent with the original expectations, since we do not expect retail employment to be systematically drawn to rail lines.

Despite these deviations from expected performance, it is clear that the rail lines typically outperformed the control lines in various categories of analysis; indeed, it was the rare instance when the reverse was true. Finally, the fact that the expected lack of difference in the Greenbelt comparison actually occurred reinforces the notion that only the imminent opening or actual operation of rail lines, not long-term anticipation, makes an important difference in development patterns in the region.

## Study Three: Station and Nonstation Areas within Rail Corridors

The first two studies have provided substantial (albeit somewhat uneven) evidence that rail corridors and station areas are associated with larger and faster growing employment levels, especially for service and government, than generally comparable nonrail areas. A third question—do station areas have higher levels of employment and faster growth rates than nonstation areas *within the corridors themselves?*—can cast light on the relative importance of the corridor versus the station area in attracting attention from planners and developers. The expectation is that the station areas will have higher levels and rates of growth of employment than the other areas in the corridor because the access advantage of the Metrorail corridor is primarily that provided by the fixed stops on the line. Other areas inside the rail corridor benefit only indirectly from it. This expectation is strongly supported by the findings in this study.

### *Methodology*

Eight rail lines (terminus to downtown) were selected and their zones divided into station area zones (those containing, or approaching within a quarter-mile of, a station) and nonstation area zones (the rest). The lines used were those with termini at Shady Grove, Glenmont, Branch Avenue, New Carrollton, Greenbelt, Addison Road, Franconia-Springfield, and Vienna. Note that the lines were defined somewhat differently from those in Study Two, where they had been limited to a single jurisdiction. The Vienna line, for example, here includes the Arlington County and District of Columbia portions as well as the Fairfax County portion. This definition was selected because differences between station areas and nonstation areas *within a corridor* are unlikely to vary much by jurisdiction. In addition, the unopened Branch Avenue and Greenbelt lines and the not-completely-opened Glenmont and Franconia-Springfield lines, excluded from Study One, were included here.

The first experiment includes all lines in an analysis of the entire region, the second includes only the six lines that are wholly or partially opened, and each of the remaining eight experiments analyzes a separate line. The experiments compare development levels (defined by the nine employment variables used in previous experiments) by using a *t*-test for the equality of means. Summary results appear in Table 3.15 and detailed results are reported in Tables A.49A to A.58B.

### *All Lines*

When taken together, station areas within the eight lines had higher employment levels for all types of employment for all three years (see

Table 3.15

## Comparison of Employment Levels and Changes: Station Areas and Nonstation Areas inside Rail Lines, Mean Zonal Values

| | Employment type | | | | |
|---|---|---|---|---|---|
| | Total | Basic | Govern-ment | Service | Retail |
| **All eight lines** | | | | | |
| Level, 1980 | + | + | + | + | + |
| Change, 1972–80 | + | | | + | + |
| Rate of change, 1972–80 | | | + | + | |
| **Six open lines** | | | | | |
| Level, 1980 | + | + | | + | + |
| Change, 1972–80 | + | | | + | |
| Rate of change, 1972–80 | + | | + | + | |
| **Shady Grove line** | | | | | |
| Level, 1980 | + | | | + | + |
| Change, 1972–80 | | | | + | |
| Rate of change, 1972–80 | | | | | |
| **Glenmont line** | | | | | |
| Level, 1980 | + | + | | + | + |
| Change, 1972–80 | + | + | | + | + |
| Rate of change, 1972–80 | + | | | + | + |
| **New Carrollton line** | | | | | |
| Level, 1980 | | | + | | |
| Change, 1972–80 | | | | | |
| Rate of change, 1972–80 | | | | | |
| **Addison Road line** | | | | | |
| Level, 1980 | | | | | |
| Change, 1972–80 | | | − | | |
| Rate of change, 1972–80 | | | | | |
| **Franconia-Springfield line** | | | | | |
| Level, 1980 | + | | + | + | + |
| Change, 1972–80 | | | | + | |
| Rate of change, 1972–80 | + | | | + | |
| **Vienna line** | | | | | |
| Level, 1980 | + | | + | + | |
| Change, 1972–80 | | | | | |
| Rate of change, 1972–80 | + | | | + | |
| **Branch Avenue line** | | | | | |
| Level, 1980 | | | | + | |
| Change, 1972–80 | | | | | |
| Rate of change, 1972–80 | | | | + | |

*(continued)*

Table 3.15 *(continued)*

| | Employment type | | | | |
|---|---|---|---|---|---|
| | Total | Basic | Govern-ment | Service | Retail |
| **Greenbelt line** | | | | | |
| Level, 1980 | + | | + | | |
| Change, 1972–80 | | | | | |
| Rate of change, 1972–80 | | | | | + |

+ = mean of rail line zones is greater than that of control line zones.
− = mean of control line zones is greater than that of rail line zones.
No entry = means are indistinguishable.

Tables A.49A and A.49B). Employment level changes in station areas exceeded those in the remaining portion of the corridors for aggregate (1972–76, 1972–80), service (all periods), and retail (1972–76, 1972–80). For many of these categories, the nonstation areas lost employment while the station areas gained, indicating a net movement of employment within the rail lines toward the station areas. Some of the movement is explained by the attractiveness of the station areas, but part of it may have been due to disruption caused by construction, which (for most of the lines) continued during the entire 1972–80 period; some firms that were originally located on or near the rail right-of-way moved during construction and did not return.

The changes in employment levels translated into faster rates of growth in the station area portion of the corridors for aggregate (1972–76), basic (1972–76, although this was reversed in the 1976–80 period), government (1972–76, 1972–80), and service (1972–80) categories.

## Six Open Lines

The elimination of the two unopened Prince George's County lines led to few changes in the comparisons although the average zonal employment levels rose, as expected (see Tables A.50A and A.50B). Station areas had more employment than nonstation areas in all categories in virtually all years. The significant changes in employment were the same as in the first experiment except that retail employment in the station areas became indistinguishable from that in the nonstation areas. The most important difference that accompanied the elimination of the two nonopened lines from the sample is that the rate of change of aggregate employment in station areas was higher than that in the rest of the corridors over the entire 1972–80 period, which had not been true in the earlier experiment. (Government and service employment rose faster in the station areas from 1972 to 1980, as in the earlier experiment.)

### Individual Line Analyses

There were wide variations between lines even within the same jurisdiction. These are each discussed separately.

### The Shady Grove Line

There were surprisingly few differences between the station areas and nonstation areas in the Shady Grove corridor except in employment levels (see Tables A.51A and A.51B). Here only aggregate (1976, 1980), government (1976), service (1976, 1980), and retail (all years) employment was higher in station areas than in the rest of the corridor. Aggregate (1972–76), government (1972–76), and service (1972–80) employment rose faster in station areas than in the rest of the corridor, but for other categories there were no differences. Only government employment (1972–76) rose at a faster rate in station areas compared to the rest of the corridor. The consistency between station areas and nonstation areas within the Shady Grove corridor is probably related to the fact that Rockville Pike runs in the same corridor and has experienced high levels of strip development, in line with the plans of Montgomery County to focus development in the entire corridor. The average nonstation zone gained 269 workers in the 1976–80 period, quite similar to the gain in station areas.

### The Glenmont Line

In contrast, Montgomery County's other line showed marked differences between the two parts of its corridor (see Tables A.52A and

A.52B). Aggregate, basic, service, and retail employment were all at higher levels in 1976 and 1980 in station areas than in the rest of the corridor, while there was no difference in any of the categories in 1972. In 1980, average aggregate employment in the station area zones was more than four times the level in the rest of the corridor zones. This difference and its timing strongly suggest important station-related impacts in this corridor.

There were also important differences in both rates and levels of change in employment. All types of employment except government grew more in station areas in 1972–76 and 1972–80 than in the rest of the corridor. The rate of growth was greater in station areas for aggregate (1972–76, 1972–80), service (1972–76, 1972–80), and retail (1972–76 and 1972–80) employment categories. In most of these categories, employment levels actually fell in the nonstation portion of the corridor, quite different from the experience in the Shady Grove corridor. Basic employment grew faster outside the station areas during the 1976–80 period, but reached a level that was still only about one-third of that of basic employment in station areas.

*The Branch Avenue Line*

This line, which runs through Southeast Washington and into southern Prince George's County, will be the last line to open, probably in the late 1990s. The data studied here indicate some differences between the planned station area zones and the rest of the corridor, but not nearly as many as in most open lines (see Tables A.53A and A.53B). Aggregate (1972, 1976), government (1972), and service (1976, 1980) employment was greater in the station areas, but for other categories and times, no distinction could be made between the two parts of the corridor. Even fewer distinctions could be made in absolute increases in employment: basic (1972–76) grew more in the station areas, but retail (1976–80) grew more outside them. Nevertheless, the rates of growth were higher for aggregate (1972–76), basic (1972–76), service (1972–76, 1972–80), and retail (1972–76) in the station areas. In these cases, the station areas grew modestly while the rest of the corridor declined. Since these distinctions cannot plausibly be related to anticipation of Metrorail (the alignment was not even confirmed until after 1980), they most likely reflect deliberate routing of Metrorail to serve activity centers already in place.

## The New Carrollton Line

This line, the only substantial and open one of the four with termini in Prince George's County, remarkably showed almost no difference between its station areas and the rest of the corridor (see Tables A.54A and A.54B). Only government employment (1976, 1980) was higher in the station areas than outside them. Even though the average station area zone apparently grew four times as much as the average nonstation area corridor zone in aggregate employment, this difference did not test out to be significant. (The variance in the two categories was quite large, making it difficult to pass any test of statistical significance.)

## The Greenbelt Line

The Greenbelt line, although not yet opened, demonstrates significant concentrations of employment in the prospective station area zones (see Tables A.55A and A.55B). Aggregate employment is over three times as great in the average station area zone as in the rest of the corridor in 1980, and is greater there than in the rest of the corridor for all three years. Similarly, basic (1972, 1976) and government (all years) employment are at higher levels in station areas than outside them. However, the absolute levels of change were indistinguishable for all periods and categories, except that basic (1976–80) grew faster outside the station areas, while retail (1972–76) grew faster inside the station areas (it declined sharply outside the station areas). Similarly, only retail (1972–76, 1972–80) employment grew at a faster rate inside the station areas than in the rest of the corridor. Thus the Greenbelt line essentially had not experienced differential effects from prospective station area development by 1980.

## The Addison Road Line

Once again there are few differences between station areas and the rest of the corridor (see Tables A.56A and A.56B). Aggregate employment was higher in 1972 in station areas, but was indistinguishable in later years. The only other differences were that government employment grew more outside the station areas in 1972–80, while retail declined at a lower rate inside the station areas during 1976–80. The station areas in the Addison Road line, unlike those in the other Prince George's lines, actually lost net employment in 1972–80 in aggregate and in all categories except service.

## The Franconia-Springfield Line

The Franconia-Springfield line, which begins in Fairfax and passes through Alexandria and Arlington on its way into the District, had more aggregate employment (all years) in the station areas (over four times the level in the nonstation zones). (See Tables A.57A and A.57B.) Government (1980), service (all years), and retail (all years) showed the same pattern. The changes in aggregate (1976–80) and service (all years) employment also were substantially greater in station areas than outside them. The rates of change in aggregate (1976–80, 1972–80) and service (1972–80) in station areas greatly exceeded those outside the station areas, which were often negative.

## The Vienna Line

The Vienna line, which leaves Fairfax County and passes through Arlington before entering the District, had characteristics similar to those in Franconia-Springfield. For all employment categories for virtually all years, station areas had higher numbers of workers than did the rest of the corridor (see Tables A.58A and A.58B). However, changes were not distinguishable between station areas and nonstation areas for any of them. The rates of change were greater in station areas for government (1972–76) and service (1976–80, 1972–80) employment, but were greater outside the station areas in retail employment (1972–76).

## Summary of Study Three

The evidence adduced here shows strong levels of development in station areas compared to nonstation areas in rail corridors. Some cases strongly suggest the influence of Metrorail, since there were no differences between the two kinds of zones in the pre-Metrorail (1972) year but major differences favoring the station area zones appeared in the later years (1976, 1980). In several cases, the station areas grew sharply while the rest of the corridor lost employment. In yet other cases, the entire line lost ground, but the station areas lost a bit less than the rest of the corridor. In only one case (Shady Grove) was there uniform comparability, and that is easily attributed to the uniqueness of the Rockville Pike corridor.

The unopened lines show trends that are similar to but weaker than those in the open lines. The fact that the trends appear at all, however, suggests that simple attribution of development to the planning and/or opening of a Metrorail station would be incorrect. Planners select activity centers as locations for their stations in many cases, and it is therefore reasonable to conclude that a good deal of the development in Metrorail station areas predates the stations.

While it is not possible ever fully to disentangle the effect of new rail stations from other factors that influence the development potential of an area, there are enough cases in Study Three where the addition of the rail station was followed by rates of growth in zones adjoining or containing it that far exceeded those of the rest of the corridor to reach the conclusion that stations do have an impact of their own in fostering local development.

**Conclusions from Three Studies**

Have the statistical tests of the data borne out the original expectations of the study? For the most part, they have done so quite convincingly. Did rail corridors grow faster than the rest of the region? The regional and inner suburb studies suggest no difference, but in Montgomery County total employment was clearly growing at a faster rate in the corridor than outside it; in Arlington, basic industry grew faster in corridors than outside of them. More convincing, however, is the evidence from the controlled experiments in Study Two, which showed that rail corridors developed much more than their controls. The balance of evidence therefore is that rail corridors do make a difference, even though within the region they are not the only places (and perhaps not even the main places) where rapid rates of development can occur.

The evidence that station areas grow faster than nonstation areas is much stronger. The inner-suburb study showed clearly that station areas have higher levels, greater gains, and faster rates of growth than nonstation areas. This finding was confirmed in many of the other studies as well, especially in Study Three in which the station area and nonstation area portions of the rail corridors were compared.

Do the categories of employment perform as expected? Here the evidence is more mixed, just as the expectations were less unambiguous. When differences between impact and nonimpact areas show up, they often conform to the prior expectations: basic employment frequently favors noncorridor or nonstation areas, although the Arlington exception is quite significant. Government employment showed little difference anywhere, although in a few places it did focus on station areas. This ambiguous finding is probably due to the general stagnation in government employment in the last decade. Service employment generally behaved as expected; it grew at a faster pace in station areas more frequently than any other type of employment. Retail employment proved to be as fickle in its location pattern as expected; it often grew at faster rates in nonstation and noncorridor areas, although in other cases it joined service employment in concentrating in station areas. Thus, as a general rule, the disaggregations of employment followed their predicted pattern.

What happens inside corridors? Here the evidence from Study Three, the eight-line study, supports the notion that station areas are centers of development (or centers of resistance to decline) within rail corridors, and that in fact it may be less the rail corridor as a whole than specific station areas that attract prospective developers. Even in corridors that were developing slowly or declining, station areas still seemed to be (relative) centers of economic activity and growth. Of course, such levels of activity can only partially be attributed to the decision to locate a station area at a particular site; many sites had significant levels of activity prior to the placing of stations, and in fact the placement of the station is often due to the planners' desire to serve existing activity centers with Metrorail.

No final conclusion can be drawn about the relative importance of prior activity and the new accessibility brought by a station in causing local development. Abundant evidence has been marshaled demonstrating that rates of growth in station areas and rail lines exceed their controls and surrounding jurisdictions, but such tendencies might still have happened in the absence of Metrorail. The prospective Greenbelt line reviewed in Study Two, however, shows no difference between the level and changes in employment in the planned rail line and its control, indicating that at least for this line, no substantial differences have occurred without Metrorail. Perhaps the opening of the Greenbelt line in the 1990s will catalyze development there, causing a gap in development activity levels to emerge between it and its control. This comparison is certainly one to watch over the coming two decades to test hypotheses about the impact of Metrorail on development. The Branch Avenue line (also unopened) reviewed in Study Three suggests, on the other hand, that planners may in fact be targeting areas that are already or soon will be centers of economic activity, relatively speaking.

The cross-currents in the development process that have been uncovered by these studies do allow the conclusion that a combination of previous activity, government planning, and new market opportunities have caused Metrorail station areas today to have higher levels, changes, and rates of growth of development than many other locations in the region. It is now more difficult to contend that these stations do not matter in the emerging pattern of regional development.

# Appendix 3.1

# Methodological Issues in the Use of *t*-Tests for Studies One, Two, and Three

Several methodological issues need to be addressed in order to justify the statistical procedures used in this chapter. They are: (1) Can the means of the paired groups specified in Studies One, Two, and Three be properly compared using a *t*-test? (2) Do the paired groups constitute appropriate impact and control areas? (3) Do the large variances in most groupings of zones complicate the findings? And (4) What implications do the special problems of skewness and bias associated with the percentage change variables have for the findings associated with them? Each of these questions is discussed below.

## The Zone System

Many of the statistical problems arise because of the nature of the zone system. The Washington Metropolitan Area Council of Governments has partitioned the region into 1,337 traffic zones. No basis for this partition is known or can be inferred, and the zones differ greatly in size (whether size is defined in terms of geographical area, population, or amount of employment). The zones do tend to be geographically larger the farther they are from the region's center, and for the most part their boundaries are important roads. Beyond this, the zone system is probably arbitrary.

## (1) The Appropriateness of the $t$-Test

Statistical tests are based on observations that have some common quality and some other factors that vary (as in a series of random draws of balls of the same size but with different colors in separate identical bags). To carry out simple statistical analyses (like $t$-tests) using "draws" from the zone system, it is necessary either to assume that zones are fundamentally comparable or to appeal to the rule of large numbers to conclude that groups of zones are comparable. Alternately, one may attempt to select zones in each group that are comparable in most dimensions, that is, to control consciously for differences. Most importantly, for the $t$-test to be applicable, the distributions of the observations in each group must approximate a normal distribution.

For Study One, large groups of zones are compared. The size of these groups makes it likely that each pair of groups has similar distributions (albeit with large variances).

For Study Two, a smaller number of zones was selected for each group, and the impact and control zones were selected so as to have many traits in common. For instance, zones in each impact/control pair were drawn from the same jurisdiction, thus controlling for many factors; the sets of selected zones usually ran parallel to each other at approximately the same distance from the center of the region, making the distributions of the zones' geographical sizes and other variables related to distance from the city center (like rents for similar parcels) comparable.

For Study Three, the zone groups were all taken from individual rail lines. Impact and control zones alternated as one moved from the terminus of the rail line to the city center (i.e., station area zones were followed by nonstation area zones, which in turn were followed by station area zones, etc.). Therefore, few major differences remained between the groups of zones other than the presence or absence of a station.

Tests for normality of distribution (the Kolomogorov D for samples over 50, the Shapiro-Wilk W for samples of size 50 or less) were conducted on each group in the three studies. The results for all variables showed that their distributions over the zones in each group approximated normality (marginally so in a few instances). It is concluded that *t*-tests for equal means for the employment variables are appropriate in principle in each of the three studies.

## (2) Impact and Control Area Selection

In addition to making sure that the comparison between groups meets the technical requirements allowing the *t*-test, it is important to select, as far as possible, impact areas that did not differ from the control area in the pre-impact period. Unfortunately this cannot be done fully.

Most notably, the impact areas (over which there is little choice) generally had higher levels of employment than the control areas prior to the time of the Metro impact. Thus, a comparison of absolute levels of employment between a group of impact zones and its group of control zones will support the hypothesis about the presence of a Metro-related impact only when, in a particular comparison, the 1972 values do not differ while the later values do. Of course, the finding of a greater level of employment in the impact area in pre-impact years as well as later does not mean that Metro had no impact, only that the results of this test cannot be used to support that hypothesis.

The change in employment variable therefore becomes important since the periods studied span the time during which impacts occurred. Even if the 1972 values for impact areas exceeded those for control areas, if the increases in employment were greater in the impact area than in the control area during the time when the impact was felt, the hypothesis of a Metro impact is supported.

The third set of variables—rates of change in employment—is important for similar reasons. If an impact area that was larger in the pre-impact period grew more than a control area simply by growing at the same rate as the control, this would somewhat weaken the support of the hypothesis of a Metro impact. Therefore the rate-of-change comparison between pre- and post-Metro years ultimately can be the most telling; if this significantly favors the impact area, then a Metro impact is strongly implied, especially if the level and change variables also test out similarly. But there are special problems with this third set of variables, considered below.

A pure impact/control experiment is in principle impossible outside a laboratory, but the three types of variables tested for each of three years or time periods provide a reasonably good approximation to such an experiment.

## (3) Large Variances

The wide variation in size of the zones leads to very large variances within each group of zones. Such large variances make it very difficult to argue statistically that the means of the groups differ; in particular, the *t*-test is very hard to pass. This is actually something of an advantage: when, despite the large variances, the groups pass the test of statistically significant differences, it is very unlikely that this is a false-positive finding.

## (4) The Problem of Percentages and Bias

The statistical tests comparing levels and absolute changes in employment have no other special problems and therefore are likely to yield valid results. But there are additional problems with the percentage change variables. Since the comparisons using these variables are important in establishing the validity of the impact/control character of the studies, it is necessary to study the biases associated with them to see if they compromise the statistical test used.

### *Percentage Rate-of-Change Comparison Biases*

There are two biases in the rate-of-change comparisons, one caused by small base-year values and one caused by the compression of negative values.

### *1. Small Base-Year Values*

Because of the wide variation in size of zones, extremely large percentage changes can occur in zones with small base-year values, overstating the change. (A parallel but less distorting effect occurs when changes in zones with large base-year employment are understated.) In the 1,337-zone universe, there are instances of increases over 1,000 percent (a zone with 10 employees in the base year and 210 four years later—a moderate absolute increase—would have a deceptively large 2,000 percent rate of change). Problems with the distribution of the percentage rate-of-change variable are more serious at the disaggregated level because many zones have extremely low base-year values for at least some of the components of employment. To correct for misleading information associated with very small values for the base year in comparisons of rates of change, zones with fewer than one hundred workers in either of the base years (1972 and 1976) were dropped from the sample for Study One. (Such zones were not dropped in Studies Two and Three where direct selection of zones reduced the incidence of this problem.) This procedure produced a sample of 970 zones (74 percent of all zones) containing 97.87 percent, 98.15 percent, and 97.27 percent of the region's total employment in 1972, 1976, and 1980, respectively. Clearly this adjustment should have no serious biasing effects while ameliorating a major data distortion.

## 2. Compression of Negative Values

The range of negative values (which account for over one-third of the values in all of the comparisons) is both truncated and compressed due to the fact that an absolute variable can increase by any percentage value but cannot decrease by more than 100 percent. The distribution of percentage changes for any grouping of zones will therefore tend to be skewed toward the positive tail.

Fortunately, the tests of normality noted above show that despite these two biases, the distribution of the percentage change variable in each of the groups of zones used in the comparisons approximates a normal distribution (in some cases just barely). The rate of change for a zone is greatly affected by the structure of the zone system—more so than the other variables—but this bias is not severe enough to render the use of the $t$-test inappropriate in making statistical comparisons.

### Problems with Distributions of Percentage Variables

For each zone of interest, the (percentage) rate of change of each absolute employment variable over each time period is calculated. For a given group of zones, one thus obtains a distribution of zonal rates of changes about their mean, which can be used to make statistical comparisons with other groups of zones. (Because of the two problems with percentage variables noted above, this group mean of the zonal rates of changes of a variable is almost always greater than the rate of change of the group total for the same variable. This latter value is the appropriate measure of central tendency for most purposes and hence is reported in the tables, while the significance tests are based on the distribution and mean discussed above.) The question arises whether for a given group of zones, the underlying distribution around the mean of the zonal percentage changes accurately reflects the characteristics of the group. In other words, is the zone system drawn in such a way that spurious findings routinely occur? (It is easy to conceive of a zone system that would greatly distort the processes of employment change, yielding results opposite to those that are known to be happening. The question is to what extent such distortion actually happens, since the WASHCOG zone system used in this study was obviously not drawn to make this happen! See Figure A3.1.) In all of the comparisons, there is only one instance in which the rate of change for the impact-zone total was less than that for the control-zone total but the $t$-test nevertheless indicated that the mean rate of change of the impact zones was larger than that of the control zones (an obvious spurious finding). In this case, the cause of the finding was a preponderance of impact-area zones with very low base-year levels of employment, meaning that small absolute increases caused high percentage increases in these zones. The fact that only one such case of obvious inconsistency occurred out of all the comparisons made in the three studies indicates that, while care must be taken in using these statistics, this problem has a very limited incidence and is not a source of general concern.

## A Final Check

The question still remains whether some consistent and apparently statistically significant Metro impacts could actually be spurious effects of unpredictable biases described above. A standard method for dealing with uncontrollable biases in statistical experiments is to judge whether the bias is for or against the hypothesis to be tested. If the bias makes the hypothesis test harder to pass, then it is considered reasonable to use the statistical test in question. If the contrary case exists, results of the test must be used more cautiously, if at all.

In the present case, the bias runs consistently contrary to the hypothesis that the means will be different, so that the statistical tests can be used with confidence. This is a consequence of the following facts, known from a detailed examination of the data.

*Fact 1.* In almost all paired groups of impact and control zones, more zones in the control groups than in the impact groups have low base-year values and/or negative changes.

Figure A3.1. **Partitioning a region can create spurious effects**

| | Impact area using zone system 1 | Impact area using zone system 2 | Control area (same in both zone systems) |
|---|---|---|---|
| Pre-impact | 2,000   10 / 10   1 | 500   600 / 400   521 | 200   600 / 400   521 |
| Post-impact | 2,200   50 / 50   5 | 600   700 / 500   545 | 220   750 / 450   631 |

| Area sums | | | |
|---|---|---|---|
| Pre-impact | 2,021 | 2,021 | 1,721 |
| Post-impact | 2,305 | 2,305 | 2,041 |
| Percentage change in area | 14 | 14 | 19 |
| Percentage change in each zone | | | |
| 1 | 10 | 20 | 10 |
| 2 | 400 | 17 | 25 |
| 3 | 400 | 25 | 13 |
| 4 | 400 | 5 | 21 |
| Mean of the zonal rates of change | 303 | 17 | 17 |

A t-test for the hypothesis that the impact area is growing faster than the control area would support the hypothesis if zone system 1 were used and not if zone system 2 were used.

*Fact 2.* Impact groups usually have higher percentage changes in employment than their control groups. That is, both the mean of the percentage changes in individual zones, and the percentage change in employment totaled over all the zones in the group, are higher for the impact group.

*Fact 3.* The difference between the mean of percentage changes in a group of impact zones and that of its control is almost always less than the difference between the percentage change in employment totaled over all zones in the impact group and that of its control.

Fact 1 means that there will be more upward bias in the mean of the percentage changes in the control zones compared to that of the impact zones because of the positive skewing of percentage-variable distributions mentioned above. Since (according to Fact 2) the impact values are still (usually) greater than the control values, the effect of the differential in biases is to reduce the difference between the means relative to a hypothetically unbiased comparison. (Such an unbiased comparison is approximated by the comparison of the aggregate percentage changes in the groups.) This is the relevance of Fact 3.

The implication of this reasoning is that the bias almost always works in favor of the null hypothesis (i.e., that the mean of the impact group of zones is not different from its control) and against the hypothesis that an impact area will have a larger mean percentage change than its control. Therefore the bias reduces the number of true and false positives in the sample, and increases the number of false negatives. The $t$-test will therefore err on the conservative side, that is, will more often fail to detect a difference favoring the impact area than it will detect such a difference incorrectly. The conclusion is that the bias is against the hypothesis to be tested, that the test is therefore sound, if a bit conservative, and that the credibility of findings that do show a statistically significantly higher mean for impact areas is actually enhanced because of this bias.

# Appendix 3.2

# Detailed Tables for Studies One, Two, and Three

## General Note

For Tables A.1–A.40, zones with fewer than 100 employees in 1972 or 1976 were dropped from the sample. For all tables, the values reported in the "Percentage changes in employment" rows are the percentage changes in employment in the group of zones taken as a whole. The significance test (which determines whether an apparent difference between impact and control values is in fact statistically significant) is done using the distribution of the percentage changes in employment in each zone in the group around the mean of these values. For more details, see Appendix 3.1.

# List of Appendix 3.2 Tables

Table A.1

**Comparison of Employment Levels and Changes: Rail Corridors versus Areas Outside Rail Corridors and Station Areas versus Nonstation Areas—Regional Total Employment, Mean Zonal Values**

|  | Rail corridors | Areas outside rail corridors | Station areas | Nonstation areas |
|---|---|---|---|---|
| Employment levels |  |  |  |  |
| 1972 | 2,119‡ | 1,007 | 2,472‡ | 1,006 |
| 1976 | 2,345‡ | 1,094 | 2,793‡ | 1,073 |
| 1980 | 2,489‡ | 1,206 | 2,968‡ | 1,176 |
| Employment changes |  |  |  |  |
| 1972–76 | 226† | 87 | 321‡ | 67 |
| 1976–80 | 143 | 112 | −9 | 31 |
| 1972–80 | 369‡ | 199 | 496‡ | 171 |
| Percentage changes in employment |  |  |  |  |
| 1972–76 | 10.7 | 8.6 | 13.0 | 6.7 |
| 1976–80 | 6.1 | 10.2 | 6.3 | 9.6 |
| 1972–80 | 17.3 | 19.7 | 20.1 | 17.0 |

† Difference between means is significant at 0.10 level, two-tailed $t$-test.
‡ Difference between means is significant at 0.05 level, two-tailed $t$-test.

Table A.2

**Comparison of Employment Levels and Changes: Rail Corridors versus Areas Outside Rail Corridors and Station Areas versus Nonstation Areas—Regional Basic Employment, Mean Zonal Values**

|  | Rail corridors | Areas outside rail corridors | Station areas | Nonstation areas |
|---|---|---|---|---|
| Employment levels |  |  |  |  |
| 1972 | 243‡ | 126 | 272‡ | 129 |
| 1976 | 263‡ | 131 | 300‡ | 132 |
| 1980 | 258‡ | 166 | 291‡ | 164 |
| Employment changes |  |  |  |  |
| 1972–76 | 19 | 4 | 28† | 3 |
| 1976–80 | −5 | 35 | −9 | 32 |
| 1972–80 | 14 | 39 | 19 | 34 |
| Percentage changes in employment |  |  |  |  |
| 1972–76 | 7.9 | 3.3 | 10.1 | 2.1 |
| 1976–80 | −1.9 | 26.8† | −2.9 | 23.9‡ |
| 1972–80 | 5.8 | 30.9 | 6.9 | 26.5 |

† Difference between means is significant at 0.10 level, two-tailed $t$-test.
‡ Difference between means is significant at 0.05 level, two-tailed $t$-test.

Table A.3

**Comparison of Employment Levels and Changes: Rail Corridors versus Areas Outside Rail Corridors and Station Areas versus Nonstation Areas—Regional Government Employment, Mean Zonal Values**

| | Rail corridors | Areas outside rail corridors | Station areas | Nonstation areas |
|---|---|---|---|---|
| **Employment levels** | | | | |
| 1972 | 966‡ | 361 | 1,181‡ | 352 |
| 1976 | 1,060‡ | 361 | 1,311‡ | 350 |
| 1980 | 1,061‡ | 362 | 1,312‡ | 350 |
| **Employment changes** | | | | |
| 1972–76 | 95† | 0 | 130‡ | −2 |
| 1976–80 | 1 | 1 | 1 | 1 |
| 1972–80 | 95 | 1 | 131‡ | −1 |
| **Percentage changes in employment** | | | | |
| 1972–76 | 9.8 | −0.1 | 11.0‡ | −0.6 |
| 1976–80 | 0.0 | 0.3 | 0.1 | 0.2 |
| 1972–80 | 9.8 | 0.3 | 11.1† | −0.4 |

† Difference between means is significant at 0.10 level, two-tailed *t*-test.
‡ Difference between means is significant at 0.05 level, two-tailed *t*-test.

Table A.4

**Comparison of Employment Levels and Changes: Rail Corridors versus Areas Outside Rail Corridors and Station Areas versus Nonstation Areas—Regional Service Employment, Mean Zonal Values**

| | Rail corridors | Areas outside rail corridors | Station areas | Nonstation areas |
|---|---|---|---|---|
| **Employment levels** | | | | |
| 1972 | 574‡ | 271 | 652‡ | 277 |
| 1976 | 664‡ | 323 | 774‡ | 322 |
| 1980 | 826‡ | 397 | 977‡ | 391 |
| **Employment changes** | | | | |
| 1972–76 | 90 | 53 | 122‡ | 45 |
| 1976–80 | 162‡ | 74 | 202‡ | 69 |
| 1972–80 | 251‡ | 126 | 324‡ | 113 |
| **Percentage changes in employment** | | | | |
| 1972–76 | 15.6 | 19.5† | 18.7 | 16.1 |
| 1976–80 | 24.4 | 22.8 | 26.2 | 21.4 |
| 1972–80 | 43.8 | 46.7 | 49.8 | 40.9 |

† Difference between means is significant at 0.10 level, two-tailed *t*-test.
‡ Difference between means is significant at 0.05 level, two-tailed *t*-test.

Table A.5

**Comparison of Employment Levels and Changes: Rail Corridors versus Areas Outside Rail Corridors and Station Areas versus Nonstation Areas—Regional Retail Employment, Mean Zonal Values**

| | Rail corridors | Areas outside rail corridors | Station areas | Nonstation areas |
|---|---|---|---|---|
| Employment levels | | | | |
| 1972 | 336 | 248 | 367‡ | 247 |
| 1976 | 358 | 278 | 407‡ | 269 |
| 1980 | 344 | 280 | 388 | 271 |
| Employment changes | | | | |
| 1972–76 | 23 | 30 | 41 | 22 |
| 1976–80 | −14 | 2 | −19 | 2 |
| 1972–80 | 9 | 32 | 21 | 25 |
| Percentage changes in employment | | | | |
| 1972–76 | 6.7 | 12.1 | 11.1 | 9.0 |
| 1976–80 | −3.8 | 0.7† | −4.7 | 0.8 |
| 1972–80 | 2.6 | 12.9 | 5.8 | 9.9 |

† Difference between means is significant at 0.10 level, two-tailed $t$-test.
‡ Difference between means is significant at 0.05 level, two-tailed $t$-test.

Table A.6

**Comparison of Employment Levels and Changes: Rail Corridors versus Areas Outside Rail Corridors and Station Areas versus Nonstation Areas—Inner Suburban Total Employment, Mean Zonal Values**

| | Rail corridors | Areas outside rail corridors | Station areas | Nonstation areas |
|---|---|---|---|---|
| Employment levels | | | | |
| 1972 | 1,633‡ | 973 | 1,921‡ | 982 |
| 1976 | 1,901‡ | 1,048 | 2,384‡ | 1,035 |
| 1980 | 2,085‡ | 1,174 | 2,643‡ | 1,152 |
| Employment changes | | | | |
| 1972–76 | 268 | 75 | 463‡ | 54 |
| 1976–80 | 184 | 126 | 259 | 116 |
| 1972–80 | 452† | 202 | 722‡ | 170 |
| Percentage changes in employment | | | | |
| 1972–76 | 16.4 | 7.7 | 24.1† | 5.5 |
| 1976–80 | 9.7 | 12.1 | 10.9 | 11.2 |
| 1972–80 | 27.6 | 20.7 | 37.6† | 17.3 |

†Difference between means is significant at 0.10 level, two-tailed $t$-test.
‡Difference between means is significant at 0.05 level, two-tailed $t$-test.

Table A.7

**Comparison of Employment Levels and Changes: Rail Corridors versus Areas Outside Rail Corridors and Station Areas versus Nonstation Areas—Inner Suburban Basic Employment, Mean Zonal Values**

| | Rail corridors | Areas outside rail corridors | Station areas | Nonstation areas |
|---|---|---|---|---|
| Employment levels | | | | |
| 1972 | 233‡ | 135 | 265‡ | 139 |
| 1976 | 252‡ | 127 | 294‡ | 132 |
| 1980 | 260‡ | 167 | 307‡ | 167 |
| Employment changes | | | | |
| 1972–76 | 19 | −7 | 29† | −7 |
| 1976–80 | 8 | 40 | 13 | 35 |
| 1972–80 | 27 | 32 | 42 | 28 |
| Percentage changes in employment | | | | |
| 1972–76 | 8.1 | −5.6 | 11.0 | −5.0 |
| 1976–80 | 3.2 | 31.2 | 4.5 | 26.8 |
| 1972–80 | 11.6 | 23.9 | 16.0 | 20.5 |

† Difference between means is significant at 0.10 level, two-tailed $t$-test.
‡ Difference between means is significant at 0.05 level, two-tailed $t$-test.

Table A.8

**Comparison of Employment Levels and Changes: Rail Corridors versus Areas Outside Rail Corridors and Station Areas versus Nonstation Areas—Inner Suburban Government Employment, Mean Zonal Values**

| | Rail corridors | Areas outside rail corridors | Station areas | Nonstation areas |
|---|---|---|---|---|
| Employment levels | | | | |
| 1972 | 722† | 329 | 920‡ | 329 |
| 1976 | 784‡ | 318 | 1,023‡ | 316 |
| 1980 | 804‡ | 314 | 1,060‡ | 311 |
| Employment changes | | | | |
| 1972–76 | 61 | −11 | 103 | −12 |
| 1976–80 | 20 | −4 | 37 | −5 |
| 1972–80 | 81 | −15 | 140† | −18 |
| Percentage changes in employment | | | | |
| 1972–76 | 8.5 | −3.4 | 11.2‡ | −3.8 |
| 1976–80 | 2.6 | −1.3 | 3.6 | −1.6 |
| 1972–80 | 11.3 | −4.6 | 15.3 | −5.4 |

† Difference between means is significant at 0.10 level, two-tailed $t$-test.
‡ Difference between means is significant at 0.05 level, two-tailed $t$-test.

Table A.9

**Comparison of Employment Levels and Changes: Rail Corridors versus Areas Outside Rail Corridors and Station Areas versus Nonstation Areas— Inner Suburban Service Employment, Mean Zonal Values**

| | Rail corridors | Areas outside rail corridors | Station areas | Nonstation areas |
|---|---|---|---|---|
| Employment levels | | | | |
| 1972 | 377‡ | 254 | 400‡ | 262 |
| 1976 | 491‡ | 314 | 596‡ | 310 |
| 1980 | 618‡ | 393 | 773‡ | 384 |
| Employment changes | | | | |
| 1972–76 | 114 | 60 | 196‡ | 49 |
| 1976–80 | 127 | 79 | 178‡ | 73 |
| 1972–80 | 241† | 139 | 373‡ | 122 |
| Percentage changes in employment | | | | |
| 1972–76 | 30.4 | 23.8 | 48.9 | 18.6 |
| 1976–80 | 25.9 | 25.2 | 29.8 | 23.7 |
| 1972–80 | 64.1 | 55.0 | 93.3 | 46.6 |

† Difference between means is significant at 0.10 level, two-tailed $t$-test.
‡ Difference between means is significant at 0.05 level, two-tailed $t$-test.

Table A.10

**Comparison of Employment Levels and Changes: Rail Corridors versus Areas Outside Rail Corridors and Station Areas versus Nonstation Areas— Inner Suburban Retail Employment, Mean Zonal Values**

| | Rail corridors | Areas outside rail corridors | Station areas | Nonstation areas |
|---|---|---|---|---|
| Employment levels | | | | |
| 1972 | 301 | 255 | 336 | 253 |
| 1976 | 374 | 289 | 471‡ | 277 |
| 1980 | 403 | 301 | 502‡ | 290 |
| Employment changes | | | | |
| 1972–76 | 73 | 34 | 136‡ | 25 |
| 1976–80 | 28 | 12 | 31 | 13 |
| 1972–80 | 102 | 45 | 166‡ | 38 |
| Percentage changes in employment | | | | |
| 1972–76 | 24.4 | 14.2 | 40.4 | 9.7 |
| 1976–80 | 7.6 | 4.0 | 6.5 | 4.7 |
| 1972–80 | 33.8 | 17.8 | 49.5 | 14.8 |

‡ Difference between means is significant at 0.05 level, two-tailed $t$-test.

Table A.11

**Comparison of Employment Levels and Changes: Rail Corridors versus Areas Outside Rail Corridors and Station Areas versus Nonstation Areas—District of Columbia Total Employment, Mean Zonal Values**

| | Rail corridors | Areas outside rail corridors | Station areas | Nonstation areas |
|---|---|---|---|---|
| Employment levels | | | | |
| 1972 | 2,586‡ | 1,188 | 2,889‡ | 1,122 |
| 1976 | 2,772‡ | 1,270 | 3,103‡ | 1,194 |
| 1980 | 2,876‡ | 1,269 | 3,215‡ | 1,206 |
| Employment changes | | | | |
| 1972–76 | 186 | 82 | 213 | 72 |
| 1976–80 | 104 | −1 | 112 | 12 |
| 1972–80 | 291 | 81 | 325 | 84 |
| Percentage changes in employment | | | | |
| 1972–76 | 7.2 | 6.9 | 7.3 | 6.4 |
| 1976–80 | 3.8 | −0.1 | 3.6 | 1.0 |
| 1972–80 | 11.2 | 6.8 | 11.2 | 7.5 |

‡ Difference between means is significant at 0.05 level, two-tailed $t$-test.

Table A.12

**Comparison of Employment Levels and Changes: Rail Corridors versus Areas Outside Rail Corridors and Station Areas versus Nonstation Areas—District of Columbia Basic Employment, Mean Zonal Values**

| | Rail corridors | Areas outside rail corridors | Station areas | Nonstation areas |
|---|---|---|---|---|
| Employment levels | | | | |
| 1972 | 253‡ | 70 | 287‡ | 79 |
| 1976 | 273‡ | 124 | 304‡ | 118 |
| 1980 | 255‡ | 103 | 279‡ | 106 |
| Employment changes | | | | |
| 1972–76 | 20 | 54 | 26 | 39 |
| 1976–80 | −18 | −20 | −25 | −11 |
| 1972–80 | 2 | 34 | 1 | 27 |
| Percentage changes in employment | | | | |
| 1972–76 | 7.9 | 77.1 | 9.1 | 49.4 |
| 1976–80 | −6.6 | −16.1 | −8.2 | −9.3 |
| 1972–80 | 0.8 | 48.6 | 0.3 | 34.2 |

‡ Difference between means is significant at 0.05 level, two-tailed $t$-test.

Table A.13

**Comparison of Employment Levels and Changes: Rail Corridors versus Areas Outside Rail Corridors and Station Areas versus Nonstation Areas— District of Columbia Government Employment, Mean Zonal Values**

|  | Rail corridors | Areas outside rail corridors | Station areas | Nonstation areas |
|---|---|---|---|---|
| Employment levels |  |  |  |  |
| 1972 | 1,199‡ | 512 | 1,379‡ | 444 |
| 1976 | 1,326‡ | 542 | 1,529‡ | 466 |
| 1980 | 1,308‡ | 544 | 1,502‡ | 474 |
| Employment changes |  |  |  |  |
| 1972–76 | 127 | 30 | 151 | 23 |
| 1976–80 | −19 | 2 | −27 | 7 |
| 1972–80 | 108 | 32 | 124 | 30 |
| Percentage changes in employment |  |  |  |  |
| 1972–76 | 10.6 | 5.9 | 10.9 | 5.2 |
| 1976–80 | −1.4 | 0.4 | −1.8 | 1.5 |
| 1972–80 | 9.0 | 6.3 | 9.0 | 12.2 |

‡ Difference between means is significant at 0.05 level, two-tailed $t$-test.

Table A.14

**Comparison of Employment Levels and Changes: Rail Corridors versus Areas Outside Rail Corridors and Station Areas versus Nonstation Areas— District of Columbia Service Employment, Mean Zonal Values**

|  | Rail corridors | Areas outside rail corridors | Station areas | Nonstation areas |
|---|---|---|---|---|
| Employment levels |  |  |  |  |
| 1972 | 764‡ | 384 | 843‡ | 371 |
| 1976 | 830‡ | 392 | 909‡ | 390 |
| 1980 | 1,025‡ | 479 | 1,130‡ | 469 |
| Employment changes |  |  |  |  |
| 1972–76 | 66 | 8 | 67 | 19 |
| 1976–80 | 195 | 87 | 221 | 79 |
| 1972–80 | 261 | 95 | 288† | 98 |
| Percentage changes in employment |  |  |  |  |
| 1972–76 | 8.6 | 1.9 | 7.9 | 5.1 |
| 1976–80 | 23.5 | 22.3 | 24.3 | 20.2 |
| 1972–80 | 34.6 | 24.7 | 34.2 | 26.4 |

† Difference between means is significant at 0.10 level, two-tailed $t$-test.
‡ Difference between means is significant at 0.05 level, two-tailed $t$-test.

Table A.15

**Comparison of Employment Levels and Changes: Rail Corridors versus Areas Outside Rail Corridors and Station Areas versus Nonstation Areas— District of Columbia Retail Employment, Mean Zonal Values**

|  | Rail corridors | Areas outside rail corridors | Station areas | Nonstation areas |
|---|---|---|---|---|
| Employment levels |  |  |  |  |
| 1972 | 369‡ | 223 | 390‡ | 228 |
| 1976 | 343‡ | 212 | 359‡ | 219 |
| 1980 | 288‡ | 143 | 302‡ | 157 |
| Employment changes |  |  |  |  |
| 1972–76 | −26 | −10 | −31 | −9 |
| 1976–80 | −54 | −69 | −57 | −63 |
| 1972–80 | −81 | −80 | −88 | −71 |
| Percentage changes in employment |  |  |  |  |
| 1972–76 | −7.1 | −4.7 | −7.9 | −3.7 |
| 1976–80 | −15.8‡ | −32.7 | −15.9‡ | −28.5 |
| 1972–80 | −21.8 | −35.9 | −22.6 | −31.2 |

‡ Difference between means is significant at 0.05 level, two-tailed $t$-test.

Table A.16

**Comparison of Employment Levels and Changes: Rail Corridors versus Areas Outside Rail Corridors and Station Areas versus Nonstation Areas— Montgomery County Total Employment, Mean Zonal Values**

|  | Rail corridors | Areas outside rail corridors | Station areas | Nonstation areas |
|---|---|---|---|---|
| Employment levels |  |  |  |  |
| 1972 | 1,803‡ | 777 | 2,084‡ | 859 |
| 1976 | 2,438‡ | 749 | 3,383‡ | 786 |
| 1980 | 2,767‡ | 863 | 3,722‡ | 927 |
| Employment changes |  |  |  |  |
| 1972–76 | 635‡ | −28 | 1,299‡ | −74 |
| 1976–80 | 329‡ | 114 | 338† | 141 |
| 1972–80 | 964‡ | 86 | 1,638‡ | 68 |
| Percentage changes in employment |  |  |  |  |
| 1972–76 | 35.2‡ | −3.7 | 62.4‡ | −8.6 |
| 1976–80 | 13.5 | 15.2 | 10.0 | 18.0 |
| 1972–80 | 53.5‡ | 11.0 | 78.6‡ | 7.9 |

† Difference between means is significant at 0.10 level, two-tailed $t$-test.
‡ Difference between means is significant at 0.05 level, two-tailed $t$-test.

Table A.17

**Comparison of Employment Levels and Changes: Rail Corridors versus Areas Outside Rail Corridors and Station Areas versus Nonstation Areas— Montgomery County Basic Employment, Mean Zonal Values**

| | Rail corridors | Areas outside rail corridors | Station areas | Nonstation areas |
|---|---|---|---|---|
| Employment levels | | | | |
| 1972 | 243 | 118 | 271‡ | 129 |
| 1976 | 279‡ | 97 | 353‡ | 107 |
| 1980 | 288‡ | 122 | 338‡ | 134 |
| Employment changes | | | | |
| 1972–76 | 37 | −21 | 82‡ | −23 |
| 1976–80 | 8 | 25 | −15 | 27 |
| 1972–80 | 45 | 4 | 67 | 5 |
| Percentage changes in employment | | | | |
| 1972–76 | 15.2 | −18.0 | 30.1 | −17.4 |
| 1976–80 | 3.0 | 25.9 | −4.2 | 25.8 |
| 1972–80 | 18.6 | 3.2 | 24.7 | 3.8 |

‡ Difference between means is significant at 0.05 level, two-tailed $t$-test.

Table A.18

**Comparison of Employment Levels and Changes: Rail Corridors versus Areas Outside Rail Corridors and Station Areas versus Nonstation Areas— Montgomery County Government Employment, Mean Zonal Values**

| | Rail corridors | Areas outside rail corridors | Station areas | Nonstation areas |
|---|---|---|---|---|
| Employment levels | | | | |
| 1972 | 525‡ | 220 | 696‡ | 227 |
| 1976 | 733‡ | 203 | 1,099‡ | 200 |
| 1980 | 894‡ | 204 | 1,257‡ | 224 |
| Employment changes | | | | |
| 1972–76 | 208‡ | −17 | 404‡ | −26 |
| 1976–80 | 161‡ | 1 | 157‡ | 24 |
| 1972–80 | 370‡ | −16 | 561‡ | −3 |
| Percent changes in employment | | | | |
| 1972–76 | 39.6 | −7.6 | 57.9 | −11.6 |
| 1976–80 | 22.1 | 0.5 | 14.3 | 11.9 |
| 1972–80 | 70.4 | −7.3 | 80.6 | −1.2 |

‡ Difference between means is significant at 0.05 level, two-tailed $t$-test.

Table A.19

**Comparison of Employment Levels and Changes: Rail Corridors versus Areas Outside Rail Corridors and Station Areas versus Nonstation Areas— Montgomery County Service Employment, Mean Zonal Values**

|  | Rail corridors | Areas outside rail corridors | Station areas | Nonstation areas |
|---|---|---|---|---|
| **Employment levels** | | | | |
| 1972 | 614‡ | 250 | 633‡ | 296 |
| 1976 | 848‡ | 277 | 1,134‡ | 296 |
| 1980 | 962‡ | 321 | 1,270‡ | 345 |
| **Employment changes** | | | | |
| 1972–76 | 234† | 26 | 502‡ | 0 |
| 1976–80 | 114 | 44 | 136 | 49 |
| 1972–80 | 348‡ | 71 | 637‡ | 49 |
| **Percentage changes in employment** | | | | |
| 1972–76 | 38.1 | 10.6 | 79.3‡ | 0.1 |
| 1976–80 | 13.5 | 15.9 | 11.9 | 16.6 |
| 1972–80 | 56.7 | 28.2 | 100.7† | 16.7 |

† Difference between means is significant at 0.10 level, two-tailed $t$-test.
‡ Difference between means is significant at 0.05 level, two-tailed $t$-test.

Table A.20

**Comparison of Employment Levels and Changes: Rail Corridors versus Areas Outside Rail Corridors and Station Areas versus Nonstation Areas— Montgomery County Retail Employment, Mean Zonal Values**

|  | Rail corridors | Areas outside rail corridors | Station areas | Nonstation areas |
|---|---|---|---|---|
| **Employment levels** | | | | |
| 1972 | 422‡ | 189 | 484‡ | 208 |
| 1976 | 578‡ | 172 | 797‡ | 183 |
| 1980 | 623‡ | 216 | 856‡ | 224 |
| **Employment changes** | | | | |
| 1972–76 | 156 | −16 | 313‡ | −25 |
| 1976–80 | 45 | 44 | 60 | 41 |
| 1972–80 | 201 | 27 | 372‡ | 16 |
| **Percentage changes in employment** | | | | |
| 1972–76 | 37.1 | −8.8 | 64.6 | −12.0 |
| 1976–80 | 7.7 | 25.5 | 7.5 | 22.4 |
| 1972–80 | 47.7 | 14.5 | 76.9‡ | 7.7 |

‡ Difference between means is significant at 0.05 level, two-tailed $t$-test.

Table A.21

**Comparison of Employment Levels and Changes: Rail Corridors versus Areas Outside Rail Corridors and Station Areas versus Nonstation Areas— Prince George's County Total Employment, Mean Zonal Values**

|  | Rail corridors | Areas outside rail corridors | Station areas | Nonstation areas |
|---|---|---|---|---|
| **Employment levels** | | | | |
| 1972 | 892 | 1,062 | 965 | 1,033 |
| 1976 | 1,053 | 1,131 | 1,232 | 1,086 |
| 1980 | 1,072 | 1,221 | 1,268 | 1,166 |
| **Employment changes** | | | | |
| 1972–76 | 161 | 69 | 268 | 54 |
| 1976–80 | 20 | 89 | 36 | 80 |
| 1972–80 | 180 | 158 | 303 | 134 |
| **Percentage changes in employment** | | | | |
| 1972–76 | 18.0 | 6.5 | 27.7† | 5.2 |
| 1976–80 | 1.8 | 7.9 | 2.9 | 7.3 |
| 1972–80 | 20.2 | 14.9 | 31.5 | 12.9 |

† Difference between means is significant at 0.10 level, two-tailed $t$-test.


Table A.22

**Comparison of Employment Levels and Changes: Rail Corridors versus Areas Outside Rail Corridors and Station Areas versus Nonstation Areas— Prince George's County Basic Employment, Mean Zonal Values**

|  | Rail corridors | Areas outside rail corridors | Station areas | Nonstation areas |
|---|---|---|---|---|
| **Employment levels** | | | | |
| 1972 | 149 | 166 | 152 | 164 |
| 1976 | 184 | 146 | 186 | 149 |
| 1980 | 170 | 174 | 192 | 169 |
| **Employment changes** | | | | |
| 1972–76 | 34† | −20 | 34 | −15 |
| 1976–80 | −14 | 27 | 6 | 20 |
| 1972–80 | 20 | 8 | 40 | 4 |
| **Percentage changes in employment** | | | | |
| 1972–76 | 22.9 | −11.8 | 22.7 | −9.3 |
| 1976–80 | −7.5 | 18.5 | 3.0 | 13.2 |
| 1972–80 | 13.7 | 4.5 | 26.4 | 2.7 |

† Difference between means is significant at 0.10 level, two-tailed $t$-test.

Table A.23

**Comparison of Employment Levels and Changes: Rail Corridors versus Areas Outside Rail Corridors and Station Areas versus Nonstation Areas— Prince George's County Government Employment, Mean Zonal Values**

|  | Rail corridors | Areas outside rail corridors | Station areas | Nonstation areas |
|---|---|---|---|---|
| Employment levels |  |  |  |  |
| 1972 | 306 | 374 | 371 | 355 |
| 1976 | 392 | 373 | 518 | 347 |
| 1980 | 355 | 425 | 464 | 396 |
| Employment changes |  |  |  |  |
| 1972–76 | 86 | −1 | 147‡ | −7 |
| 1976–80 | −38 | 52 | −54 | 49 |
| 1972–80 | 49 | 51 | 93 | 41 |
| Percentage changes in employment |  |  |  |  |
| 1972–76 | 28.2† | −0.3 | 39.6 | −2.1 |
| 1976–80 | −9.6 | 14.1 | −10.4 | 14.0 |
| 1972–80 | 15.9 | 13.7 | 25.1 | 11.6 |

† Difference between means is significant at 0.10 level, two-tailed *t*-test.
‡ Difference between means is significant at 0.05 level, two-tailed *t*-test.

Table A.24

**Comparison of Employment Levels and Changes: Rail Corridors versus Areas Outside Rail Corridors and Station Areas versus Nonstation Areas— Prince George's County Service Employment, Mean Zonal Values**

|  | Rail corridors | Areas outside rail corridors | Station areas | Nonstation areas |
|---|---|---|---|---|
| Employment levels |  |  |  |  |
| 1972 | 143 | 210† | 141 | 205 |
| 1976 | 167 | 255‡ | 174 | 247 |
| 1980 | 224 | 290 | 258 | 277 |
| Employment changes |  |  |  |  |
| 1972–76 | 24 | 45 | 34 | 42 |
| 1976–80 | 57 | 35 | 84 | 31 |
| 1972–80 | 81 | 80 | 118† | 72 |
| Percentage changes in employment |  |  |  |  |
| 1972–76 | 16.8 | 21.6 | 23.9 | 20.3 |
| 1976–80 | 34.1 | 13.5 | 48.1 | 12.4 |
| 1972–80 | 56.7 | 38.1 | 83.4† | 35.2 |

† Difference between means is significant at 0.10 level, two-tailed *t*-test.
‡ Difference between means is significant at 0.05 level, two-tailed *t*-test.

Table A.25

**Comparison of Employment Levels and Changes: Rail Corridors versus Areas Outside Rail Corridors and Station Areas versus Nonstation Areas— Prince George's County Retail Employment, Mean Zonal Values**

|  | Rail corridors | Areas outside rail corridors | Station areas | Nonstation areas |
|---|---|---|---|---|
| **Employment levels** | | | | |
| 1972 | 293 | 312 | 301 | 309 |
| 1976 | 310 | 357 | 353 | 344 |
| 1980 | 324 | 332 | 353 | 325 |
| **Employment changes** | | | | |
| 1972–76 | 16 | 45 | 53 | 35 |
| 1976–80 | 14 | −25 | 0 | −19 |
| 1972–80 | 30 | 20 | 53 | 16 |
| **Percentage changes in employment** | | | | |
| 1972–76 | 5.6 | 14.4† | 17.5 | 11.3 |
| 1976–80 | 4.5 | −7.0 | 0.0 | −5.5 |
| 1972–80 | 10.3 | 6.4 | 17.5 | 5.1 |

† Difference between means is significant at 0.10 level, two-tailed $t$-test.

Table A.26

**Comparison of Employment Levels and Changes: Rail Corridors versus Areas Outside Rail Corridors and Station Areas versus Nonstation Areas— Arlington Total Employment, Mean Zonal Values**

|  | Rail corridors | Areas outside rail corridors | Station areas | Nonstation areas |
|---|---|---|---|---|
| **Employment levels** | | | | |
| 1972 | 3,261‡ | 990 | 4,070‡ | 995 |
| 1976 | 3,146‡ | 969 | 3,905‡ | 986 |
| 1980 | 3,358‡ | 940 | 4,262‡ | 917 |
| **Employment changes** | | | | |
| 1972–76 | −115 | −21 | −166 | −9 |
| 1976–80 | 211 | −29 | 357 | −69 |
| 1972–80 | 97 | −50 | 191 | −78 |
| **Percentage changes in employment** | | | | |
| 1972–76 | −3.5 | −2.1 | −4.1 | −1.0 |
| 1976–80 | 6.7 | −3.0 | 9.1 | −7.0 |
| 1972–80 | 2.9 | −5.1 | 4.7 | −7.9 |

‡ Difference between means is significant at 0.05 level, two-tailed $t$-test.

Table A.27

**Comparison of Employment Levels and Changes: Rail Corridors versus Areas Outside Rail Corridors and Station Areas versus Nonstation Areas— Arlington Basic Employment, Mean Zonal Values**

|  | Rail corridors | Areas outside rail corridors | Station areas | Nonstation areas |
|---|---|---|---|---|
| Employment levels |  |  |  |  |
| 1972 | 364 | 63 | 475† | 60 |
| 1976 | 375† | 59 | 468† | 73 |
| 1980 | 381† | 56 | 470† | 75 |
| Employment changes |  |  |  |  |
| 1972–76 | 11 | −4 | −7 | 12 |
| 1976–80 | 7 | −3 | 2 | 2 |
| 1972–80 | 18 | −7 | −5 | 14 |
| Percentage changes in employment |  |  |  |  |
| 1972–76 | 3.0 | −6.0 | −1.5 | 20.2 |
| 1976–80 | 1.8 | −5.5 | 0.4 | 3.1 |
| 1972–80 | 4.9 | −11.2† | −1.1 | 23.9 |

† Difference between means is significant at 0.10 level, two-tailed *t*-test.

Table A.28

**Comparison of Employment Levels and Changes: Rail Corridors versus Areas Outside Rail Corridors and Station Areas versus Nonstation Areas— Arlington Government Employment, Mean Zonal Values**

|  | Rail corridors | Areas outside rail corridors | Station areas | Nonstation areas |
|---|---|---|---|---|
| Employment levels |  |  |  |  |
| 1972 | 2,091† | 526 | 2,594‡ | 567 |
| 1976 | 1,841† | 454 | 2,279† | 495 |
| 1980 | 1,773† | 391 | 2,239‡ | 412 |
| Employment changes |  |  |  |  |
| 1972–76 | −250 | −72 | −314 | −72 |
| 1976–80 | −68 | −63 | −41 | −83 |
| 1972–80 | −318 | −135 | −355 | −155 |
| Percentage changes in employment |  |  |  |  |
| 1972–76 | −11.9 | −13.6 | −12.1 | −12.7 |
| 1976–80 | −3.7 | −13.9 | −1.8 | −16.7 |
| 1972–80 | −15.2 | −25.7 | −13.7 | −27.3 |

† Difference between means is significant at 0.10 level, two-tailed *t*-test.
‡ Difference between means is significant at 0.05 level, two-tailed *t*-test.

Table A.29

**Comparison of Employment Levels and Changes: Rail Corridors versus Areas Outside Rail Corridors and Station Areas versus Nonstation Areas— Arlington Service Employment, Mean Zonal Values**

|  | Rail corridors | Areas outside rail corridors | Station areas | Nonstation areas |
|---|---|---|---|---|
| **Employment levels** | | | | |
| 1972 | 523‡ | 219 | 647‡ | 210 |
| 1976 | 642‡ | 280 | 798‡ | 263 |
| 1980 | 905‡ | 301 | 1,172‡ | 268 |
| **Employment changes** | | | | |
| 1972–76 | 119 | 61 | 151 | 53 |
| 1976–80 | 263 | 21 | 375‡ | 4 |
| 1972–80 | 382 | 82 | 525‡ | 58 |
| **Percentage changes in employment** | | | | |
| 1972–76 | 22.7 | 27.7 | 23.3 | 25.5 |
| 1976–80 | 40.9 | 7.5 | 46.9 | 1.6 |
| 1972–80 | 72.9 | 37.3 | 81.2 | 27.5 |

‡ Difference between means is significant at 0.05 level, two-tailed $t$-test.

Table A.30

**Comparison of Employment Levels and Changes: Rail Corridors versus Areas Outside Rail Corridors and Station Areas versus Nonstation Areas— Arlington Retail Employment, Mean Zonal Values**

|  | Rail corridors | Areas outside rail corridors | Station areas | Nonstation areas |
|---|---|---|---|---|
| **Employment levels** | | | | |
| 1972 | 283 | 182 | 354‡ | 158 |
| 1976 | 289† | 176 | 360‡ | 155 |
| 1980 | 299 | 192 | 381‡ | 163 |
| **Employment changes** | | | | |
| 1972–76 | 6 | −6 | 5 | −3 |
| 1976–80 | 10 | 16 | 21 | 7 |
| 1972–80 | 16 | 10 | 26 | 4 |
| **Percentage changes in employment** | | | | |
| 1972–76 | 2.0 | −3.4 | 1.5 | −1.9 |
| 1976–80 | 3.5 | 9.3† | 5.8 | 4.8 |
| 1972–80 | 5.6 | 5.5 | 7.4 | 2.8 |

† Difference between means is significant at 0.10 level, two-tailed $t$-test.
‡ Difference between means is significant at 0.05 level, two-tailed $t$-test.

Table A.31

**Comparison of Employment Levels and Changes: Rail Corridors versus Areas Outside Rail Corridors and Station Areas versus Nonstation Areas—Alexandria Total Employment, Mean Zonal Values**

| | Rail corridors | Areas outside rail corridors | Station areas | Nonstation areas |
|---|---|---|---|---|
| Employment levels | | | | |
| 1972 | 961 | 823 | 915 | 872 |
| 1976 | 1,072 | 968 | 951 | 1,030 |
| 1980 | 1,091 | 1,175 | 1,280 | 1,097 |
| Employment changes | | | | |
| 1972–76 | 111 | 144 | 36 | 159 |
| 1976–80 | 19 | 207 | 329 | 67 |
| 1972–80 | 130 | 351 | 365 | 226 |
| Percentage changes in employment | | | | |
| 1972–76 | 11.6 | 17.5† | 3.9 | 18.2† |
| 1976–80 | 1.8 | 21.4 | 34.6‡ | 6.5 |
| 1972–80 | 13.6 | 42.6 | 39.9 | 25.9 |

† Difference between means is significant at 0.10 level, two-tailed $t$-test.
‡ Difference between means is significant at 0.05 level, two-tailed $t$-test.

Table A.32

**Comparison of Employment Levels and Changes: Rail Corridors versus Areas Outside Rail Corridors and Station Areas versus Nonstation Areas—Alexandria Basic Employment, Mean Zonal Values**

| | Rail corridors | Areas outside rail corridors | Station areas | Nonstation areas |
|---|---|---|---|---|
| Employment levels | | | | |
| 1972 | 216 | 119 | 163 | 159 |
| 1976 | 198 | 146 | 154 | 173 |
| 1980 | 197 | 161 | 200 | 169 |
| Employment changes | | | | |
| 1972–76 | −18 | 27† | −9 | 13 |
| 1976–80 | −2 | 14 | 46 | −4 |
| 1972–80 | −20 | 42 | 37 | 9 |
| Percentage changes in employment | | | | |
| 1972–76 | −8.4 | 22.9† | −5.7 | 8.3 |
| 1976–80 | −0.8 | 9.8 | 30.3 | −2.3 |
| 1972–80 | −9.1 | 34.9 | 22.8 | 5.8 |

† Difference between means is significant at 0.10 level, two-tailed $t$-test.

Table A.33

**Comparison of Employment Levels and Changes: Rail Corridors versus Areas Outside Rail Corridors and Station Areas versus Nonstation Areas— Alexandria Government Employment, Mean Zonal Values**

|  | Rail corridors | Areas outside rail corridors | Station areas | Nonstation areas |
|---|---|---|---|---|
| Employment levels |  |  |  |  |
| 1972 | 416† | 176 | 405 | 239 |
| 1976 | 564† | 122 | 488 | 255 |
| 1980 | 488† | 122 | 620† | 174 |
| Employment changes |  |  |  |  |
| 1972–76 | 148 | −54 | 83 | 16 |
| 1976–80 | 76 | 0 | 131 | −82 |
| 1972–80 | 72 | −54 | 214 | −65 |
| Percentage changes in employment |  |  |  |  |
| 1972–76 | 35.7 | −30.5 | 20.5 | 6.9 |
| 1976–80 | −13.5 | −0.2 | 26.9‡ | −31.9 |
| 1972–80 | 17.3 | −30.6 | 52.9 | −27.2 |

† Difference between means is significant at 0.10 level, two-tailed $t$-test.
‡ Difference between means is significant at 0.05 level, two-tailed $t$-test.

---

Table A.34

**Comparison of Employment Levels and Changes: Rail Corridors versus Areas Outside Rail Corridors and Station Areas verus Nonstation Areas— Alexandria Service Employment, Mean Zonal Values**

|  | Rail corridors | Areas outside rail corridors | Station areas | Nonstation areas |
|---|---|---|---|---|
| Employment levels |  |  |  |  |
| 1972 | 185 | 308† | 203 | 272 |
| 1976 | 186 | 415‡ | 175 | 361† |
| 1980 | 219 | 538‡ | 248 | 449 |
| Employment changes |  |  |  |  |
| 1972–76 | 1 | 108‡ | −28 | 89† |
| 1976–80 | 33 | 122‡ | 74 | 88 |
| 1972–80 | 34 | 230 | 45 | 178 |
| Percentage changes in employment |  |  |  |  |
| 1972–76 | 0.3 | 34.9 | −13.9 | 32.9 |
| 1976–80 | 18.0 | 29.5 | 42.1 | 24.4 |
| 1972–80 | 18.3 | 74.8 | 22.2 | 65.4 |

† Difference between means is significant at 0.10 level, two-tailed $t$-test.
‡ Difference between means is significant at 0.05 level, two-tailed $t$-test.

Table A.35

**Comparison of Employment Levels and Changes: Rail Corridors versus Areas Outside Rail Corridors and Station Areas versus Nonstation Areas— Alexandria Retail Employment, Mean Zonal Values**

|  | Rail corridors | Areas outside rail corridors | Station areas | Nonstation areas |
|---|---|---|---|---|
| Employment levels |  |  |  |  |
| 1972 | 143 | 221 | 144 | 201 |
| 1976 | 124 | 284† | 134 | 241 |
| 1980 | 188 | 354 | 211 | 305 |
| Employment changes |  |  |  |  |
| 1972–76 | −19 | 63‡ | −10 | 40 |
| 1976–80 | 63 | 70 | 78 | 64 |
| 1972–80 | 44 | 133 | 68 | 104 |
| Percentage changes in employment |  |  |  |  |
| 1972–76 | −13.3 | 28.5 | −6.8 | 19.7 |
| 1976–80 | 50.9 | 113.5 | 125.6 | 95.2 |
| 1972–80 | 30.8 | 60.4† | 47.2 | 51.6 |

† Difference between means is significant at 0.10 level, two-tailed $t$-test.
‡ Difference between means is significant at 0.05 level, two-tailed $t$-test.

Table A.36

**Comparison of Employment Levels and Changes: Rail Corridors versus Areas Outside Rail Corridors and Station Areas versus Nonstation Areas— Fairfax Total Employment, Mean Zonal Values**

|  | Rail corridors | Areas outside rail corridors | Station areas | Nonstation areas |
|---|---|---|---|---|
| Employment levels |  |  |  |  |
| 1972 | 619 | 1,109 | 656 | 1,092 |
| 1976 | 943 | 1,297 | 1,084 | 1,275 |
| 1980 | 1,240 | 1,485 | 1,436 | 1,461 |
| Employment changes |  |  |  |  |
| 1972–76 | 324 | 188 | 428 | 182 |
| 1976–80 | 297 | 188 | 352 | 186 |
| 1972–80 | 621 | 376 | 780 | 368 |
| Percentage changes in employment |  |  |  |  |
| 1972–76 | 52.3 | 16.9 | 65.3 | 16.7 |
| 1976–80 | 31.5 | 14.5 | 32.5 | 14.6 |
| 1972–80 | 100.2 | 33.9 | 119.3 | 33.7 |

Table A.37

**Comparison of Employment Levels and Changes: Rail Corridors versus Areas Outside Rail Corridors and Station Areas versus Nonstation Areas— Fairfax Basic Employment, Mean Zonal Values**

|  | Rail corridors | Areas outside rail corridors | Station areas | Nonstation areas |
|---|---|---|---|---|
| **Employment levels** | | | | |
| 1972 | 181 | 139 | 217 | 137 |
| 1976 | 165 | 149 | 206 | 145 |
| 1980 | 245 | 229 | 299 | 224 |
| **Employment changes** | | | | |
| 1972–76 | −15 | 9 | −12 | 8 |
| 1976–80 | 79 | 80 | 94 | 79 |
| 1972–80 | 64 | 90 | 82 | 87 |
| **Percentage changes in employment** | | | | |
| 1972–76 | −8.5 | 6.8 | −5.3 | 6.2 |
| 1976–80 | 48.0 | 53.9 | 45.4 | 54.2 |
| 1972–80 | 35.4 | 64.4 | 37.7 | 63.7 |

Table A.38

**Comparison of Employment Levels and Changes: Rail Corridors versus Areas Outside Rail Corridors and Station Areas versus Nonstation Areas— Fairfax Government Employment, Mean Zonal Values**

|  | Rail corridors | Areas outside rail corridors | Station areas | Nonstation areas |
|---|---|---|---|---|
| **Employment levels** | | | | |
| 1972 | 100 | 387† | 96 | 379† |
| 1976 | 133 | 393† | 150 | 384† |
| 1980 | 146 | 341‡ | 169 | 333‡ |
| **Employment changes** | | | | |
| 1972–76 | 32 | 6 | 54 | 5 |
| 1976–80 | 13 | −52 | 19 | −51 |
| 1972–80 | 45 | −46 | 73 | −46 |
| **Percentage changes in employment** | | | | |
| 1972–76 | 32.3 | 1.5 | 55.7 | 1.3 |
| 1976–80 | 9.7 | −13.3 | 12.8 | −13.3 |
| 1972–80 | 45.2 | −12.0 | 75.7 | −12.2 |

† Difference between means is significant at 0.10 level, two-tailed $t$-test.
‡ Difference between means is significant at 0.05 level, two-tailed $t$-test.

Table A.39

**Comparison of Employment Levels and Changes: Rail Corridors versus Areas Outside Rail Corridors and Station Areas versus Nonstation Areas— Fairfax Service Employment, Mean Zonal Values**

|  | Rail corridors | Areas outside rail corridors | Station areas | Nonstation areas |
|---|---|---|---|---|
| Employment levels |  |  |  |  |
| 1972 | 168 | 294 | 155 | 291 |
| 1976 | 268 | 392 | 267 | 388 |
| 1980 | 467 | 550 | 498 | 545 |
| Employment changes |  |  |  |  |
| 1972–76 | 99 | 98 | 112 | 97 |
| 1976–80 | 199 | 159 | 231 | 157 |
| 1972–80 | 299 | 257 | 343 | 254 |
| Percentage changes in employment |  |  |  |  |
| 1972–76 | 59.2 | 33.4 | 71.9 | 33.3 |
| 1976–80 | 74.5 | 40.5 | 86.6 | 40.5 |
| 1972–80 | 177.8‡ | 87.4 | 220.8‡ | 87.2 |

‡ Difference between means is significant at 0.05 level, two-tailed $t$-test.

Table A.40

**Comparison of Employment Levels and Changes: Rail Corridors versus Areas Outside Rail Corridors and Station Areas versus Nonstation Areas— Fairfax Retail Employment, Mean Zonal Values**

|  | Rail corridors | Areas outside rail corridors | Station areas | Nonstation areas |
|---|---|---|---|---|
| Employment levels |  |  |  |  |
| 1972 | 170 | 289 | 187 | 284 |
| 1976 | 377 | 363 | 461 | 356 |
| 1980 | 382 | 365 | 469 | 358 |
| Employment changes |  |  |  |  |
| 1972–76 | 207† | 74 | 274‡ | 72 |
| 1976–80 | 5 | 2 | 9 | 1 |
| 1972–80 | 212 | 76 | 283† | 73 |
| Percentage changes in employment |  |  |  |  |
| 1972–76 | 121.9 | 25.7 | 146.9 | 25.4 |
| 1976–80 | 1.4 | 0.5 | 1.9 | 0.4 |
| 1972–80 | 124.9 | 26.3 | 151.5 | 25.9 |

† Difference between means is significant at 0.10 level, two-tailed $t$-test.
‡ Difference between means is significant at 0.05 level, two-tailed $t$-test.

Table A.41A

**Employment Levels and Changes: Rail Lines Compared to Control Areas—
All Lines in Region, Total and Basic Employment, Mean Zonal Values**

|  | Total employment | | Basic employment | |
|---|---|---|---|---|
|  | Rail corridors | Control corridors | Rail corridors | Control corridors |
| Employment levels | | | | |
| 1972 | 1,310 | 1,176 | 193 | 140 |
| 1976 | 1,633 | 1,123 | 215† | 120 |
| 1980 | 1,869† | 1,230 | 222† | 126 |
| Employment changes | | | | |
| 1972–76 | 322‡ | −53 | 22 | −19 |
| 1976–80 | 223 | 107 | 5 | 6 |
| 1972–80 | 548‡ | 53 | 28 | −13 |
| Percentage changes in employment | | | | |
| 1972–76 | 24.6 | −4.5 | 11.7 | −14.2 |
| 1976–80 | 13.7 | 9.5 | 2.4‡ | 5.6 |
| 1972–80 | 41.8‡ | 4.6 | 14.4 | −9.4 |

† Difference between means is significant at 0.10 level, two-tailed *t*-test.
‡ Difference between means is significant at 0.05 level, two-tailed *t*-test.

Table A.41B

**Employment Levels and Changes: Rail Lines Compared to Control Areas—
All Lines in Region, Government, Service, and Retail Employment,
Mean Zonal Values**

|  | Government employment | | Service employment | | Retail employment | |
|---|---|---|---|---|---|---|
|  | Rail corridors | Control corridors | Rail corridors | Control corridors | Rail corridors | Control corridors |
| Employment levels | | | | | | |
| 1972 | 401 | 391 | 402 | 313 | 313 | 331 |
| 1976 | 500 | 293 | 536 | 371 | 380 | 337 |
| 1980 | 573 | 364 | 655‡ | 416 | 417 | 321 |
| Employment changes | | | | | | |
| 1972–76 | 99‡ | −98 | 133 | 58 | 67 | 6 |
| 1976–80 | 69 | 71 | 115 | 45 | 33† | −16 |
| 1972–80 | 169‡ | −26 | 249 | 103 | 101† | −10 |
| Percentage changes in employment | | | | | | |
| 1972–76 | 24.7 | −25.1 | 33.1 | 18.7 | 21.5 | 1.9 |
| 1976–80 | 13.7 | 24.4 | 21.3 | 12.1 | 8.9 | −4.8 |
| 1972–80 | 41.7 | −6.8 | 61.4 | 32.9 | 32.3 | −3.0 |

† Difference between means is significant at 0.10 level, two-tailed *t*-test.
‡ Difference between means is significant at 0.05 level, two-tailed *t*-test.

Table A.42A

**Employment Levels and Changes: Rail Lines Compared to Control Areas—All Lines except Vienna (Fairfax) and Its Control, Total and Basic Employment, Mean Zonal Values**

| | Total employment | | Basic employment | |
|---|---|---|---|---|
| | Rail corridors | Control corridors | Rail corridors | Control corridors |
| Employment levels | | | | |
| 1972 | 1,405 | 1,164 | 200 | 159 |
| 1976 | 1,747‡ | 1,041 | 223† | 121 |
| 1980 | 1,973‡ | 1,104 | 219† | 111 |
| Employment changes | | | | |
| 1972–76 | 342† | −123 | 23 | −37 |
| 1976–80 | 225 | 63 | −3 | −9 |
| 1972–80 | 567‡ | −60 | 20 | −47 |
| Percentage changes in employment | | | | |
| 1972–76 | 24.4† | −10.6 | 11.7 | −23.8 |
| 1976–80 | 12.9 | 6.0 | −1.6‡ | −8.1 |
| 1972–80 | 40.4‡ | −5.1 | 10.0† | −30.0 |

† Difference between means is significant at 0.10 level, two-tailed $t$-test.
‡ Difference between means is significant at 0.05 level, two-tailed $t$-test.

Table A.42B

**Employment Levels and Changes: Rail Lines Compared to Control Areas—All Lines except Vienna (Fairfax) and Its Control, Government, Service, and Retail Employment, Mean Zonal Values**

| | Government employment | | Service employment | | Retail employment | |
|---|---|---|---|---|---|---|
| | Rail corridors | Control corridors | Rail corridors | Control corridors | Rail corridors | Control corridors |
| Employment levels | | | | | | |
| 1972 | 436 | 401 | 431 | 289 | 337 | 315 |
| 1976 | 545 | 278 | 569 | 352 | 409 | 288 |
| 1980 | 621 | 373 | 683‡ | 351 | 448 | 268 |
| Employment changes | | | | | | |
| 1972–76 | 109† | −122 | 138 | 63 | 71† | −26 |
| 1976–80 | 76 | 94 | 114‡ | −1 | 39† | −20 |
| 1972–80 | 185† | −27 | 252† | 62 | 110‡ | −46 |
| Percentage changes in employment | | | | | | |
| 1972–76 | 25.2 | −30.5 | 32.0 | 22.0 | 21.1 | −8.4 |
| 1976–80 | 13.9 | 34.0 | 20.0 | −0.5 | 9.5 | −7.0 |
| 1972–80 | 42.6 | −6.8 | 58.4 | 21.4 | 32.6† | −14.9 |

† Difference between means is significant at 0.10 level, two-tailed $t$-test.
‡ Difference between means is significant at 0.05 level, two-tailed $t$-test.

Table A.43A

**Employment Levels and Changes: Rail Line Compared to Control Area—Shady Grove Line, Total and Basic Employment, Mean Zonal Values**

| | Total employment | | Basic employment | |
|---|---|---|---|---|
| | Rail corridor | Control corridor | Rail corridor | Control corridor |
| Employment levels | | | | |
| 1972 | 1,955‡ | 622 | 224‡ | 60 |
| 1976 | 2,598‡ | 537 | 276‡ | 65 |
| 1980 | 3,012‡ | 495 | 260‡ | 50 |
| Employment changes | | | | |
| 1972–76 | 643‡ | −125 | 52 | 5 |
| 1976–80 | 413‡ | −41 | −16 | −15 |
| 1972–80 | 1,057‡ | −167 | 36 | −10 |
| Percentage changes in employment | | | | |
| 1972–76 | 32.9† | −18.9 | 23.5 | 8.0 |
| 1976–80 | 15.9 | −7.7 | −5.9 | −22.7 |
| 1972–80 | 54.1‡ | −25.2 | 16.2 | −16.5 |

† Difference between means is significant at 0.10 level, two-tailed $t$-test.
‡ Difference between means is significant at 0.05 level, two-tailed $t$-test.

Table A.43B

**Employment Levels and Changes: Rail Line Compared to Control Area—Shady Grove Line, Government, Service, and Retail Employment, Mean Zonal Values**

| | Government employment | | Service employment | | Retail employment | |
|---|---|---|---|---|---|---|
| | Rail corridor | Control corridor | Rail corridor | Control corridor | Rail corridor | Control corridor |
| Employment levels | | | | | | |
| 1972 | 704‡ | 95 | 604‡ | 221 | 422 | 285 |
| 1976 | 944‡ | 76 | 852‡ | 195 | 525 | 200 |
| 1980 | 1,153‡ | 83 | 1,010‡ | 174 | 588‡ | 186 |
| Employment changes | | | | | | |
| 1972–76 | 240 | −19 | 247 | −26 | 102 | −84 |
| 1976–80 | 208† | 7 | 158† | −21 | 63 | −13 |
| 1972–80 | 449‡ | −11 | 405† | −47 | 166† | −98 |
| Percentage changes in employment | | | | | | |
| 1972–76 | 34.1 | −20.0 | 41.0† | −11.9 | 24.4‡ | −29.8 |
| 1976–80 | 22.1 | 9.9 | 18.5 | −10.6 | 12.1 | −6.7 |
| 1972–80 | 63.8 | −12.1 | 67.0‡ | −21.2 | 39.4† | −34.5 |

†Difference between means is significant at 0.10 level, two-tailed $t$-test.
‡Difference between means is significant at 0.05 level, two-tailed $t$-test.

Table A.44A

**Employment Levels and Changes: Rail Line Compared to Control Area—
Glenmont Line, Total and Basic Employment, Mean Zonal Values**

| | Total employment | | Basic employment | |
|---|---|---|---|---|
| | Rail corridor | Control corridor | Rail corridor | Control corridor |
| Employment levels | | | | |
| 1972 | 1,117 | 662 | 196‡ | 60 |
| 1976 | 1,490 | 537 | 184 | 65 |
| 1980 | 1,615 | 495 | 219† | 50 |
| Employment changes | | | | |
| 1972–76 | 373 | −125 | −12 | 5 |
| 1976–80 | 125† | −41 | 35 | −15 |
| 1972–80 | 498 | −167 | 23 | −10 |
| Percentage changes in employment | | | | |
| 1972–76 | 33.3 | −18.9 | −5.9 | 8.0 |
| 1976–80 | 8.4 | −7.7 | 18.9† | −22.7 |
| 1972–80 | 44.6 | −25.2 | 11.8 | −16.5 |

† Difference between means is significant at 0.10 level, two-tailed $t$-test.
‡ Difference between means is significant at 0.05 level, two-tailed $t$-test.

Table A.44B

**Employment Levels and Changes: Rail Line Compared to Control Area—
Glenmont Line, Government, Service, and Retail Employment,
Mean Zonal Values**

| | Government employment | | Service employment | | Retail employment | |
|---|---|---|---|---|---|---|
| | Rail corridor | Control corridor | Rail corridor | Control corridor | Rail corridor | Control corridor |
| Employment levels | | | | | | |
| 1972 | 156 | 95 | 457 | 221 | 308 | 285 |
| 1976 | 119 | 76 | 660 | 195 | 526 | 200 |
| 1980 | 191 | 83 | 671† | 174 | 534 | 186 |
| Employment changes | | | | | | |
| 1972–76 | −37 | −19 | 203 | −26 | 218 | −84 |
| 1976–80 | 72 | 7 | 11 | −21 | 8† | −13 |
| 1972–80 | 34 | −11 | 213 | −47 | 226† | −98 |
| Percentage changes in employment | | | | | | |
| 1972–76 | −23.7 | −20.0 | 44.4 | −11.9 | 70.9 | −29.8 |
| 1976–80 | 60.1 | 9.9 | 1.6 | −10.6 | 1.6 | −6.7 |
| 1972–80 | 22.1 | −12.1 | 46.7 | −21.2 | 73.6 | −34.5 |

† Difference between means is significant at 0.10 level, two-tailed $t$-test.

Table A.45A

**Employment Levels and Changes: Rail Line Compared to Control Area— New Carrollton Line, Total and Basic Employment, Mean Zonal Values**

|  | Total employment | | Basic employment | |
|---|---|---|---|---|
|  | Rail corridor | Control corridor | Rail corridor | Control corridor |
| Employment levels |  |  |  |  |
| 1972 | 739 | 1,546 | 202 | 409 |
| 1976 | 787 | 1,485 | 243 | 307 |
| 1980 | 908 | 1,493 | 178 | 334 |
| Employment changes |  |  |  |  |
| 1972–76 | 48 | −61 | 41 | −101 |
| 1976–80 | 120 | 8 | −65 | 26 |
| 1972–80 | 168 | −53 | −24 | −75 |
| Percentage changes in employment |  |  |  |  |
| 1972–76 | 6.5 | −4.0 | 20.4 | −24.9 |
| 1976–80 | 15.3 | 0.6 | −26.8 | 8.7 |
| 1972–80 | 22.8† | −3.4 | −11.9† | −18.3 |

† Difference between means is significant at 0.10 level, two-tailed *t*-test.

Table A.45B

**Comparison of Employment Levels and Changes: Rail Line Compared to Control Area—New Carrollton Line, Government, Service, and Retail Employment, Mean Zonal Values**

|  | Government employment | | Service employment | | Retail employment | |
|---|---|---|---|---|---|---|
|  | Rail corridor | Control corridor | Rail corridor | Control corridor | Rail corridor | Control corridor |
| Employment levels |  |  |  |  |  |  |
| 1972 | 50 | 209‡ | 134 | 504‡ | 353 | 423 |
| 1976 | 48 | 201‡ | 140 | 620‡ | 355 | 355 |
| 1980 | 42 | 185‡ | 190 | 615‡ | 498 | 358 |
| Employment changes |  |  |  |  |  |  |
| 1972–76 | −2 | −8 | 6 | 116 | 2 | −67 |
| 1976–80 | −6 | −16 | 49 | −5 | 142 | 3 |
| 1972–80 | −8 | −24 | 56 | 110 | 144† | −64 |
| Percentage changes in employment |  |  |  |  |  |  |
| 1972–76 | −4.0 | −4.0 | 5.0 | 23.0 | 0.6 | −15.9 |
| 1976–80 | −12.9 | −8.0† | 35.0 | 0.9 | 40.1 | 0.9 |
| 1972–80 | −16.4 | −11.6 | 41.7 | 21.9 | 41.0‡ | −15.2 |

† Difference between means is significant at 0.10 level, two-tailed *t*-test.
‡ Difference between means is significant at 0.05 level, two-tailed *t*-test.

Table A.46A

**Employment Levels and Changes: Rail Line Compared to Control Area—
Greenbelt Line, Total and Basic Employment, Mean Zonal Values**

| | Total employment | | Basic employment | |
|---|---|---|---|---|
| | Rail corridor | Control corridor | Rail corridor | Control corridor |
| Employment levels | | | | |
| 1972 | 833 | 798 | 171† | 81 |
| 1976 | 1,096 | 915 | 220‡ | 69 |
| 1980 | 1,182 | 994 | 223‡ | 40 |
| Employment changes | | | | |
| 1972–76 | 263 | 117 | 49 | −11 |
| 1976–80 | 85 | 78 | 2 | −29 |
| 1972–80 | 349 | 196 | 51 | −41 |
| Percentage changes in employment | | | | |
| 1972–76 | 31.6 | 14.7 | 28.8 | −14.4 |
| 1976–80 | 7.8 | 8.6 | 1.0† | −41.9 |
| 1972–80 | 41.9 | 24.6 | 30.1 | −50.3 |

† Difference between means is significant at 0.10 level, two-tailed $t$-test.
‡ Difference between means is significant at 0.05 level, two-tailed $t$-test.

Table A.46B

**Employment Levels and Changes: Rail Line Compared to Control Area—
Greenbelt Line, Government, Service, and Retail Employment, Mean Zonal Values**

| | Government employment | | Service employment | | Retail employment | |
|---|---|---|---|---|---|---|
| | Rail corridor | Control corridor | Rail corridor | Control corridor | Rail corridor | Control corridor |
| Employment levels | | | | | | |
| 1972 | 223‡ | 56 | 161 | 280 | 277 | 380 |
| 1976 | 385 | 55 | 205 | 337 | 284 | 453 |
| 1980 | 414 | 215 | 267 | 384 | 278 | 354 |
| Employment changes | | | | | | |
| 1972–76 | 162 | −1 | 43 | 57 | 7 | 72 |
| 1976–80 | 28 | 159 | 61 | 47 | −6† | −99 |
| 1972–80 | 191 | 158 | 105 | 104 | 1 | −26 |
| Percentage changes in employment | | | | | | |
| 1972–76 | 72.9 | −1.8 | 27.0 | 20.5 | 2.7 | 19.2† |
| 1976–80 | 7.3 | 288.5 | 30.0 | 14.0 | −2.4† | −21.9 |
| 1972–80 | 85.5 | 281.6 | 65.2 | 37.4 | 0.3 | −6.9 |

† Difference between means is significant at 0.10 level, two-tailed $t$-test.
‡ Difference between means is significant at 0.05 level, two-tailed $t$-test.

Table A.47A

**Employment Levels and Changes: Rail Line Compared to Control Area—
East Falls Church Line, Total and Basic Employment, Mean Zonal Values**

|  | Total employment | | Basic employment | |
|---|---|---|---|---|
|  | Rail corridor | Control corridor | Rail corridor | Control corridor |
| **Employment levels** | | | | |
| 1972 | 1,528 | 1,726 | 188 | 98 |
| 1976 | 1,557 | 1,353 | 165‡ | 48 |
| 1980 | 1,728 | 1,594 | 171‡ | 24 |
| **Employment changes** | | | | |
| 1972–76 | 29 | −373 | −23 | −50 |
| 1976–80 | 171 | 241 | 6 | −24 |
| 1972–80 | 200 | −132 | −17 | −74 |
| **Percentage changes in employment** | | | | |
| 1972–76 | 1.9 | −21.6 | −11.9 | −50.9 |
| 1976–80 | 10.9 | 17.8 | 3.4 | −50.3 |
| 1972–80 | 13.1 | −7.7 | 8.8‡ | −75.6 |

‡ Difference between means is significant at 0.05 level, two-tailed *t*-test.

Table A.47B

**Comparison of Employment Levels and Changes: Rail Line Compared to
Control Area—East Falls Church Line, Government, Service, and Retail
Employment, Mean Zonal Values**

|  | Government employment | | Service employment | | Retail employment | |
|---|---|---|---|---|---|---|
|  | Rail corridor | Control corridor | Rail corridor | Control corridor | Rail corridor | Control corridor |
| **Employment levels** | | | | | | |
| 1972 | 582 | 1,266 | 484‡ | 168 | 273 | 193 |
| 1976 | 610 | 799 | 527 | 301 | 254 | 204 |
| 1980 | 553 | 1,065 | 728† | 289 | 274 | 215 |
| **Employment changes** | | | | | | |
| 1972–76 | 28 | −467 | 43 | 133 | −19 | 11 |
| 1976–80 | −57 | 266 | 201† | −12 | 20 | 11 |
| 1972–80 | −29 | −201 | 244 | 121 | 1 | 22 |
| **Percentage changes in employment** | | | | | | |
| 1972–76 | 4.8‡ | −36.9 | 8.9 | 79.2 | −7.0 | 5.5 |
| 1976–80 | −9.3 | 33.4 | 38.2 | −4.1 | 8.0 | 5.2 |
| 1972–80 | −5.0† | −15.8 | 50.6 | 71.9 | 0.3 | 11.0 |

† Difference between means is significant at 0.10 level, two-tailed *t*-test.
‡ Difference between means is significant at 0.05 level, two-tailed *t*-test.

Table A.48A

**Employment Levels and Changes: Rail Line Compared to Control Area—
Vienna Line, Total and Basic Employment, Mean Zonal Values**

|  | Total employment | | Basic employment | |
|---|---|---|---|---|
|  | Rail corridor | Control corridor | Rail corridor | Control corridor |
| **Employment levels** | | | | |
| 1972 | 427 | 1,210‡ | 129 | 88 |
| 1976 | 563 | 1,346‡ | 143 | 117 |
| 1980 | 814 | 1,574 | 251 | 169 |
| **Employment changes** | | | | |
| 1972–76 | 136 | 136 | 15 | 29 |
| 1976–80 | 200 | 228 | 95 | 52 |
| 1972–80 | 352 | 364 | 81 | 111 |
| **Percentage changes in employment** | | | | |
| 1972–76 | 31.9 | 11.3 | 10.9 | 33.1 |
| 1976–80 | 35.5 | 16.9 | 66.4 | 44.0 |
| 1972–80 | 82.4 | 30.1 | 62.8 | 126.1 |

‡ Difference between means is significant at 0.05 level, two-tailed $t$-test.

Table A.48B

**Employment Levels and Changes: Rail Line Compared to Control Area—
Vienna Line, Government, Service, and Retail Employment, Mean Zonal Values**

|  | Government employment | | Service employment | | Retail employment | |
|---|---|---|---|---|---|---|
|  | Rail corridor | Control corridor | Rail corridor | Control corridor | Rail corridor | Control corridor |
| **Employment levels** | | | | | | |
| 1972 | 78 | 366‡ | 137 | 379‡ | 84 | 376‡ |
| 1976 | 78 | 333‡ | 227 | 424 | 115 | 472‡ |
| 1980 | 84 | 341‡ | 372 | 597 | 108 | 467‡ |
| **Employment changes** | | | | | | |
| 1972–76 | 0 | −33 | 90 | 45 | 31 | 96† |
| 1976–80 | 6 | 8 | 124 | 173 | −17 | −5 |
| 1972–80 | 6 | −25 | 223 | 218 | 16 | 91† |
| **Percentage changes in employment** | | | | | | |
| 1972–76 | 0.0 | −9.1 | 65.7 | 11.8 | 36.9 | 25.6 |
| 1976–80 | 7.7 | 2.5 | 54.6 | 40.8 | −14.8 | −1.1‡ |
| 1972–80 | 7.7 | −6.9 | 162.8 | 57.4 | 19.0 | 24.1 |

† Difference between means is significant at 0.10 level, two-tailed $t$-test.
‡ Difference between means is significant at 0.05 level, two-tailed $t$-test.

Table A.49A

**Employment Levels and Changes inside Rail Corridors: Station Areas Compared to Nonstation Areas—All Lines, Total and Basic Employment, Mean Zonal Values**

|  | Total employment | | Basic employment | |
|---|---|---|---|---|
|  | Station areas | Nonstation areas | Station areas | Nonstation areas |
| Employment levels | | | | |
| 1972 | 1,794‡ | 846 | 235‡ | 128 |
| 1976 | 2,072‡ | 766 | 266‡ | 120 |
| 1980 | 2,252‡ | 814 | 256‡ | 134 |
| Employment changes | | | | |
| 1972–76 | 277‡ | −87 | 30 | −9 |
| 1976–80 | 169 | 48 | −11 | 13 |
| 1972–80 | 449‡ | −40 | 19 | 4 |
| Percentage changes in employment | | | | |
| 1972–76 | 15.5‡ | −10.3 | 12.7‡ | −7.1 |
| 1976–80 | 8.2 | 6.2 | −4.2 | 11.1‡ |
| 1972–80 | 24.9 | −4.7 | 8.0 | 3.1 |

‡ Difference between means is significant at 0.05 level, two-tailed $t$-test.

Table A.49B

**Employment Levels and Changes inside Rail Corridors: Station Areas Compared to Nonstation Areas—All Lines, Government, Service, and Retail Employment, Mean Zonal Values**

|  | Government employment | | Service employment | | Retail employment | |
|---|---|---|---|---|---|---|
|  | Station areas | Nonstation areas | Station areas | Nonstation areas | Station areas | Nonstation areas |
| Employment levels | | | | | | |
| 1972 | 804‡ | 249 | 449‡ | 272 | 306‡ | 197 |
| 1976 | 863‡ | 219 | 585‡ | 260 | 358‡ | 168 |
| 1980 | 894‡ | 218 | 744‡ | 287 | 357‡ | 176 |
| Employment changes | | | | | | |
| 1972–76 | 59 | −33 | 135‡ | −15 | 52‡ | −30 |
| 1976–80 | 26 | −1 | 156‡ | 28 | −2 | 7 |
| 1972–80 | 86 | −33 | 292‡ | 13 | 51† | −23 |
| Percentage changes in employment | | | | | | |
| 1972–76 | 7.3† | −13.0 | 30.2 | −5.4 | 17.3 | −15.4 |
| 1976–80 | 3.0 | −0.3 | 26.6 | 10.6 | −0.5 | 4.4 |
| 1972–80 | 10.6† | −13.3 | 64.8‡ | 4.5 | 16.8 | −11.7 |

† Difference between means is significant at 0.10 level, two-tailed $t$-test.
‡ Difference between means is significant at 0.05 level, two-tailed $t$-test.

Table A.50A

**Employment Levels and Changes inside Rail Corridors: Station Areas Compared to Nonstation Areas—Open Lines, 1980, Total and Basic Employment, Mean Zonal Values**

|  | Total employment | | Basic employment | |
|---|---|---|---|---|
|  | Station areas | Nonstation areas | Station areas | Nonstation areas |
| Employment levels |  |  |  |  |
| 1972 | 1,828‡ | 894 | 235† | 130 |
| 1976 | 2,115‡ | 813 | 263‡ | 120 |
| 1980 | 2,367‡ | 856 | 272‡ | 128 |
| Employment changes |  |  |  |  |
| 1972–76 | 287‡ | −92 | 28 | −11 |
| 1976–80 | 238 | 42 | 7 | 8 |
| 1972–80 | 527‡ | −50 | 36 | −3 |
| Percentage changes in employment |  |  |  |  |
| 1972–76 | 15.7‡ | −10.2 | 12.0‡ | −8.7 |
| 1976–80 | 11.2 | 5.2 | 2.8 | 6.4‡ |
| 1972–80 | 28.6‡ | −5.5 | 15.2 | −3.0 |

† Difference between means is significant at 0.10 level, two-tailed $t$-test.
‡ Difference between means is significant at 0.05 level, two-tailed $t$-test.

Table A.50B

**Employment Levels and Changes inside Rail Corridors: Station Areas Compared to Nonstation Areas—Open Lines, 1980, Government, Service, and Retail Employment, Mean Zonal Values**

|  | Government employment | | Service employment | | Retail employment | |
|---|---|---|---|---|---|---|
|  | Station areas | Nonstation areas | Station areas | Nonstation areas | Station areas | Nonstation areas |
| Employment levels |  |  |  |  |  |  |
| 1972 | 751‡ | 287 | 514‡ | 292 | 327‡ | 186 |
| 1976 | 790‡ | 264 | 676‡ | 261 | 385‡ | 168 |
| 1980 | 830 | 257 | 857‡ | 293 | 398‡ | 178 |
| Employment changes |  |  |  |  |  |  |
| 1972–76 | 39 | −27 | 162‡ | −34 | 58 | −20 |
| 1976–80 | 44 | −7 | 176‡ | 32 | 10 | 10 |
| 1972–80 | 83 | −34 | 339‡ | −2 | 68 | −10 |
| Percentage changes in employment |  |  |  |  |  |  |
| 1972–76 | 5.2 | −9.2 | 31.6 | −11.5 | 17.6 | −10.8 |
| 1976–80 | 5.5 | −2.8 | 25.9 | 12.3 | 2.5 | 6.0 |
| 1972–80 | 11.0† | −11.8 | 65.7‡ | −0.7 | 20.6 | −5.4 |

† Difference between means is significant at 0.10 level, two-tailed $t$-test.
‡ Difference between means is significant at 0.05 level, two-tailed $t$-test.

Table A.51A

**Employment Levels and Changes inside Rail Corridors: Station Areas Compared to Nonstation Areas—Shady Grove Line, Total and Basic Employment, Mean Zonal Values**

| | Total employment | | Basic employment | |
|---|---|---|---|---|
| | Station areas | Nonstation areas | Station areas | Nonstation areas |
| Employment levels | | | | |
| 1972 | 2,272 | 1,355 | 190 | 127 |
| 1976 | 2,887‡ | 1,185 | 252 | 148 |
| 1980 | 3,150‡ | 1,455 | 247 | 186 |
| Employment changes | | | | |
| 1972–76 | 613† | −169 | 62 | 21 |
| 1976–80 | 263 | 269 | −6 | 38 |
| 1972–80 | 877 | 100 | 56 | 59 |
| Percentage changes in employment | | | | |
| 1972–76 | 27.0 | −12.5 | 32.7 | 16.6 |
| 1976–80 | 9.1 | 22.7 | −2.3 | 25.4 |
| 1972–80 | 38.5 | 7.4 | 29.6 | 46.3 |

† Difference between means is significant at 0.10 level, two-tailed *t*-test.
‡ Difference between means is significant at 0.05 level, two-tailed *t*-test.

Table A.51B

**Employment Levels and Changes inside Rail Corridors: Station Areas Compared to Nonstation Areas—Shady Grove Line, Government, Service, and Retail Employment, Mean Zonal Values**

| | Government employment | | Service employment | | Retail employment | |
|---|---|---|---|---|---|---|
| | Station areas | Nonstation areas | Station areas | Nonstation areas | Station areas | Nonstation areas |
| Employment levels | | | | | | |
| 1972 | 757 | 405 | 802 | 534 | 522‡ | 288 |
| 1976 | 943† | 297 | 1,077‡ | 457 | 613‡ | 282 |
| 1980 | 1,012 | 461 | 1,279‡ | 530 | 611‡ | 277 |
| Employment changes | | | | | | |
| 1972–76 | 186† | −107 | 274 | −77 | 90 | −6 |
| 1976–80 | 69 | 163 | 202 | 72 | −2 | −5 |
| 1972–80 | 255 | 57 | 477† | −4 | 88 | −11 |
| Percentage changes in employment | | | | | | |
| 1972–76 | 24.6† | −26.5 | 32.7 | −16.6 | 17.3 | −2.1 |
| 1976–80 | 7.3 | 55.1 | 18.8 | 15.4 | −0.3 | −1.8 |
| 1972–80 | 33.7 | 14.0 | 59.5 | −0.8 | 16.9 | −3.8 |

† Difference between means is significant at 0.10 level, two-tailed *t*-test.
‡ Difference between means is significant at 0.05 level, two-tailed *t*-test.

Table A.52A

**Employment Levels and Changes inside Rail Corridors: Station Areas Compared to Nonstation Areas—Glenmont Line, Total and Basic Employment, Mean Zonal Values**

| | Total employment | | Basic employment | |
|---|---|---|---|---|
| | Station areas | Nonstation areas | Station areas | Nonstation areas |
| Employment levels | | | | |
| 1972 | 986 | 866 | 181 | 152 |
| 1976 | 1,704‡ | 371 | 270‡ | 46 |
| 1980 | 1,747† | 429 | 243† | 83 |
| Employment changes | | | | |
| 1972–76 | 718‡ | −495 | 89‡ | −105 |
| 1976–80 | 42 | 58 | −26 | 37 |
| 1972–80 | 761‡ | −437 | 62† | −68 |
| Percentage changes in employment | | | | |
| 1972–76 | 72.8‡ | −57.1 | 49.3 | −69.6 |
| 1976–80 | 2.5 | 15.6 | −9.8 | 80.7‡ |
| 1972–80 | 77.2‡ | −50.3 | 34.6 | −45.0 |

† Difference between means is significant at 0.10 level, two-tailed $t$-test.
‡ Difference between means is significant at 0.05 level, two-tailed $t$-test.

Table A.52B

**Employment Levels and Changes inside Rail Corridors: Station Areas Compared to Nonstation Areas—Glenmont Line, Government, Service, and Retail Employment, Mean Zonal Values**

| | Government employment | | Service employment | | Retail employment | |
|---|---|---|---|---|---|---|
| | Station areas | Nonstation areas | Station areas | Nonstation areas | Station areas | Nonstation areas |
| Employment levels | | | | | | |
| 1972 | 112 | 116 | 381 | 381 | 312 | 219 |
| 1976 | 137 | 35 | 694† | 201 | 602† | 89 |
| 1980 | 196 | 58 | 703† | 195 | 604† | 94 |
| Employment changes | | | | | | |
| 1972–76 | 25 | −81 | 314‡ | −179 | 290‡ | −128 |
| 1976–80 | 58 | 23 | 9 | −6 | 1 | 4 |
| 1972–80 | 83 | −58 | 323‡ | −186 | 291‡ | −124 |
| Percentage changes in employment | | | | | | |
| 1972–76 | 22.2 | −69.7 | 82.4† | −47.2 | 93.0‡ | −58.9 |
| 1976–80 | 42.4 | 65.0 | 1.3 | −3.2 | 0.2 | 4.6 |
| 1972–80 | 74.1 | −50.0 | 84.9† | −48.9 | 93.5‡ | −57.0 |

† Difference between means is significant at 0.10 level, two-tailed $t$-test.
‡ Difference between means is significant at 0.05 level, two-tailed $t$-test.

Table A.53A

**Employment Levels and Changes inside Rail Corridors: Station Areas Compared to Nonstation Areas—Branch Avenue Line, Total and Basic Employment, Mean Zonal Values**

| | Total employment | | Basic Employment | |
|---|---|---|---|---|
| | Station areas | Nonstation areas | Station areas | Nonstation areas |
| Employment levels | | | | |
| 1972 | 1,274† | 545 | 159 | 83 |
| 1976 | 1,429‡ | 339 | 185 | 41 |
| 1980 | 1,263 | 501 | 150 | 61 |
| Employment changes | | | | |
| 1972–76 | 154 | −205 | 26† | −42 |
| 1976–80 | −165 | 162 | −35 | 19 |
| 1972–80 | −11 | −44 | −10 | −23 |
| Percentage changes in employment | | | | |
| 1972–76 | 12.1† | −37.7 | 16.1‡ | −50.3 |
| 1976–80 | −11.6 | 47.6 | −19.1 | 45.6 |
| 1972–80 | −0.9 | −8.0 | −6.1 | −27.6 |

† Difference between means is significant at 0.10 level, two-tailed $t$-test.
‡ Difference between means is significant at 0.05 level, two-tailed $t$-test.

Table A.53B

**Employment Levels and Changes inside Rail Corridors: Station Areas Compared to Nonstation Areas—Branch Avenue Line, Government, Service, and Retail Employment, Mean Zonal Values**

| | Government employment | | Service employment | | Retail employment | |
|---|---|---|---|---|---|---|
| | Station areas | Nonstation areas | Station areas | Nonstation areas | Station areas | Nonstation areas |
| Employment levels | | | | | | |
| 1972 | 729† | 194 | 135 | 83 | 250 | 184 |
| 1976 | 811 | 108 | 163‡ | 53 | 269 | 137 |
| 1980 | 722 | 169 | 169† | 84 | 221 | 186 |
| Employment changes | | | | | | |
| 1972–76 | 82 | −86 | 27 | −29 | 19 | −47 |
| 1976–80 | −88 | 61 | 6 | 32 | −48 | 50† |
| 1972–80 | −6 | −25 | 33 | 2 | −29 | 2 |
| Percentage changes in employment | | | | | | |
| 1972–76 | 11.3 | −44.3 | 20.0‡ | −35.7 | 7.6† | −25.8 |
| 1976–80 | −10.9 | 56.4 | 3.9 | 59.6 | −17.8 | 36.5 |
| 1972–80 | −0.9 | −12.9 | 24.6† | 2.6 | −11.5 | 1.3 |

† Difference between means is significant at 0.10 level, two-tailed $t$-test.
‡ Difference between means is significant at 0.05 level, two-tailed $t$-test.

Table A.54A

**Employment Levels and Changes inside Rail Corridors: Station Areas Compared to Nonstation Areas—New Carrollton Line, Total and Basic Employment, Mean Zonal Values**

| | Total employment | | Basic employment | |
|---|---|---|---|---|
| | Station areas | Nonstation areas | Station areas | Nonstation areas |
| **Employment levels** | | | | |
| 1972 | 617 | 398 | 101 | 116 |
| 1976 | 734 | 526 | 163 | 190 |
| 1980 | 784 | 434 | 131 | 86 |
| **Employment changes** | | | | |
| 1972–76 | 117 | 128 | 61 | 74 |
| 1976–80 | 49 | −92 | −32 | −104 |
| 1972–80 | 166 | 36 | 29 | −30 |
| **Percentage changes in employment** | | | | |
| 1972–76 | 18.9 | 32.3 | 61.1 | 64.1 |
| 1976–80 | 6.7 | −17.5 | −19.8 | −54.9 |
| 1972–80 | 26.9 | 9.1 | 29.1 | −26.0 |

Table A.54B

**Employment Levels and Changes inside Rail Corridors: Station Areas Compared to Nonstation Areas—New Carrollton Line, Government, Service, and Retail Employment, Mean Zonal Values**

| | Government employment | | Service employment | | Retail employment | |
|---|---|---|---|---|---|---|
| | Station areas | Nonstation areas | Station areas | Nonstation areas | Station areas | Nonstation areas |
| **Employment levels** | | | | | | |
| 1972 | 217 | 44 | 81 | 63 | 218 | 175 |
| 1976 | 302† | 41 | 76 | 83 | 193 | 212 |
| 1980 | 311† | 35 | 122 | 82 | 220 | 231 |
| **Employment changes** | | | | | | |
| 1972–76 | 85 | −3 | −5 | 21 | −24 | 37 |
| 1976–80 | 9 | −6 | 46 | −1 | 26 | 19 |
| 1972–80 | 94 | −9 | 41 | 19 | 2 | 56 |
| **Percentage changes in employment** | | | | | | |
| 1972–76 | 39.2 | −7.7 | −6.7 | 33.0 | −11.2 | 21.1 |
| 1976–80 | 3.0 | −14.6 | 61.2 | −1.9 | 13.6 | 9.3 |
| 1972–80 | 43.4 | −21.2 | 50.4 | 30.5 | 0.8 | 32.4 |

† Difference between means is significant at 0.10 level, two-tailed $t$-test.

Table A.55A

**Employment Levels and Changes inside Rail Corridors: Station Areas Compared to Nonstation Areas—Greenbelt Line, Total and Basic Employment, Mean Zonal Values**

| | Total employment | | Basic employment | |
| --- | --- | --- | --- | --- |
| | Station areas | Nonstation areas | Station areas | Nonstation areas |
| Employment levels | | | | |
| 1972 | 1,954‡ | 740 | 296† | 136 |
| 1976 | 2,264‡ | 710 | 338† | −146 |
| 1980 | 2,289‡ | 742 | 232 | 181 |
| Employment changes | | | | |
| 1972–76 | 310 | −30 | 41 | 11 |
| 1976–80 | 24 | 33 | −106 | 35† |
| 1972–80 | 334 | 2 | −64 | 45 |
| Percentage changes in employment | | | | |
| 1972–76 | 15.9 | −4.1 | 14.0 | 7.8 |
| 1976–80 | 1.1 | 4.6 | −31.3 | 23.6 |
| 1972–80 | 17.1 | 0.3 | −21.7 | 33.3 |

† Difference between means is significant at 0.10 level, two-tailed $t$-test.
‡ Difference between means is significant at 0.05 level, two-tailed $t$-test.

Table A.55B

**Employment Levels and Changes inside Rail Corridors: Station Areas Compared to Nonstation Areas—Greenbelt Line, Government, Service, and Retail Employment, Mean Zonal Values**

| | Government employment | | Service employment | | Retail employment | |
| --- | --- | --- | --- | --- | --- | --- |
| | Station areas | Nonstation areas | Station areas | Nonstation areas | Station areas | Nonstation areas |
| Employment levels | | | | | | |
| 1972 | 1,167‡ | 107 | 289 | 251 | 200 | 246 |
| 1976 | 1,334‡ | 66 | 344 | 318 | 248 | 178 |
| 1980 | 1,347‡ | 74 | 495 | 326 | 213 | 161 |
| Employment changes | | | | | | |
| 1972–76 | 166 | −40 | 54 | 67 | 48† | −68 |
| 1976–80 | 13 | 7 | 152 | 8 | −34 | −16 |
| 1972–80 | 179 | −33 | 206 | 75 | 13 | −84 |
| Percentage changes in employment | | | | | | |
| 1972–76 | 14.2 | −37.7 | 18.7 | 26.6 | 24.1‡ | −27.5 |
| 1976–80 | 1.0 | 10.8 | 44.1 | 2.4 | −13.9 | −9.3 |
| 1972–80 | 15.4 | −31.0 | 71.1 | 29.7 | 6.9† | −34.3 |

† Difference between means is significant at 0.10 level, two-tailed $t$-test.
‡ Difference between means is significant at 0.05 level, two-tailed $t$-test.

Table A.56A

**Employment Levels and Changes inside Rail Corridors: Station Areas Compared to Nonstation Areas—Addison Road Line, Total and Basic Employment, Mean Zonal Values**

| | Total employment | | Basic employment | |
|---|---|---|---|---|
| | Station areas | Nonstation areas | Station areas | Nonstation areas |
| Employment levels | | | | |
| 1972 | 411† | 136 | 34 | 11 |
| 1976 | 290 | 188 | 31 | 0 |
| 1980 | 391 | 173 | 12 | 0 |
| Employment changes | | | | |
| 1972–76 | −121 | 52 | −4 | −11 |
| 1976–80 | 101 | −15 | −18 | 0 |
| 1972–80 | −19 | 37 | −23 | −11 |
| Percentage changes in employment | | | | |
| 1972–76 | −29.4 | 38.2 | −12.7 | −100 |
| 1976–80 | 34.9 | −8.0 | −60.0 | 0 |
| 1972–80 | −4.8 | 27.2 | −65.1 | −100 |

† Difference between means is significant at 0.10 level, two-tailed $t$-test.

Table A.56B

**Employment Levels and Changes inside Rail Corridors: Station Areas Compared to Nonstation Areas—Addison Road Line, Government, Service, and Retail Employment, Mean Zonal Values**

| | Government employment | | Service employment | | Retail employment | |
|---|---|---|---|---|---|---|
| | Station areas | Nonstation areas | Station areas | Nonstation areas | Station areas | Nonstation areas |
| Employment levels | | | | | | |
| 1972 | 186 | 67 | 59 | 20 | 129† | 38 |
| 1976 | 118 | 82 | 51 | 63 | 89 | 42 |
| 1980 | 144 | 106 | 175 | 50 | 59 | 16 |
| Employment changes | | | | | | |
| 1972–76 | −68 | 15 | −7 | 43 | −41 | 4 |
| 1976–80 | 26 | 23 | 123 | −12 | −30 | −26 |
| 1972–80 | −41 | 39† | 116 | 30 | −70 | −21 |
| Percentage changes in employment | | | | | | |
| 1972–76 | −36.6 | 23.1 | −12.6 | 215.0 | −31.5 | 11.8 |
| 1976–80 | 22.3 | 28.5 | 240.0 | −19.8 | −33.7‡ | −61.2 |
| 1972–80 | −22.4 | 58.2 | 197.1 | 152.5 | −54.6 | −56.6 |

† Difference between means is significant at 0.10 level, two-tailed $t$-test.
‡ Difference between means is significant at 0.05 level, two-tailed $t$-test.

Table A.57A

**Employment Levels and Changes inside Rail Corridors: Station Areas Compared to Nonstation Areas—Franconia-Springfield Line, Total and Basic Employment, Mean Zonal Values**

| | Total employment | | Basic employment | |
|---|---|---|---|---|
| | Station areas | Nonstation areas | Station areas | Nonstation areas |
| Employment levels | | | | |
| 1972 | 3,147† | 896 | 398 | 160 |
| 1976 | 3,118† | 1,031 | 379 | 170 |
| 1980 | 3,562‡ | 797 | 395 | 153 |
| Employment changes | | | | |
| 1972–76 | −29 | 94 | −19 | 5 |
| 1976–80 | 443† | −234 | 15 | −17 |
| 1972–80 | 414 | −140 | −3 | −12 |
| Percentage changes in employment | | | | |
| 1972–76 | −0.9 | 9.76 | −4.8 | 1.8 |
| 1976–80 | 14.2† | −22.7 | 4.1 | −10.2 |
| 1972–80 | 13.2‡ | −15.1 | −0.9 | −9.5 |

† Difference between means is significant at 0.10 level, two-tailed *t*-test.
‡ Difference between means is significant at 0.05 level, two-tailed *t*-test.

Table A.57B

**Employment Levels and Changes inside Rail Corridors: Station Areas Compared to Nonstation AReas—Franconia-Springfield Line, Government, Service, and Retail Employment, Mean Zonal Values**

| | Government employment | | Service employment | | Retail employment | |
|---|---|---|---|---|---|---|
| | Station areas | Nonstation areas | Station areas | Nonstation areas | Station areas | Nonstation areas |
| Employment levels | | | | | | |
| 1972 | 2,101 | 483 | 434‡ | 149 | 213‡ | 107 |
| 1976 | 1,914 | 581 | 594‡ | 176 | 230‡ | 103 |
| 1980 | 1,980† | 363 | 911‡ | 156 | 274‡ | 123 |
| Employment changes | | | | | | |
| 1972–76 | −186 | 75 | 159† | 18 | 17 | −5 |
| 1976–80 | 66 | −218 | 317‡ | −19 | 44 | 21 |
| 1972–80 | −121 | −143 | 477‡ | −0.5 | 61 | 16 |
| Percentage changes in employment | | | | | | |
| 1972–76 | −8.9 | 14.8 | 36.7 | 12.1 | 8.0 | −4.9 |
| 1976–80 | 3.4 | −37.5 | 53.6 | −11.1 | 19.2 | 20.3 |
| 1972–80 | −5.8 | −28.3 | 109.9‡ | −0.3 | 28.7 | 14.4 |

† Difference between means is significant at 0.10 level, two-tailed *t*-test.
‡ Difference between means is significant at 0.05 level, two-tailed *t*-test.

Table A.58A

**Employment Levels and Changes inside Rail Corridors: Station Areas Compared to Nonstation Areas—Vienna Line, Total and Basic Employment, Mean Zonal Values**

| | Total employment | | Basic employment | |
|---|---|---|---|---|
| | Station areas | Nonstation areas | Station areas | Nonstation areas |
| Employment levels | | | | |
| 1972 | 1,871‡ | 434 | 330‡ | 76 |
| 1976 | 2,018‡ | 454 | 281‡ | 48 |
| 1980 | 2,464‡ | 566 | 357 | 65 |
| Employment changes | | | | |
| 1972–76 | 146 | 20 | −48 | −28 |
| 1976–80 | 387 | 112 | 68 | 17 |
| 1972–80 | 539 | 132 | 18 | −11 |
| Percentage changes in employment | | | | |
| 1972–76 | 7.8 | 4.6 | −14.8 | −37.1 |
| 1976–80 | 18.7‡ | 24.7 | 23.7 | 35.1 |
| 1972–80 | 27.9 | 30.4 | 5.3 | −15.2 |

‡ Difference between means is significant at 0.05 level, two-tailed *t*-test.

Table A.58B

**Employment Levels and Changes inside Rail Corridors: Station Areas Compared to Nonstation Areas—Vienna Line, Government, Service, and Retail Employment, Mean Zonal Values**

| | Government employment | | Service employment | | Retail employment | |
|---|---|---|---|---|---|---|
| | Station areas | Nonstation areas | Station areas | Nonstation areas | Station areas | Nonstation areas |
| Employment levels | | | | | | |
| 1972 | 511‡ | 53 | 739‡ | 180 | 290† | 124 |
| 1976 | 599‡ | 42 | 852‡ | 230 | 285† | 134 |
| 1980 | 623‡ | 37 | 1,181‡ | 311 | 303 | 153 |
| Employment changes | | | | | | |
| 1972–76 | 88 | −11 | 112 | 49 | −5 | 9 |
| 1976–80 | 6 | −5 | 304 | 82 | 9 | 18 |
| 1972–80 | 97 | −16 | 420 | 131 | 3 | 28 |
| Percentage changes in employment | | | | | | |
| 1972–76 | 17.2† | −21.4 | 15.2 | 27.6 | −1.8 | 7.7† |
| 1976–80 | 1.0 | −11.5 | 34.7‡ | 35.5 | 3.0 | 13.9 |
| 1972–80 | 18.4 | −30.5 | 55.2† | 72.9 | 1.1 | 22.6 |

† Difference between means is significant at 0.10 level, two-tailed *t*-test.
‡ Difference between means is significant at 0.05 level, two-tailed *t*-test.

*Four*

# Regional and Urban Modeling: A Review of the Literature

The long search for a practical modeling methodology for urban areas has followed several paths of study. The earliest models were simple and highly abstract and eventually failed the test of practicality (as also did the more recent models in this tradition developed by the New Urban Economics school). They were succeeded by other, more practical approaches such as pure empiricism (the EMPIRIC work), gravity models (the Lowry tradition), and the Wilsonian entropy-maximizing framework. Except for some highly abstract work of little practical utility, the field of urban modeling now seems to be converging on a set of interactive models with a common theoretical base in utility-maximizing theory.

## Approaches to Urban Economic Modeling

Urban modeling efforts by economists have often been purely theoretical attempts to formulate systematic explanations for the location decisions of firms, households, and farms, the resulting urban/rural split, and the urban structure itself.

### The New Urban Economics Models

One approach—rooted in the work of von Thunen (1898) and Weber (1929) and developed further, in the New Urban Economics tradition, by Alonso (1964), Muth (1969), Henderson (1985), and Wheaton (1979b)—typically provides only the most general, stylized vision of urban form and intrametropolitan location. Such models are of little practical use for planners, forecasters, or developers. Their simplifying assumptions (such as work trip costs increasing as a linear function of distance from the CBD) limit their usefulness for understanding modern planning problems. Much more complex theoretical models are needed to simulate today's city accurately, and it has been quite difficult to modify the New Urban Economic models to resemble reality.

There have been extensive efforts based on such models to estimate empirically urban production functions and gradients of employment, population density, and land value (Kau et al., 1983) and to model household location decisions (Curran, Carlson, and Ford, 1982). The results of these efforts, however, have generally been of low statistical reliability, and they reflect, at best, a limited slice of urban activities. Hence they have not led to practical applications to the urban development process.

### Economic Base Studies

Other students of land use have attempted to investigate urban activity with a simpler vision of location decisions. This work, which can be traced at least to the community economic base studies of Charles Tiebout (1962), was initially concerned with the character rather than the location of economic activities. Modelers attempted to classify economic activity into basic and nonbasic sectors (and often into finer levels as well), and then to predict nonbasic activity levels from basic activity, which was generally assumed to be a given (or determined exogenously to the urban area by, for example, growth in GNP).

For many urban and regional scholars, such forecasts were far too aggregated to provide information about emerging urban forms. Nevertheless, the simplification of the metropolitan economy in economic base studies led to a fruitful approach to the question of where people and nonbasic economic activities locate *within* a given metropolis. In this analysis, the line of causation of urban change begins with infrastructure and basic employment as givens. These lead to residential location decisions, which in turn determine the locations of nonbasic activities serving these residences.

Some economists who branched off from the New Urban Economics joined in the move toward disaggregated modeling using multiple economic and demographic variables to determine zone location decisions in an urban area. But research teams rapidly found the data requirements for such models to be overwhelming. This discovery led these teams to consider sample-based microsimulation as a reasonable solution to the data problem. While subject to oft-expressed reservations about sampling procedures and their ability to reflect accurately the heterogeneous population of an urban area, these models offer more potential for implementation and use by practitioners than their unwieldly precursors (Ingram, 1979; Putman, 1983).

### The EMPIRIC Model[1]

The EMPIRIC model was developed to forecast future development in zones in cities by using a large amount of data and little theory. The model has been calibrated in many cities, but has never proven very successful as a forecasting tool.

The goal of the EMPIRIC modelers was to create a recursive forecasting model utilizing a large volume of independent variables (called *locator* variables) to forecast the zonal portion of regional growth for each of several dependent variables (called *located* variables). Exogenous forecasts of regional growth totals supplied estimates of changes in key variables for the region as a whole, which were then divided up among the zones according to the endogenously forecasted shares. The model's structure was based on the idea (Hill et al., 1966, as cited by Putman, 1979) that "the development patterns of urban activities are interrelated in a systematic manner." This extremely vague—if correct—formulation meant that the model developers were going to let the numbers do the talking.

Unfortunately, numbers do not talk fluently. To calibrate the model, a wide range of sets of independent variables were used until high $R^2$s were achieved. Two major difficulties accompanied this apparently successful effort. One is the lack of structural equations from which to derive the set of single equations (effectively reduced-form equations), which means that little policy-making insight can be gained from EMPIRIC. The appearance of counterintuitive signs (Putman, 1976a) in many of the estimations of the model reflects this lack of an underlying theory of causation. The other difficulty is that EMPIRIC is ineffective in medium-range forecasting. Its success in short-term forecasting occurred largely because urban areas, like elephants, move slowly; most of what is there today is there tomorrow. If rapid changes occur within

---

[1]Much of what follows is based on Putman, 1979.

a few zones, those changes are likely to be minor perturbations within the urban system as a whole. Thus, EMPIRIC-based forecasts are theoretically suspect. It is in the final analysis contradictory to perform policy-simulation experiments, that is, to try to find out what kind of *changes* in urban form various policies might induce, using a model whose strength is its ability to reflect the *continuity* of urban form.

## The Lowry and Entropy-Maximizing Models

Two major streams of modeling appeared within this general research problem during the 1960s, EMPIRIC (discussed above) and the Lowry-type models (Putman, 1979). The Lowry path seems to have been the more fruitful in theoretical content, ultimate estimability, and, most importantly (given the interest that gave rise to these models), for policy-simulation experiments.

### *The Lowry Models*

Lowry-type models attempt to predict zonal changes based only upon certain principles of spatial interaction; they do not use explicit individual decision-making principles. They have been the most successful models in practice despite their initial lack of a sound basis in social science theory (recent work suggests such a basis, as we shall see).

Early Lowry-type models described spatial interaction in terms of a straightforward analogy from physics: the gravity model. Reflecting the Newtonian proposition that the force exerted by one body on another is directly proportional to the product of their masses and inversely proportional to the square of the distance between them, the interaction between two locations is specified as proportional to the product of land-use intensity in the two sites (their "masses") and inversely proportional to the difficulty of traveling between the two sites (the "distance between them"). A simple equation reflecting this proposition is:

$$Q_{ij} = \frac{K L_{oi} L_{dj}}{f(T_{ij})}$$

where

$Q_{ij}$ = level of traffic interaction between zones $i$ and $j$;
$K$ = some constant to adjust for the arbitrary scales and magnitudes attached to other variables;
$L_{oi}$ = land-use intensity at the point of trip origin;
$L_{dj}$ = land-use intensity at the point of trip destination (usually employment); and
$f(T_{ij})$ = some function of the transport impedances.

Typically, $f$ is a power function $f(T_{ij}) = T_{ij}^{\alpha}$, an exponential function $f(T_{ij}) = \exp(\beta T_{ij})$, or a Tanner function $f(T_{ij}) = T_{ij}^{\alpha} \times \exp(\beta T_{ij})$.

Lowry's original (1964) residential location model was really a simple version of the gravity model. Residential location in zone $i$, $N_i$, is a scaling factor $k$ times a weighted sum composed of the number of workers employed in each zone, $E_j$, times a function $p_{ij}$ reflecting the probability of those workers living in zone $i$, or

$$N_i = k \sum_j E_j p_{ij}. \qquad [1]$$

The probability function has definite gravity model characteristics, since the $p_{ij}$ typically reflects the impedance, or travel difficulty, between the zones. Lowry's original formulation was simply a declining power function

$$p_{ij} = d_{ij}^{-1.33} \ (d_{ij} \geq 1.0),$$

where $d_{ij}$ = distance between points $i$ and $j$.

The Lowry formulation allowed the addition of attractiveness factors as well as impedance factors; this is analogous to the "mass" element of the Newtonian model.

### Entropy-Maximizing Models

An alternative formulation of spatial relationships emerged with the entropy-maximizing framework of Wilson (1970b; 1974). Where gravity models use land-use intensity (or levels) as an analog to mass, the entropy-maximizing framework focuses on individuals, assessing the probability of individuals making a particular journey and then obtaining the interaction as a statistical average (Wilson, 1974). Thus, the entropy-maximizing approach follows not from a specific individual behavioral rationale but from the notion of a macro-state description that encompasses the maximum number of possible micro states. In economic terms, gravity could be thought of as a macro concept, entropy-maximizing as a micro concept.

A simple residential location model may be derived from entropy-maximizing concepts as follows:

$$T_{ij} = A_i B_j O_i E_j F(c_{ij}),$$

where

$T_{ij}$ = trips between zones $i$ and $j$, or number of persons living in zone $i$ and working in zone $j$;
$O_i$ = trip origins, or employed persons living in zone $i$;
$E_j$ = trip destinations, or persons employed in zone $j$;
$A_i$ = balancing factor for trip origins;
$B_j$ = balancing factor for trip destinations; and
$F(c_{ij})$ = impedance function.

It is possible to replace the trip origins $O_i$ by a measure of attractiveness of the origin zone, $W_i$. This eliminates the need for the origins balancing factor $A_i$, giving:

$$T_{ij} = B_j W_i E_j F(c_{ij}) \qquad [2]$$

To meet the constraint that $\sum_k T_{kj} = E_j$ we set:

$$B_j = \frac{1}{\sum_k W_k F(c_{kj})}.$$

Substituting this expression back into equation 2 yields:

$$T_{ij} = E_j \frac{W_i F(c_{ij})}{\sum_k W_k F(c_{kj})}. \qquad [3]$$

If the term $W_i F (c_{ij})$ is called an "accessibility attractiveness" measure, then the fraction in equation 3 is a relative measure of the accessibility-attractiveness of zone $i$ to zone $j$ compared to all other zones, $k$. Further, it is clear that the total number of employed persons residing in zone $i$ is:

$$N_i = \sum_j T_{ij} .$$

Substitution gives:

$$N_i = \sum_j E_j \frac{W_i F (c_{ij})}{\sum_k W_k F (c_{kj})} .$$

This is equivalent to saying,

$$N_i = \sum_j E_j p_{ij} ,$$

which is exactly the Lowry-model equation 1, where $p_{ij}$ is the probability that a person will work in zone $j$ and live in zone $i$.

Despite its innocuous appearance, this revised Lowry formulation has important ramifications. Among other things, it affords workable solutions to the problems of calibrating these models and procedures for linking them directly to transport network packages.

### Further Developments from Entropy Maximizing

Several important developments followed upon the emergence of entropy maximizing. First, the method made model calibration relatively more tractable by greatly reducing data requirements (Putman and Ducca, 1978a, 1978b). This allowed extensive calibration work on employment, transportation, and residential location models to proceed for some forty cities in several countries, notably the United States and Great Britain (Putman, 1986b).

Second, the entropy-maximizing framework proved to be a general form that yields not only the basic Lowry gravity models but many other Lowry-related systems as well (Black, 1981; Putman, 1983). This unification of disparate methods is suggestive of an underlying model reflecting human behavior in a fashion that is more theoretically appealing than analogies to Newtonian mechanics or molecular interaction.

The third important development associated with entropy-maximization modeling is in fact the convergence of modeling based on individual behavioral principles with models derived from the entropy-maximizing frameworks. Seminal work on the individual behavioral modeling of urban form began with McFadden (1973).

In this formulation, which has developed from an important trend in econometric modeling in general, a binomial (or, in more generalized form, a multinomial) logit function is specified that describes the probabilities that an individual of type $n$ will locate in zone $i$, given that she or he works in zone $j$. This is measured as a function of the relative attractiveness of zone $i$ compared to the general or average attractiveness of all zones in the region. Then, with appropriate data about the relative portion of the population taken by each type of individual, as well as their work locations, these share values can lead to reasonable estimates of residential location by zone, and hence of demographic and density values for each zone's population.

Let us consider the theoretical structure of the McFadden family of models (Putman, 1983). Those scholars using utility-maximizing choice models consider a set of individual decision makers choosing among a given set of alternatives. The utility of each alternative, to the chooser, is composed of a deterministic component and a stochastic or random component. The deterministic component is so described because it is the (presumably) predictable or explainable portion of the individual's utility function and is held in common with all other individuals of the same type. The stochastic component is the unexplained and/or individual-specific portion of the individual's utility function. Thus:

$$u_{ij}^* = u_{ij} + \varepsilon_{ij},$$

where

$u_{ij}^*$ = the perceived utility of alternative $j$ to decision makers $i$;

$u_{ij}$ = the deterministic component of utility which is common to all decision makers of type $i$; and

$\varepsilon_{ij}$   = the stochastic component of utility representing individual differences (i.e., personal tastes and preferences) in decision makers $i$, as well as unexplained aspects of alternatives $j$.

It is usually assumed that:

$$u_{ij} = \sum_k a_k X_{ij}^k ,$$

where

$X_{ij}^k$   = attribute $k$ of choice alternative $j$ for decision makers $i$; and
$a_k$   = utility coefficients common to all decision makers $i$ which serve to weight and scale the attributes.

If the appropriate assumptions are made about the distributions of the $ij$, then it is possible to derive the following expression for $P_{j|i}$, the probability that the decision makers $i$ will chose alternative $j$:

$$P_{j|i} = \frac{\exp (\sum_k a_k X_{ij}^k)}{\sum_j \exp (\sum_k a_k X_{ij}^k)}$$

(See Wilson et al., 1981, and Anas, 1982, for more complete presentations.)

Let us return to the entropy-maximizing formulation. From a practical point of view, residence location models derived from entropy-maximizing principles are usually stated as:

$$N_i = \sum_j E_j B_j f(c_{ij}) , \qquad [4]$$

where

$N_i$   = persons choosing to reside in zone $i$;
$E_j$   = persons working in zone $j$;
$c_{ij}$   = generalized cost of travel between zone $i$ and zone $j$; and
$B_j$   = a balancing factor.

In most applications, $f(c_{ij})$ has equaled $\exp(-\beta c_{ij})$ and thus:

$$B_j = [\sum_i \exp(-\beta c_{ij})]^{-1}$$

Hence we may redefine:

$$N_i = \sum_j E_j P_{i|j}, \qquad [5]$$

where

$$P_{i|j} = \frac{\exp(-\beta c_{ij})}{\sum_i \exp(-\beta c_{ij})}. \qquad [6]$$

The substantive implication of equations 5 and 6 is that given place of work, an employee's choice of place of residence is determined solely by the relative travel cost to any such potential place of residence. This is, of course, a gross oversimplification of reality. An improved statement may be had by augmenting equation 4 with a measure of residence zone attractiveness, often expressed as a set of attribute descriptors of the potential places of residence along with a set of coefficients to weight and/or scale them. This results in:

$$N_i = \sum_j E_j B_j \prod_k X_{ik}^{a_k} f(c_{ij}),$$

with:

$$B_j = [\sum_i \prod_k X_{ik}^{a_k} f(c_{ij})]^{-1}.$$

Now:

$$P_{ij} = \frac{(\prod_k X_{ik}^{a_k}) f(c_{ij})}{\sum_i (\prod_k X_{ik}^{a_k}) f(c_{ij})}. \qquad [7]$$

If one lets $f(c_{ij}) = c_{ij}^{\alpha}$, where under most circumstances $\alpha \leq 0$, and then takes the natural logarithm of the numerator of equation 7, one gets:

$$\ln [(\prod_k X_{ik}^{a_k}) c_{ij}^{\alpha}] = (\sum_k a_k \ln X_{ik}) + \alpha \ln c_{ij}.$$

Then, transforming back by exponentiating and substituting into equation 7, one has:

$$P_{ij} = \frac{\exp (\alpha \ln c_{ij} + \sum_k a_k \ln X_{ik})}{\sum_i \exp (\alpha \ln c_{ij} + \sum_k a_k \ln X_{ik})},$$

thus demonstrating that a singly constrained model derived via the entropy-maximizing approach can be easily transformed into a multi-nomial logit model formulation for determining residence location given place of work. Anas (1983) has shown that the behavioral choice (stochastic utility-maximizing) and the maximum entropy (information-minimizing) approaches are in fact identical, and that the two approaches applied to the same set of data will yield identical parameter estimates for the multinomial logit model.

Thus, by traveling the somewhat suspect path of natural-science-based theoretical structures, we have arrived at a point where all of these models turn out to be reduced forms of a general, *social* science, *human* behavioral model. This is indeed an important scientific development and demonstrates the theoretical usefulness of the previous Lowry-derived modeling work. The failure of the EMPIRIC-based work to lead back to some key theoretical formulation and the parallel failure of the New Urban Economics modeling work to lead forward to empirically verifiable work both show how the process of scientific discovery leaves many theories and much work in its wake.

### Interactive Modeling: Bringing Theory and Data Together

The interaction of land-use models (mainly residential and employment location models, with some housing stock supply models) with transit models has been explored in the work of the Urban Simulation Laboratory at the University of Pennsylvania. A detailed account of that work is available in Putman (1986b, 1991). The Integrated Transportation and Land-Use Package (ITLUP) is briefly described here, followed by a discussion of a few leading issues stimulated by that work.

## ITLUP: The State of the Art

Many regional modeling systems have been designed but few have proven applicable to more than one setting. ITLUP, on the other hand, is transferable. It has been calibrated and used to make forecasts in twelve cities with many different zone systems. It has been used in historical research (a successful calibration and analysis was performed with data from nineteenth-century Philadelphia), and it has been used for urban regions outside the United States (successful calibrations and forecasts were performed for cities in Yugoslavia and Taiwan).

The model has undergone constant development since 1971. The current version contains four principal models plus a number of submodels. The four principal models are: (1) EMPAL, for employment location; (2) DRAM, for simultaneous residential location and trip distribution; (3) MSPLIT for mode split calculation; and (4) NETWRK, for trip assignment. ITLUP operates recursively. In each recursion, the sequence of operation of the principal models of ITLUP is quite straightforward: EMPAL, DRAM, MSPLIT, NETWRK. For this discussion, the problem of system initialization will be neglected and it will be assumed that the model package is calculating the $n$th recursion, from time $t$ to time $t + 1$.

The recursion begins with the execution of EMPAL. To forecast the location of employment of type $k$ in zone $j$ at time $t + 1$, EMPAL uses the following input variables: employment of type $k$ in all zones at time $t$; population of all types in all zones at time $t$; total area per zone for all zones; and zone-to-zone travel cost between zone $j$ and all other zones at time $t$. The parameters used are derived from time $t$ and time $t - 1$ data. The model requires exogenous regional employment forecasts for time $t + 1$.

Following the employment location forecasts produced by EMPAL, a set of residence location forecasts is produced by DRAM. To forecast the location of residents of type $h$ in zone $i$ at time $t + 1$, DRAM uses the following input variables: residents of all $h$ types in zone $i$ at time $t$; land used for residential purposes in zone $i$ at time $t$; the percentage of the developable land in zone $i$ which has already been developed at time $t$; the vacant developable land in zone $i$ at time $t$; zone-to-zone travel costs between zone $i$ and all other zones at time $t + 1$; and employment of all $k$ types in all zones at time $t + 1$. The parameters used are derived from time $t$ data. The model requires exogenous regional population forecasts for time $t + 1$.

Following the residence location forecasts produced by DRAM, it is necessary to split trips by mode and to assign vehicle trips to the transportation network(s). The origin-destination work trip matrix is produced in DRAM simultaneously with residence location. DRAM also produces matrices of work-to-shop and home-to-shop trips. These three trip matrices must be expanded to represent total trips and then converted from trip probabilities (the form in which they are calculated) to actual person and/or vehicle trips. These trips are then split into trips by mode in MSPLIT, yielding transit-person trips plus automobile vehicle trips. The automobile trips are then assigned, using NETWRK, to a highway network for time $t + 1$. The output of NETWRK is a set of zone-to-zone highway travel times (costs) on the time $t + 1$ network. These highway times are then combined with the transit times to yield a composite time (cost) matrix.

The major submodels are briefly described in the following sections.

*Employment Location—EMPAL*

EMPAL is a modified version of the standard singly constrained spatial interaction model. There are three modifications: (1) A multivariate, multiparametric attractiveness function is used; (2) a separate, weighted, lagged variable is included outside the spatial interaction formulation; and (3) a constraint procedure is included in the model, allowing zone- and/or sector-specific constraints. The model is normally used for three to five employment sectors whose parameters are individually estimated.

*Household (Residence) Location—DRAM*

DRAM is a modified version of the standard singly constrained spatial interaction model. There are two modifications: (1) A multivariate, multiparametric attractiveness function is used; and (2) a consistent, balanced constraint procedure is included in the model, allowing zone- and/or sector-specific constraints. The model is normally used for four household types (actually income groups) whose parameters are individually estimated. Trip generation and distribution are calculated in DRAM simultaneously with household location by calculating and storing trip-probability matrices during the household location calculations.

*Mode Split—MSPLIT*

The trip matrices produced in DRAM are split into trip matrices for each available mode in MSPLIT (see Appendix 4.1). This model uses a multinomial logit formulation to do the mode split calculation.

*Trip Assignment—NETWRK*

Trips are assigned to a capacity-constrained network in NETWRK using an incremental tree-by-tree assignment with random origin selection. Stochastic multipath and user equilibrium assignment algorithms are also available.

**Issues in Interactive Modeling**

ITLUP is an interactive system of nonlinear models run recursively. These features pose important issues for this type of work.

*Nonlinearity*

ITLUP contains a demand-side residence location model, a nonbasic employment location model, and a transportation network assignment model. Most demand-side location models allocate an exogenously determined regional activity total to the region's zones or network links. Initially this is accomplished by calculating what portion of the region's total will be allocated to each zone or link. This process is linear; in the absence of any constraining mechanism these models respond to an $X$ percent change in a regional total by an $X$ percent change in each zone's or link's allocation. Consequently, one must constrain, for example, population or employment densities (on the zones) or volume/capacity ratios (on the links) to produce more realistic local responses to regional growth or decline or changes in trip totals. If one then links together such constrained and hence nonlinear location and trip assignment models, their interactions can reproduce complex real-world phenomena.

One such interaction yields what appear to be appropriate asymmetries in subarea response to regional growth. A series of ITLUP simulations examined the spatial distribution consequences of regional growth increments (both positive and negative). Most subareas generally followed the regional rates, but some were found to "overrespond" to regional growth and "underrespond" to regional decline, while others did just the opposite. Closer examination of the simulation results revealed these responses to be jointly determined by the attractiveness of the zones and by the capacities of the transport facility links serving them. In particular, the zones that overresponded to regional growth had adequate network capacity to carry the trips generated by new locators responding to the zones' attractiveness, without critical increases in link congestion (Putman, 1983, chap. 9).

*Equilibrium and Oscillation in*
*Iterative Model Systems*

Typically a model (or set of models) is run repeatedly; each iteration represents some unit of time, the output of the $n$th recursion is input to the $n + 1$'th recursion, and there are externally generated control totals representing regional growth or decline from one time period to the next. If the control totals are set equal to the totals of the base-year variables and the model is run for eight to ten recursions, one of two things is likely to happen.

The first possibility is that eventually there will be no change in spatial patterns from one recursion to the next. That is, an equilibrium will be reached, with numerical values that are solely the result of the model's equations. How realistic is such an equilibrium solution?

In one experiment, the model's first recursion forecasts turned out to be the best estimates of the future years' spatial patterns. As the model was driven toward equilibrium by further recursions, the forecasted spatial patterns matched the known future-year spatial patterns less and less closely.

Putman (1986b) suggests that at any instant the patterns of activities in an urban area (and the dynamics of the urban system) imply a potential equilibrium toward which the system is tending, but this equilibrium can only be reached if, from that instant onward, all external shocks to the system cease and all "behavior" patterns remain constant. Since these two conditions will never be true, the potential equilibrium will never be reached in reality.

Indeed, a network equilibrium model may give worse forecasts of actual network flows than some more traditional network models. Similar caution should be observed for system equilibria as well as integrated models of urban systems.

The other likely outcome of repeated recursions of an interactive model is that it will oscillate rather than converge to a stable solution (Putman, 1986b). This surprising system response can result from interactions of otherwise unexceptional model behaviors. For example, large increments in regional control totals for the location models can produce large changes in network congestion that lead in turn to large location changes, and so on. Oscillations can also be due to an all-or-nothing trip assignment algorithm; even when the assignment method is of the incremental tree-by-tree form with capacity constraints, critical links in the network can congest rapidly and produce system oscillation. This system behavior can be damped by methods of marginal trip assignment combined with limiting regional changes per iteration to smaller ranges.

*Time Series Problems*

Model parameters often must be estimated without any lagged variables. Such model structures are ignorant of the past; they cannot distinguish between two zones of similar present attributes, one of which has been growing and the other declining. In two model application exercises, even though the models calibrated well, the forecasts underpredicted zones that had been declining. A related problem is that of parameter variation over time. Many approaches to this problem that have some promise in theory are not practical in application for want of sufficient data (Martin, Thrift, and Bennett, 1978). One possible remedy for this situation comes from the sampling approach of behavioral-choice modeling work, which might lead to means for calibrating models on intercensal years. If this were possible, it is conceivable that better time series data will become available—thus, eventually, providing the basis for a better understanding of the temporal behavior of urban spatial patterns.

For now, the most feasible approach to resolving the issue of temporal dynamics involves the use of cross-sectoral or "static" models in dynamic frameworks (Batty and March, 1978). Yet there are many theoretical as well as practical questions to be resolved regarding the dynamics of these model systems. Even if the analysis is limited to simpler models, the reformulation of standard models into difference equation form can lead to very complex system behavior. Numerical experiments based on such models have yielded particularly interesting results regarding spatial patterns of activities in urban areas (Beaumont, Clarke, and Wilson, 1981); variations in selected parameters for a fixed data set and a fixed equation structure resulted in radically different urban patterns. In a subsequent set of simulation experiments with the ITLUP model system, Putman showed how variations in selected variables (input data set) for a fixed equation structure and fixed parameters could also result in markedly different urban patterns. Thus, it appears that there is a whole new avenue of exploration of the dynamics of urban models and systems of models (Putman, 1986a).

*Other Issues*

Other work with integrated location, land use, and transportation system modeling has included the analysis of the interactions of simplified model forms (Berechman, 1980), theoretical studies of combined network equilibrium and urban systems models (Fisk, Boyce, and Brown, 1981), and a set of more empirical efforts to test a variety of integrated model system configurations on a number of different urban areas (Devereux, Echenique, and Flowerdew, 1982; Mackett, 1979; Nakamura, Hayashi, and Niyamoto, 1983; Sarna and Hutchinson, 1979; and Wegener, 1982). These works demonstrate the importance of adopting a systems view of the location-transportation problem, and the importance of dealing with model-to-model interactions.

## Conclusion

The early urban modeling efforts, from von Thunen to Lowry, represented an important beginning in understanding the interactions of urban phenomena. Their limited success was due partly to the sheer technical difficulty of data handling and calculation in the precomputer era, which greatly limited the scope and complexity of early models. A more serious problem, however, was that the theories on which this pioneering work was based, notably the assumption that the downtown was a unique attractor, were simply unrealistic. A later attempt to circumvent this problem by avoiding theory almost entirely and relying on computer number-crunching capabilities to find patterns in data, EMPIRIC, produced useful snapshots of urban processes, but poor forecasts.

Tiebout's economic-base theory provided a workable method for forecasting levels of economic activity in urban areas, and Lowry's gravity model formulation gave the key to dealing with the issue of the attraction of activities from one location to another. Despite its origin in a physics analogy, the gravity model turns out to embody genuine insights into social phenomena; this is attested to partly by the sound social-science theoretical justifications later provided by entropy-maximizing theory and utility theory, but primarily by the extensive practical forecasting successes of models in this tradition.

These two principles allow the construction of models that usefully reproduce quite complex real-world phenomena, and underlie the interactive regional model ITLUP, used in the present project as an essential source of contextual data, as well as the small-area model LOCDEV, described in the following chapters.

# Appendix 4.1

# Trip Mode Choice (Mode-Split) Modeling

A significant improvement of ITLUP, used for the first time in the current project, is the introduction of a mode-split procedure to ITLUP. This procedure, MSPLIT, operates after the employment (EMPAL) and residence (DRAM) location modules and allocates the residence-work trips among the available transportation modes. We discuss here the mode choices that occur after DRAM has run (i.e., the post-DRAM mode-split choice).[1]

Mode choice calculations are carried out in three phases. First, a work-to-home trip matrix is derived from the simultaneous residential location/trip distribution process in DRAM. Second, the market share captured by each alternative mode between all employment zone and residential zone pairs is estimated by a mode choice model. Third, the trip matrix is factored by each market share matrix to estimate trip matrices by mode. Four types of mode choice models are considered here: diversion curve; multiple regression; aggregate logit; and dis-aggregate logit.

Early approaches to mode-split include the diversion curve, multiple regression, and aggregate logit methods. These are all *macrolevel* techniques because they rely on aggregate data for model calibration, and make behavioral predictions for groups of travelers.

Diversion curve models are constructed simply by plotting the percentage of trip-interchange travelers choosing one mode *(Y)* against a zonal- or interchange-specific choice variable *(X)* and connecting these points to produce a line or curve. In forecasting, the modal market share is estimated using the predicted choice variable in conjunction with the estimated mathematical function of the plotted curve.

The diversion curves constructed for Toronto in the early 1960s are an example of this approach (Black, 1981). In this case, eighty work trip curves were developed to split trips between transit and automobile. The choice variables were relative travel costs, relative travel time, relative travel service, and income.

The multiple regression model has been used in a more sophisticated way to explain the variation in the percentage of trip-interchange travelers choosing a particular mode through the use of zonal- or interchange-specific choice variables. The general equation, following Stopher and Meyburg (1975), is:

$$T_{ij}^m / \sum_m T_{ij}^m = \beta_0 + \beta_1 C_1 + \beta_2 C_2 + \ldots + \beta_n C_n ,$$

where

---

[1] The following review is based on Keith, 1983.

$T_{ij}^{m}$        = number of trips between zones $i$ and $j$ choosing mode $m$;

$\beta_0, \ldots, \beta_n$ = empirically derived parameters; and

$C_1, \ldots, C_n$ = zonal or interchange-specific choice variables.

The least squares method is employed to calibrate the model. In forecasting, the modal market share is estimated by using the predicted choice variable(s) in conjunction with the estimated equation parameters.

Such multiple regression models were constructed for the Twin Cities (Minnesota) area in the early 1960s (Stopher and Meyburg, 1975). In this study, trip purpose models (work, school, other) were developed to split trips between transit and the automobile. The choice variables were travel time ratios, parking cost, income, residential density, and employment density.

While the two previous models are essentially deterministic (i.e., an a priori mode split is estimated), the aggregate logit model is embedded in a probabilistic framework. This model states that the probability of trip-interchange travelers choosing mode $i$ is directly proportional to the utility of the mode (a function of zonal and interchange-specific choice variables) and inversely proportional to the utility of all available modes. The general equation structure (logit function), following Williams (1977), is:

$$p_{ij}^{m} = \frac{\exp(U_m)}{\sum\limits_{m} \exp(U_m)},$$

where

$p_{ij}^{m}$  =  probability of trips between zones $i$ and $j$ choosing mode $m$; and

$U_m$  =  utility of mode $m$.

This equation structure can be derived either through individual choice behavior theory (utility-maximization theory), the basis of the disaggregate logit model, or entropy-maximization theory, the basis of Wilson's family of spatial interaction models (Anas, 1983). A mathematical search procedure can be used to estimate parameter values. The modal market share is estimated by using the predicted utility functions in conjunction with the equation structure.

Such a mode-split model was constructed for the SELNEC Transportation Study in the late 1960s. A general model was developed to predict the probability of trips choosing transit and the automobile. The equation structure, following Wilson et al. (1969), is:

$$p_{ij}^{m} = \frac{\exp(\tau c_{ij}^{m})}{\exp(\tau c_{ij}^{T}) + \exp(\tau c_{ij}^{A})},$$

where

$p_{ij}^{m}$     = probability of trips between zones $i$ and $j$ choosing mode $m$;
$c_{ij}^{T}$     = generalized cost of travel between zones $i$ and $j$ by transit;
$c_{ij}^{A}$     = generalized cost of travel between zones $i$ and $j$ by automobile; and
$\tau$     = empirically derived mode choice function parameter.

The utility of each mode is the product of its associated trip-interchange generalized cost and a weight (parameter) that measures the sensitivity to the cost (an aggregate sensitivity). These early approaches have been superseded for the most part by the disaggregate logit model. Unlike the aggregate models, the disaggregate logit model is a *microlevel* technique that is calibrated with disaggregate data describing the mode choice behavior of individual travelers. These data are in the form of individual trip records. Each record contains information describing the traveler, each alternative modal option, the actual mode chosen, and the other characteristics of the trip. The probability of the traveler choosing each available mode is estimated.

The general equation structure for the disaggregate logit model is the same as that for the aggregate logit model and is, following Spear (1977),

$$p_{t}^{m} = \frac{\exp(U_{mt})}{\sum\limits_{m} \exp(U_{mt})}, \qquad [1]$$

where

$p_{t}^{m}$     = probability of traveler $t$ choosing mode $m$; and
$U_{mt}$     = utility of mode $m$ to traveler $t$.

The utility of a mode to a traveler is expressed in a linear, additive form. That is,

$$U_{mt} = ß_0 + ß_1c_1 + ß_2c_2 + \ldots + ß_nc_n,$$

where

$ß_0 \ldots ß_n$ = empirically derived parameters; and
$c_1 \ldots c_n$ = choice variables.

Each choice variable included attempts to represent a certain portion of the total desirability (utility) of the mode to the traveler. The type of variables typically used are characteristics of the traveler (socioeconomic variables), characteristics of the modes (level of service variables), and characteristics of the urban spatial structure (land-use variables). More than one variable of each type may be included (e.g., travel time and travel cost). The parameter associated with each variable measures the traveler sensitivity to that choice attribute (a disaggregate sensitivity); it is an indicator of the relative importance of that variable to the measurement of total utility. The constant, frequently referred to as the bias coefficient, is used to represent the effect of variables that influence the mode choice decision but are not included in the utility function. This could include variables that are difficult to measure, such as comfort and convenience.

The maximum likelihood technique is commonly used for model calibration. In forecasting, given the utility of each mode, the probability of the traveler choosing each available alternative is estimated by placing the utility function values into the logit function (equation 1). This function ensures that the probability associated with each mode will be between zero and one, and that the sum of all probabilities will be equal to one.

The disaggregate logit is superior to earlier methods owing to six major characteristics.

1. The model is based on individual choice behavior theory (utility-maximization theory) rather than on population averages, thus allowing individual behavior patterns to affect the regional outcomes directly.

2. The model is embedded in a probabilistic framework, so that predictions are stated in terms of estimated probabilities.

3. The model is calibrated using observations of individual mode

choice behavior. The implication is threefold. First, the amount of data needed to obtain statistically reliable estimates is small. Second, all of the information contained in the data set is used; that is, the model is capable of exploiting the total variation in the travelers, the modes, the urban spatial structure, and the choices made. Third, the parameter and bias coefficient estimates are not affected by the problems associated with the use of group (aggregate) data.

4. The model can be aggregated in a number of different ways. Since the model estimates the probability of the traveler choosing each of the available modes, aggregate demand is derived by summing the estimated probabilities over the entire population of interest. The population of interest can reflect such phenomena as socioeconomic groups, mode availability (choice set) groups, and geographic location. This property adds a great deal of flexibility to forecasting and policy analysis.

5. The model has considerable analysis potential. This property is due to three interrelated items. First, since the model is based on individual choice behavior theory and is calibrated with observations of individual mode choice behavior, it is more likely to contain true causal relationships rather than associative ones. Thus, prediction should be more accurate. Second, a large number of choice variables may easily be included in the utility function. Specifically, these variables can focus on the various level-of-service attributes of the mode. Third, as mentioned above, aggregation can be performed in a number of different ways.

6. The model has great spatial and temporal transferability potential. Since the model is based on individual choice behavior theory and is calibrated with observations of individual mode choice behavior and, in addition, does not depend on any specific zone system, a model calibrated for one area or time period should be transferable to another area or time period with a high degree of confidence. This property is, of course, conditional on the travel behavior of individuals being relatively similar between the two areas or time periods.

Along with these desirable properties, there are a number of concerns associated with the disaggregate logit model. These can be divided into the three general areas of model development (data collection, model specification, and model calibration), aggregate prediction, and transferability. The model does not represent travel behavior perfectly (see Ben-Akiva, 1977; Koppleman 1977; and Talvitie and Kirshner, 1978). In principle, aggregate demand is derived by summing the estimated probabilities of each traveler in the population of interest. Unfortunately, detailed data for each individual are usually not available, and aggregate demand must be derived by using limited information on the distribution of the choice variables. This introduces aggregation error into the prediction.

In response to this problem, a number of alternative aggregation procedures have been proposed. Koppleman (1977) developed a taxonomy of these procedures: enumeration, summation/integration, statistical differences, classification (market segmentation), and naive. Each of these has different information requirements for the distribution of the choice variables, different levels of complexity, and different levels of expected error. In general, as the expected error decreases, both the information requirements and the complexity increase; trade-offs exist between these procedures.

According to principle six, the disaggregate logit model has substantial transferability potential. However, the empirical validity of this principle is unclear, and conflicting results have appeared in the literature. On one hand, Talvitie and Kirshner (1978) have rejected the hypothesis that the model is transferable. On the other hand, both Watson and Westin (1973) and Atherton and Ben-Akiva (1976) have accepted this hypothesis.

Keith (1983) reviewed approximately twenty basic models to evaluate this model form. The specification associated with each model ranged from very simple to very sophisticated. Their differences can be described, in a general fashion, in terms of three criteria: market segmentation, dependent variables, and utility functions.

Each specification predicts the mode choice behavior for a particular type of traveler. These market segments are formed by stratifying the total set of travelers by one or more factors. These factors include trip purpose, characteristics of the household, characteristics of the trip ends. The trip purpose of interest is home-based work; however, other purposes can be used as strata, such as home-based-other and non-home-based. The household characteristics include such items as income level, automobile availability or ownership, and life cycle and occupation. The trip-end characteristics include destinations such as the central business district (CBD), trip orientation, and suburban trips.

Each specification contains two or more modes from which the traveler may choose. These dependent variables are divided into two general groups: public and private. Public modes include bus and rail services. Private modes include the automobile, and occasionally the automobile at different levels of occupancy.

Each specification contains a unique set of utility functions, one for each mode. The most common choice variables employed are: in-vehicle travel time, out-of-vehicle travel time, and out-of-pocket travel cost (level of service); auto availability or ownership and income (socioeconomic); and land-use density and CBD trip orientation (land use).

The specification for four of the models examined is displayed in Table 4.1. The model developed by Peat, Marwick, Mitchell and Company (PMM) was calibrated using a San Diego data set (Peat et al., 1972). The model developed by Charles River Associates (CRA) was calibrated using a Pittsburgh data set (CRA, 1982). The model developed by Cambridge Systematic, Incorporated (CSI), was calibrated using a Washington, D.C., data set (Atherton and Ben-Akiva, 1976). The model developed by the University of California, Urban Travel Demand Forecasting Project (UTDFP), was calibrated using a San Francisco Bay Area set (McFadden, 1978b).

Table A4.1

**Examples of Mode Choice Model Specifications**

| Model | Market segmentation | Dependent variables | Utility functions (choice variables and bias coefficients) |
|---|---|---|---|
| 1. PMM | Work trip purpose<br>CBD trip orientation<br>non-CBD trip orientation | Automobile driver (1)[a]<br>Automobile passenger (2) | Transformed household income (1)[b]<br>Difference (automobile-transit) in excess travel time (3)<br>Difference (automobile-transit) in line-haul travel time (3)<br>Difference (automobile-transit) in out-of-pocket travel cost (3)<br>Bias coefficient (1)<br>Bias coefficient (2) |
| 2. CRA | Work trip purpose | Automobile driver (1)<br>Transit (2) | Transit walk time (1)<br>Difference (automobile-transit) in in-vehicle travel time (1)<br>Difference (automobile-transit) in out-of-pocket travel cost (1)<br>Automobiles per worker in the household (1)<br>Bias coefficient (1) |
| 3. CSI | Work trip purpose | Automobile driver (1)<br>Carpool (2)<br>Transit (3) | Out-of-pocket travel cost divided by household income (1,2,3)<br>In-vehicle travel time (1,2,3)<br>Out-of-vehicle travel time divided by distance (1,2,3)<br>Automobiles available per licensed driver (1)<br>Automobiles available per licensed driver (2)<br>CBD trip orientation (1)<br>CBD trip orientation (2)<br>Government worker (1)<br>Disposable income (1,2)<br>One way distance times employees per commercial area (2)<br>Number of workers in family (2)<br>Breadwinner (1)<br>Bias coefficient (1)<br>Bias coefficient (2) |

| Model | Market segmentation | Dependent variables | Utility functions (choice variables and bias coefficients) |
|---|---|---|---|
| 4. UTDFP | Work trip purpose | Automobile driver (1) | Out-of-pocket travel cost divided by posttax wage (1,2,3,4) |
| | | Carpool (2) | Automobile on-vehicle travel time (1,2,4) |
| | | Bus, walk access (3) | Transit on-vehicle travel time (3,4) |
| | | Bus, automobile access (4) | Walk time (3,4) |
| | | | Transfer wait time (3,4) |
| | | | Number of transfers (3,4) |
| | | | Headway of first bus (3,4) |
| | | | Family income (1), three of these variables are included |
| | | | Number of persons in household who can drive (1) |
| | | | Number of persons in household who can drive (2) |
| | | | Number of persons in household who can drive (4) |
| | | | Head-of-household (1) |
| | | | Employment density at work location (1) |
| | | | Home location in or near CBD (1) |
| | | | Automobiles per driver with a ceiling of one (1) |
| | | | Automobiles per driver with a ceiling of one (2) |
| | | | Automobiles per driver with a ceiling of one (4) |
| | | | Bias coefficient (1) |
| | | | Bias coefficient (2) |
| | | | Bias coefficient (4) |

[a]Dependent variable label.
[b]Dependent variable(s) with which choice variable or bias coefficient is associated.

# Five

# The Local Development Model (LOCDEV): A Structural Specification, Estimation, and Analysis for the Washington, D.C., Region

Development advances swiftly at some station areas in a region and lags at others. What factors account for these variations? Can they be modeled in such a way that development around stations is explainable by a small, manageable set of variables, or is development strictly a function of random, independent, and unmodelable interventions by developers and/or planners? This chapter will demonstrate that a small set of variables, which represents regionwide accessibility to the station area and certain economic characteristics of station areas, explains a major share of the differences in development among station areas. This outcome allows model users to make policy suggestions based on the findings of small-area modeling experiments.

The Local Development (LOCDEV) model presented here consists of three development equations that are estimated based on cross-sectional data from fifty-two rapid-transit station areas in the Washington, D.C., region. The development (or dependent) variables are aggregate employment, retail employment, and commercial floor space levels. These variables are excellent indicators of nonresidential development in an area.

## The LOCDEV Model

The LOCDEV equations draw on the spatial interaction modeling tradition in that they combine an accessibility measure with a set of site-characteristic attractiveness variables to estimate the level of development activity at a station area. Site characteristics in LOCDEV

**Figure 5.1. The Local Development (LOCDEV) Model: Structural Specifications**

Aggregate Employment Equation

$$E_i = a_1 + b_1A_{1i} + c_1V_{li} + d_1V_{bi} + e_1M_i + f_1P_i + g_1C_i$$

where

| | |
|---|---|
| $E$ | = aggregate employment; |
| $A_1$ | = relative accessibility index (median income weights); |
| $V_l$ | = value per square foot of land; |
| $V_b$ | = value per square foot of commercial floor space; |
| $M$ | = average monthly residential mortgage payment; |
| $P$ | = population; |
| $C$ | = commercial share of land uses; |
| $i$ | = station area designation, $i = 1, 52$; |
| $a_1$ | = intercept; and |
| $b_1 - g_1$ | = coefficients of independent variables. |

Retail Employment Equation

$$T_i = a_2 + b_2A_{2i} + c_2F_i + d_2P_i + e_2C_i$$

where

| | |
|---|---|
| $T$ | = retail employment; |
| $A_2$ | = accessibility index (total income weights); |
| $F$ | = commercial floor space level; |
| $P$ | = population; |
| $C$ | = commercial share of land uses; |
| $i$ | = station area of interest, $i = 1, 52$; |
| $a_2$ | = intercept; and |
| $b_2 - e_2$ | = coefficients of independent variables. |

Commercial Floor Space Equation

$$LF = a_3 + b_3LA_{1i} + c_3LV_{li} + d_3LV_{oi} + e_3LC_i$$

where

| | |
|---|---|
| $L$ | = logarithm of variable; |
| $F$ | = commercial floor space; |
| $A_1$ | = accessibility index (median income weights); |
| $V_l$ | = value per square foot of land; |
| $V_o$ | = value per square foot of commercial office floor space; |
| $C$ | = commercial share of land use; |
| $a_3$ | = intercept; and |
| $b_3 - e_3$ | = coefficients of independence variables. |

are economic variables that are related to actual or potential market activities in station areas.

These development equations differ in their specific sets of independent variables, functional forms, and calibration parameters, but all have in common the general form:

Development variable = $f$ (accessibility, site characteristics).

The three equations are calibrated independently of each other using ordinary least squares estimation techniques.

### The Sample

Active station areas in the Washington region comprise the universe of interest. An active station area is defined as the area within a quarter-mile of the center of a station that opened by 1986. Twelve of the sixty-four such stations were dropped from the sample because of their peculiarities (e.g., Pentagon and Arlington Cemetery) or because of data problems. The final set contains fifty-two station areas, listed in Table 5.1.

### The Model Specifications

Three equations, grouped together in Figure 5.1, are also discussed below. Each contains a relative accessibility term and a set of economic variables that describe each station area in terms of both its real estate characteristics and the economic actors resident there.

### Relative Accessibility

To estimate the relative accessibility of locations throughout the region to a station area, it is first necessary to partition the region into zones and create a matrix of trip times between pairs of zones. This was done using the Metropolitan Washington Council of Governments' 182-zone traffic district partition of the region. The relative accessibility index for each of these zones was computed according to the following formula:

$$A_i = \frac{\sum_j Y_j \exp(-\alpha B_{ij})}{\sum_i \sum_j Y_j \exp(-\alpha B_{ij})},$$

Table 5.1

**Metrorail Stations Used in Studies, by Jurisdiction**

| **District of Columbia** | **Montgomery County** |
|---|---|
| Archives | Bethesda |
| Benning Road | Grosvenor |
| Brookland | Rockville |
| Capitol South | Shady Grove |
| Cleveland Park | Silver Spring |
| Deanwood | Takoma Park |
| Dupont Circle | Twinbrook |
| Eastern Market | White Flint |
| Farragut West | |
| Federal Center SW | **Prince George's County** |
| Federal Triangle | |
| Foggy Bottom | Addison Road |
| Fort Totten | Capitol Heights |
| Friendship Heights | Cheverly |
| Gallery Place | Landover |
| Judiciary Square | |
| L'Enfant Plaza | **Arlington County** |
| McPherson Square | |
| Metro Center | Ballston |
| Minnesota Avenue | Clarendon |
| Potomac Avenue | Courthouse |
| Rhode Island Avenue | Crystal City |
| Smithsonian | Pentagon City |
| Stadium–Armory | Rosslyn |
| Tenleytown | Virginia Square |
| Union Station | |
| Van Ness | **Alexandria** |
| Woodley Park | |
| | Braddock Road |
| **Fairfax County** | Eisenhower Avenue |
| | King Street |
| Dunn Loring | |
| Huntington | |

where

$Y_j$ = activity weight in district $j$;

$\alpha$ = calibration parameter; and

$B_{ij}$ = the average travel time to zone $i$ from zone $j$ (the average of automobile and transit time).

The numerator of this expression is the absolute accessibility of the region to a specific zone; it is defined as the sum over all zones of an activity-weighted function of the impedance between each origin zone ( $j$ ) and the destination zone ( $i$ ). The relative accessibility index is this value taken as a share of total regional accessibility (the sum of all absolute accessibilities). The set of all 182 relative accessibility indices necessarily sums to one. The destination zones of interest here are, of course, those containing rapid-transit stations.

## The Employment Equation

*The level of employment* indicates the general level of development in a given small area even though it does not specify the type or quality of development. The model specification for total employment in station areas is

$$E_i = a_1 + b_1 A_{1i} + c_1 V_{li} + d_1 V_{bi} + e_1 M_i + f_1 P_i + g_1 C_i,$$

where

| | |
|---|---|
| $E$ | = aggregate employment; |
| $A_1$ | = relative accessibility index (median income weights); |
| $V_l$ | = value per square foot of land; |
| $V_b$ | = value per square foot of commercial floor space; |
| $M$ | = average monthly residential mortgage payment; |
| $P$ | = population; |
| $C$ | = commercial share of land uses; |
| $i$ | = station area designation, $i = 1, \dots 52$; |
| $a_1$ | = intercept; and |
| $b_1 - g_1$ | = coefficients of independent variables. |

The estimated version of this equation, reported in Table 5.2 with more statistical information, is:

$$E_i = -30573 + 5438068 A_{1i} + 114 V_{li} + 122 V_{bi} - 9.8 M_i - 1.3 P_i + 10.3 C_i.$$

The equation explains over two-thirds of the variation in total employment among station areas ( $R^2 = 0.6721$ ). Furthermore, the independent variables are significant predictors of total employment. Accessibility, land value, and commercial building value are strongly

Table 5.2

## Local Development (LOCDEV) Model: Estimated Structural Equations

Independent variables

**Dependent variable: Total employment** (adj $R^2$ = 0.6721, α = 0.04)

| | Intercept | Access[a] | Land value | Commercial building value | Avg. monthly mortgage payment | Population | Commercial share of land uses |
|---|---|---|---|---|---|---|---|
| | -30,573.43† | 5,438,068.39† | 113.50† | 121.99† | -9.80 | -1.31† | 10.29 |
| | (-2.722)[b] | (3.197) | (6.384) | (2.484) | (-1.559) | (-1.750) | (0.196) |
| | (0.0092)[c] | (0.0025) | (0.0001) | (0.0168) | (0.1280) | (0.0870) | (0.8457) |

**Dependent variable: Sales (retail employment)** (adj $R^2$ = 0.4466, α = 0.155)

| | Intercept | Access[d] | Commercial floor space, 1980 | Population | Commercial share of land uses |
|---|---|---|---|---|---|
| | -1,093.48 | 163,855.91† | 0.00010289† | -0.118389 | 16.69† |
| | (-1.482) | (1.836) | (2.802) | (-1.184) | (2.118) |
| | (0.1451) | (0.0726) | (0.0073) | (0.2423) | (0.0395) |

**Dependent variable: Floor space (log)** (adj $R^2$ = 0.7883, α = 2.0)

| | Intercept | Log access[d] | Log land value | Log office floor space value | Log commercial share of land uses |
|---|---|---|---|---|---|
| | 5.2023† | 53.8186† | 0.7523† | 0.4463† | 1.2462† |
| | (4.809) | (1.717) | (7.074) | (1.813) | (6.363) |
| | (0.0001) | (0.0935) | (0.0001) | (0.0771) | (0.0001) |

[a]Weight is median income.
[b]t-statistics.
[c]Significance level.
[d]Weight is total district income.
†Significant at 0.10 level, two-tailed test.

and positively related to aggregate employment (based on their *t*-statistics), while local population also proved important with the expected negative sign (in general, the greater the population in the vicinity of a station area, the less land is available for nonresidential uses, including employment).

## The Retail Employment Equation

*The retail sector* is of special interest since its activities are far more oriented toward the public and are expected to be more sensitive to individual consumer accessibility than basic, government, and service activity.

The ideal variable to use to represent the retail sector is sales, but such data are extremely difficult to obtain. Thus, retail employment is used instead. The shortcoming of this variable is that the sales/employee ratio can vary dramatically among different kinds of retail activity. For example, this retail employment variable will be undervalued for a station area containing a preponderance of retail activities with a high sales-to-employee ratio. If, however, the distribution of retail activities according to the sales/employee ratio is quite similar between station areas (even if the level of activity is quite different), this bias would be much smaller.

The retail employment equation is specified:

$$T_i = a_2 + b_2 A_{2i} + c_2 F_i + d_2 P_i + e_2 C_i ,$$

where

| | |
|---|---|
| $T$ | = retail employment; |
| $A_2$ | = accessibility index (total income weights); |
| $F$ | = commercial floor space level; |
| $P$ | = population; |
| $C$ | = commercial share of land uses; |
| $i$ | = station area of interest, $i = 1, \ldots , 52$; |
| $a_2$ | = intercept; and |
| $b_2\text{–}e_2$ | = coefficients of independent variables. |

The estimated version of the model, which is presented in Table 5.2 in more statistical detail, is:

$$T_i = -1093 + 163856 A_{2i} + 0.000103 F_i - 0.12 P_i + 16.7 C_i.$$

The equation explains just under half of the variation in retail employment among station areas ($R^2 = 0.4482$). This level of explained variation, while lower than that achieved in the employment equation, is quite good for a compact model of this sort (see Chapter 2 for a review of studies in the same category that explained much less). Most variables were strongly significant. Access once again turned out to be very important, as was commercial floor space and the share of the station area with commercial uses. Population was not significant in this case, but the sign and size of its coefficient were reasonable and roughly comparable to that in the employment equation.

*The Commercial Floor Space Equation*

*Commercial floor space* is a direct indicator of the level of private economic development in a station area. The double-logarithmic functional form provides a statistically sounder model than the simple linear model in this case, based on the usual indicators ($t$-statistics and $R^2$ levels).

The model specification is:

$$LF = a_3 + b_3 LA_{1i} + c_3 LV_{li} + d_3 LV_{oi} + e_3 C_i,$$

where

| | |
|---|---|
| $L$ | = logarithm of variable; |
| $F$ | = commercial floor space; |
| $A_1$ | = accessibility index (median income weight); |
| $V_l$ | = value per square foot of land; |
| $V_o$ | = value per square foot of commercial office floor space; |
| $C$ | = commercial share of land use; |
| $i$ | = station area of interest, $i = 1, \ldots, 52$; |
| $a_3$ | = intercept; and |
| $b_3 - e_3$ | = coefficients of independent variables. |

The estimated model, reported in more detail in Table 5.2, is:

$$LF = 5.2 + 53.819 LA_{1i} + 0.75 LV_{li} + 0.45 LV_{oi} + 1.25 C_i.$$

Almost 80 percent of the variation in the logged floor space variable is explained by the set of independent variables ($R^2 = 0.7883$). Again, accessibility is quite important, as are the values both of land and of office building floor space and the commercial share of land uses in the station area.

## *LOCDEV's Quality*

The three models explain a great deal of the variation among station areas with several significant independent variables. This finding means that further statistical analysis based on the models is reasonable.

### Responsiveness of the Development Variables

The sensitivity of the development measures (the dependent variables) to changes in the factors affecting development (the independent variables) can provide important information about the relative importance of the independent variables in affecting development. The responsiveness can be measured by calculating the *elasticity* of the development term with respect to each independent variable. Elasticity, a measure of how much change is caused in the dependent variable by a change in a specific independent variable, is the ratio of percentage change in the dependent variable to percentage change in that independent variable. An elasticity of 0.8, for instance, indicates that a 1.6 percent increase in the dependent variable results from a 2 percent increase in the independent variable. If the elasticity is less than one, as in this example, the relationship between the variables is termed relatively inelastic; if the elasticity is greater than one, the relationship is called relatively elastic. There is a simple physical analogy. Suppose the independent variable is the amount of force applied to a rubber band and the dependent variable is the length the band stretches. For a given force, the more elastic the band, the farther it stretches.

For the relative accessibility index, calculating elasticities is quite complex because of the composite and nonlinear character of the variable. The methodology of these calculations is described in Appendix 5.1 and a representative set of them is presented there in Table A5.1. Because of the double-logarithmic form of the commercial floor space equation, the elasticity of the dependent variable with respect to each nonaccess variable is equal to the coefficient of that variable in the equation. For the aggregate employment and retail employment equations, which are linear, the elasticities of nonaccess variables are calculated using the standard midpoint formula:

$$\text{ELAS} = \frac{dY / \overline{Y}}{dX / \overline{X}},$$

where

| | |
|---|---|
| $Y$ | = dependent variable (development variable); |
| $X$ | = independent variable (factor affecting development); |
| $d$ | = change in variable; and |
| $-$ | = mean. |

These elasticities are reported in Table 5.3. Responses to prices tend to be inelastic but substantial. Aggregate employment and commercial floor space grow 6.5 and 7.5 percent respectively for each 10 percent increase in land value; employment grows 4.6 percent for each 10 percent increase in the value of commercial floor space; and commercial floor space grows 4.5 percent for every 10 percent increase in the value of office building floor space. In the same vein, retail employment grows 3.1 percent for every 10 percent increase in commercial floor space in a station area. These estimates indicate that relatively high prices for land and building space in a station area will lead to high-density activity (i.e., very high levels of commercial floor space development); low-density activity, as reflected in lower absolute levels of commercial floor space, would not be profitable in such a location. These values also reflect the fact that development itself helps cause higher property values in station areas.

Development responds negatively to the economic variables that describe the residents of station areas. Employment drops 5.1 percent for every 10 percent increase in the average mortgage payment in a station area, and 3.1 percent for every 10 percent increase in population in a station area. Retail employment also drops 3.0 percent for a 10 percent increase in population.

These calculations are based on cross-sectional data, so it should not be inferred that growth in residential property values or population *over time* at a particular station would reduce retail employment there. These results suggest, rather, that retail activity can grow faster in areas with relatively fewer and/or poorer residents because developers meet fewer obstacles to their plans in such areas.

Table 5.3

**Elasticities of Development Variables with Respect to Independent Variables: LOCDEV Structural Equations**

|  | Aggregate employment | Retail employment | Commercial floor space |
|---|---|---|---|
| Land value | 0.65 | — | 0.75 |
| Commercial building value | 0.46 | — | — |
| Office building value | — | — | 0.45 |
| Commercial floor space | — | 0.31 | — |
| Commercial share of land use | 0.04 | 0.70 | 1.25 |
| Average monthly mortgage payment | −0.51 | — | — |
| Population | −0.31 | 0.30 | — |
| Impedance [a] | −1.98 | −8.57 | −0.07 |

[a] For more details about these values, see Appendix 5.1.

The commercial share of land use in the station area also plays an important role in development. Retail employment rises 7.0 percent and commercial floor space 12.5 percent for every 10 percent increase in this variable. (Since this variable is itself a percentage, it should be noted that a 10 percent increase in, say, a 30 percent share means a share of 33 percent, not 40 percent.) Of all the site characteristic variables, only the commercial share of land use has an elasticity greater than unity. Turning to the responsiveness of the dependent variables to change in impedance (measured in terms of trip time, and the main component of the relative accessibility index), it is clear that aggregate and retail employment both respond more elastically to impedance reductions than to any of the site characteristic variables (see Tables 5.3 and A5.1). This finding is consistent with the old real estate nostrum that the three key factors affecting real estate values are location, location, and location. Commercial floor space, on the other hand, is more sensitive to land values and office space values than it is to impedance. For further discussion of the relationship between impedance and development, see Appendix 5.1.

## Model Accuracy: Residual Analysis

The percent of explained variation ($R^2$) and the significance test of model parameters ($t$-values) are basic measures of goodness of fit and model validity. LOCDEV performs well in terms of these measures.

Another avenue for testing the model is to analyze the residual patterns of its equations.

Residuals are the differences between the observed values of the dependent variable and those that are "predicted" by the model parameters when run using the original values of the independent variables in the historical data set. One measure of the accuracy of a model is its ability to reproduce these historical, observed values of the dependent variables when such a run is performed. Residuals can be examined both in the aggregate to assess the model's overall reliability, and observation-by-observation to see if there are specific types of observations for which the model is especially strong or weak.

### Aggregate Residuals

Two measures of aggregate residuals are the root mean square error (RMSE) and the absolute mean error (AME). The first is the square root of the sum of the squares of the residuals and the second is the mean of the absolute values of the residuals. The RMSE tends to be greater than the AME, especially when some of the residuals are large (in absolute terms). The AME is essentially a simple average; the RMSE emphasizes outlying residuals because of the squaring procedure. These measures are presented in Table 5.4 for LOCDEV and provide an overall sense of the accuracy of the model.

The mean percent errors are rather large, which is not surprising given the level of explanation achieved by each equation. The AME values are 54 percent for employment, 74 percent for sales, and 60 percent for floor space. (An interpretation of this is that the predicted values for the dependent variable will typically miss the true value by these percentages.) The RMSE values are even larger. These error levels suggest that the structural model is useful for indicating the direction and general magnitude of the impacts of independent variables on the development variables, but that precise estimates of dependent variables cannot be made. This finding suggests that many factors affecting development in small areas are not captured in the model; indeed, many such factors are inherently unmodelable.

### Correlations of Residuals and Variables

It is useful to examine the relationship between the residuals and the independent and dependent variables. If the residuals are highly correlated with independent variables, then the equation is seriously biased.

Table 5.4

**Aggregate Residuals for LOCDEV Structural Model**

|  | Equation | | |
|---|---|---|---|
|  | Aggregate employ- ment | Retail employ- ment | Commercial floor space (in thousands) |
| Adj $R^2$ | 0.67 | 0.44 | 0.79 |
| Mean of dependent variable (MDV) | 8,350 | 829 | 2,997 |
| Root mean square error (RMSE) | 6,537 | 918 | 4,718 |
| Absolute mean error (AME) | 4,539 | 613 | 1,790 |
| Mean percentage error (RMSE/MDV) | 78 | 111 | 157 |
| Mean percentage error (AME/MDV) | 54 | 74 | 60 |

If they are highly correlated with dependent variables, then the model may tend to compress (understate) large values and give estimates of the dependent variable that are too low. This can happen if independent variables that properly scale the dependent variable are omitted from the equation's structure; the error term is forced to take up the slack. Residuals can be large for large values of the dependent variable without implying bias, however, so it is important also to consider the correlation between the residual *as a percentage of the dependent variable* and the dependent variable as well as that between the simple residual and the dependent variable.

A review of the correlations shows that there are no cases of high correlations between residuals and independent variables. The only questionable instance is the correlation between land value and the residual in the employment equation, and even this has the rather low value of 0.3 (see Table 5.5). There are significant correlations between the residuals and the dependent variables, but the corresponding correlations between residuals as percentages of the dependent variables and the dependent variables themselves are much lower (and in some cases have an opposite sign; see Table 5.6). These relationships give only modest cause for concern over bias.

### Individual Residuals

Examination of the individual residuals can pinpoint categories of observations that are consistently well predicted, underestimated, or over-

Table 5.5

**Correlations of Residuals to Independent Variables: LOCDEV Structural Model**

| | Aggregate employment | Retail employment[b] | Commercial floor space[b] |
|---|---|---|---|
| Access | 0.0 (1.0)[a] | — | — |
| Land value | −0.31 (0.02) | — | — |
| Commercial building value | 0.0 (1.0) | — | — |
| Commercial share of land uses | −0.03 (0.85) | — | — |
| Average monthly mortgage payment | −0.01 (0.97) | — | — |
| Population | 0.07 (0.60) | — | — |

[a]Probability of no significance.
[b]All variables had value 0.0 (1.0).

Table 5.6

**Correlations of Residuals to Dependent Variables: LOCDEV Structural Model**

| | Residuals | Residuals/dependent variable |
|---|---|---|
| Aggregate employment | 0.54 (0.00)[a] | 0.16 (0.26) |
| Retail employment | 0.73 (0.00) | 0.19 (0.18) |
| Commercial floor space | 0.44 (0.00) | −0.09 (0.54) |

[a]Probability of no significance.

estimated. Some important patterns emerge from such a search. Stations in the District of Columbia tend to have the best correspondence between observed and predicted values of their development variables (see Table 5.7). All ten of the "good" stations for the employment equation and nine out of the eleven "good" stations for commercial floor space were in the District. In addition, three out of the seven

Table 5.7

**Stations for Which the Absolute Value of Residual/Observed**
**Is 0.25 or Less**

| | Aggregate employment | Retail employment | Commercial floor space |
|---|---|---|---|
| District stations | | | |
| Judiciary Square | X | X | |
| Foggy Bottom | X | X | X |
| Capitol South | X | | |
| Federal Center SW | X | | |
| Metro Center | X | | |
| Van Ness | X | | X |
| Tenleytown | X | | X |
| McPherson Square | X | | |
| Gallery Place | X | | X |
| Smithsonian | X | X | |
| Cleveland Park | | | X |
| Gallery Place | | | |
| Fort Totten | | | X |
| Federal Triangle | | | X |
| Benning Road | | | X |
| Friendship Heights | | | X |
| Non-District stations | | | |
| White Flint | | X | X |
| Silver Spring | | X | |
| Ballston | | | X |
| Courthouse | | X | |
| Rosslyn | | X | |

"good" stations for the retail employment equation were in the District. Even in the District, however, most stations did not pass the rather stringent 25 percent or less test for accuracy of the predicted values. It is noteworthy that the "good" stations have been open the longest (since the late 1970s); presumably the market forces modeled by LOCDEV have had more time to bring about their expected effect (positive or negative) at these sites.

The simplest explanation for this finding is that the model performs especially well for stations with high levels of existing development and for which future development can represent only small percentage increments, and less well for stations at a low and/or early level of development. In short, it does a good job reinforcing our knowledge about what is

Table 5.8

## Stations with Large Overestimates of Development Variables (Over 100 percent)

| Station area | Aggregate employment | Retail employment | Commercial floor space |
|---|---|---|---|
| Montgomery County (and adjacent District stations) | | | |
| Shady Grove | O | O | |
| Rockville | | | O |
| Twinbrook | | O | |
| White Flint | O | | |
| Grosvenor | O | O | |
| Bethesda | | O | |
| Tenleytown | | O | |
| Van Ness | | O | |
| Cleveland Park | | O | |
| Woodley Park | O | O | |
| Takoma Park | O | O | |
| | | | |
| Prince George's County (and adjacent District stations) | | | |
| Landover | | | O |
| Cheverly | O | | O |
| Deanwood | | O | |
| Minnesota Avenue | | O | |
| Addison Road | O | O | |
| | | | |
| Other District stations | | | |
| Fort Totten | O | O | |
| Rhode Island | O | O | |
| Union Station | | O | |
| Metro Center | | | O |
| Stadium-Armory | | O | |
| Potomac Avenue | O | O | |
| Federal Triangle | | O | |
| | | | |
| Arlington County | | | |
| Ballston | | O | |
| Virginia Square | O | O | |
| Courthouse | O | O | |
| | | | |
| Alexandria | | | |
| Eisenhower | | O | |
| King Street | O | | O |
| Braddock Road | O | | |
| | | | |
| Fairfax County | | | |
| Huntington | O | | |
| Dunn Loring | | | O |

Table 5.9

**Stations with Large Underestimates of Development Variables (Over 100 percent)[a]**

| Station area | Aggregate employment | Retail employment | Commercial floor space |
|---|---|---|---|
| Montgomery County (and adjacent District stations) | | | |
| Rockville | | | U |
| Bethesda | | | U |
| Takoma Park | | | U |
| Cleveland Park | U | | |
| | | | |
| Prince George's County (and adjacent District stations) | | | |
| Landover | U | U | |
| Deanwood | U | | U |
| Minnesota Avenue | U | | U |
| Capitol Heights | U | U | |
| Benning Road | U | U | |
| | | | |
| Other District stations | | | |
| Brookland | U | | |
| Stadium-Armory | U | | |
| Federal Triangle | | | U |
| | | | |
| Arlington County | | | |
| Pentagon City | U | U | |
| Rosslyn | | | U |
| | | | |
| Fairfax County | | | |
| Dunn Loring | | U | |

[a]Such underestimates are possible because the model can predict negative values even for variables such as aggregate employment which cannot actually have negative values.

mainly in place already, and not as good a job in those areas where development is, has been, or is likely to become more problematical.

Large residuals (reflecting weak model performance) at the station-area level are scattered widely among the jurisdictions. Nevertheless, there is a tendency for Montgomery County stations (and nearby District stations located on lines extending into this county) to be overestimated. The Prince George's County (and nearby District) stations suffer from large errors, with a slightly greater tendency to be underestimated than overestimated (10 values of the dependent variable were underestimated by over 100 percent, while 7 were overestimated by

Table 5.10

**Aggregate Employment Equation: Residuals as Percentage of Aggregate Employment in 1980, Selected Station Areas by Jurisdiction**

| Station name | Employment in 1980 | Very low | Low | Good | High | Very high |
|---|---|---|---|---|---|---|
| District of Cloumbia | | | | | | |
| Archives | 20,683 | . | . | . | 65 | . |
| Benning Road | 248 | −1,190 | . | . | . | . |
| Brookland | 881 | −214 | . | . | . | . |
| Capitol South | 13,658 | . | . | 12 | . | . |
| Cleveland Park | 781 | −383 | . | . | . | . |
| Deanwood | 105 | −1,486 | . | . | . | . |
| Dupont Circle | 18,041 | . | −31 | . | . | . |
| Eastern Market | 1,679 | . | . | . | 85 | . |
| Farragut West | 55,969 | . | −48 | . | . | . |
| Federal Center SW | 17,418 | . | −39 | . | . | . |
| Federal Triangle | 27,366 | . | . | 18 | . | . |
| Foggy Bottom | 15,773 | . | . | −11 | . | . |
| Fort Totten | 209 | . | . | . | . | 3,950 |
| Friendship Heights | 4,268 | . | . | . | 46 | . |
| Gallery Place | 17,290 | . | . | . | 25 | . |
| Judiciary Square | 21,948 | . | . | −1 | . | . |
| L'Enfant Plaza | 33,992 | . | −62 | . | . | . |
| McPherson Square | 42,874 | . | . | −17 | . | . |
| Metro Center | 32,424 | . | . | 22 | . | . |
| Minnesota Avenue | 442 | −485 | . | . | . | . |
| Potomac Avenue | 326 | . | . | . | . | 534 |
| Rhode Island Avenue | 380 | . | . | . | . | 1,211 |
| Smithsonian | 15,930 | . | . | −12 | . | . |
| Stadium-Armory | 2,414 | −111 | . | . | . | . |
| Tenleytown | 1,131 | . | . | 7 | . | . |
| Union Station | 12,479 | . | −57 | . | . | . |
| Van Ness | 1,764 | . | . | −12 | . | . |
| Woodley Park | 1,092 | . | . | . | . | 688 |
| Montgomery County | | | | | | |
| Bethesda | 7,536 | . | −32 | . | . | . |
| Grosvenor | 147 | . | . | . | . | 2,721 |
| Rockville | 2,741 | . | −59 | . | . | . |
| Shady Grove | 303 | . | . | . | . | 2,624 |
| Silver Spring | 7,951 | . | −50 | . | . | . |
| Takoma Park | 636 | . | . | . | . | 178 |
| Twinbrook | 1,448 | . | . | . | 87 | . |
| White Flint | 3,061 | . | . | . | . | 163 |

(continued)

Table 5.10 *(continued)*

| Station name | Employment in 1980 | Very low | Low | Good | High | Very high |
|---|---|---|---|---|---|---|
| **Prince George's County** | | | | | | |
| Addison Road | 216 | . | . | . | . | 2,078 |
| Capitol Heights | 234 | −1,518 | . | . | . | . |
| Cheverly | 396 | . | . | . | . | 157 |
| Landover | 570 | −515 | . | . | . | . |
| **Arlington County** | | | | | | |
| Ballston | 4,027 | . | . | . | 32 | . |
| Clarendon | 2,102 | . | . | . | 72 | . |
| Courthouse | 2,584 | . | . | . | . | 269 |
| Crystal City | 20,090 | . | −31 | . | . | . |
| Pentagon City | 1,252 | −280 | . | . | . | . |
| Rosslyn | 8,381 | . | . | . | 52 | . |
| Virginia Square | 2,169 | . | . | . | . | 279 |
| **Alexandria** | | | | | | |
| Braddock Road | 1,000 | . | . | . | . | 597 |
| Eisenhower Avenue | 3,622 | . | −27 | . | . | . |
| King Street | 937 | . | . | . | . | 298 |
| **Fairfax County** | | | | | | |
| Dunn Loring | 769 | . | . | . | . | 479 |
| Huntington | 438 | . | . | . | . | 883 |

over 100 percent for these station areas; see Tables 5.8 and 5.9). The distributions of all of the residual/dependent variable percentages appear in Tables 5.10–5.12.

The difference between the Montgomery and Prince George's stations suggests another explanation for large swings in residuals. The model does not include variables that directly reflect nonmarket factors. Some station areas with great capacity for growth based on the independent variables included in the model may nevertheless develop slowly because of other factors. According to this line of reasoning, the economic forces conducive to development along the Montgomery County Shady Grove line have not yet brought into being the level of development they justify on a strictly market basis. On the other hand, in certain station areas in Prince George's County, the economic pressures for development reflected in the independent variables in the model are not sufficient even to account for current levels of development, while in others (where overestimations occur) the development potential is as strong as in Montgomery County. The mixture of over-

Table 5.11

**Retail Employment Equation: Residuals as Percentage of Retail Employment in 1980, Selected Station Areas by Jurisdiction**

| Station name | Retail employment in 1980 | Very low | Low | Good | High | Very high |
|---|---|---|---|---|---|---|
| District of Columbia | | | | | | |
| Archives | 1,019 | . | . | . | 34 | . |
| Benning Road | 53 | −973 | . | . | . | . |
| Brookland | 146 | . | . | . | 39 | . |
| Capitol South | 805 | . | −68 | . | . | . |
| Cleveland Park | 215 | . | . | . | . | 166 |
| Deanwood | 17 | . | . | . | . | 238 |
| Dupont Circle | 2,471 | . | −63 | . | . | . |
| Eastern Market | 495 | . | −71 | . | . | . |
| Farragut West | 4,597 | . | −44 | . | . | . |
| Federal Center SW | 408 | . | . | . | . | 106 |
| Federal Triangle | 950 | . | . | . | 87 | . |
| Foggy Bottom | 1,331 | . | . | −7 | . | . |
| Fort Totten | 61 | . | . | . | . | 828 |
| Friendship Heights | 1,417 | . | −32 | . | . | . |
| Gallery Place | 4,414 | . | −57 | . | . | . |
| Judiciary Square | 1,521 | . | . | −24 | . | . |
| L'Enfant Plaza | 672 | . | −74 | . | . | . |
| McPherson Square | 2,470 | . | . | . | 34 | . |
| Metro Center | 6,878 | . | −55 | . | . | . |
| Minnesota Avenue | 41 | . | . | . | . | 982 |
| Potomac Avenue | 125 | . | . | . | . | 210 |
| Rhode Island Avenue | 33 | . | . | . | . | 2,095 |
| Smithsonian | 517 | . | . | −15 | . | . |
| Stadium-Armory | 6 | −2,677 | . | . | . | . |
| Tenleytown | 252 | . | . | . | . | 232 |
| Union Station | 314 | . | . | . | . | 323 |
| Van Ness | 314 | . | . | . | . | 244 |
| Woodley Park | 255 | . | . | . | . | 145 |
| Montgomery County | | | | | | |
| Bethesda | 1,702 | . | . | . | . | 135 |
| Grosvenor | 17 | . | . | . | . | 1,380 |
| Rockville | 412 | . | −59 | . | . | . |
| Shady Grove | 130 | . | . | . | . | 987 |
| Silver Spring | 1,852 | . | . | −8 | . | . |
| Takoma Park | 210 | . | . | . | 99 | . |
| Twinbrook | 405 | . | . | . | . | 106 |
| White Flint | 1,280 | . | . | −20 | . | . |
| Prince George's County | | | | | | |
| Addison Road | 10 | . | . | . | . | 5,347 |

*(continued)*

Table 5.11 *(continued)*

| Station name | Retail employment in 1980 | Very low | Low | Good | High | Very high |
|---|---|---|---|---|---|---|
| Prince George's County *(continued)* | | | | | | |
| Capitol Heights | 37 | −1,075 | . | . | . | . |
| Cheverly | 224 | . | −96 | . | . | . |
| Landover | 389 | −141 | . | . | . | . |
| | | | | | | |
| Arlington County | | | | | | |
| Ballston | 385 | . | . | . | . | 168 |
| Clarendon | 783 | . | . | . | 40 | . |
| Courthouse | 238 | . | . | . | . | 200 |
| Crystal City | 870 | . | −34 | . | . | . |
| Pentagon City | 92 | −665 | . | . | . | . |
| Rosslyn | 817 | . | . | −11 | . | . |
| Virginia Square | 441 | . | . | . | . | 212 |
| | | | | | | |
| Alexandria | | | | | | |
| Braddock Road | 278 | . | . | . | 54 | . |
| Eisenhower Avenue | 82 | . | . | . | . | 719 |
| King Street | 461 | . | . | . | 68 | . |
| | | | | | | |
| Fairfax County | | | | | | |
| Dunn Loring | 112 | −208 | . | . | . | . |
| Huntington | 97 | . | . | . | 51 | . |

and underestimates in Prince George's County suggests that the county has a lower level of objective conditions conducive to development than Montgomery County. Such a finding is consistent with the conventional wisdom that Prince George's County has only begun to overcome its status (and resulting image) as an economically less-developed part of the region.

### Summary and Conclusions

There are two sets of final comments on this chapter. The first deals with what LOCDEV has to say to policymakers about the relationship between transportation, land use, and public policy. The second concerns modeling prospects for small areas.

### *Development Lessons from LOCDEV*

The LOCDEV equations estimated above are structural cross-sectional models. They explain the majority of the variations in development

Table 5.12

**Commercial Floor Space Equation: Residuals as a Percentage
of Commercial Floor Space in 1985, Selected Station Areas
by Jurisdiction**

| Station name | Commercial floor space (in thousands) | Very low | Low | Good | High | Very high |
|---|---|---|---|---|---|---|
| **District of Columbia** | | | | | | |
| Archives | 3,608 | . | . | . | . | 124 |
| Benning Road | 30 | . | . | −5 | . | . |
| Capitol South | 569 | . | −29 | . | . | . |
| Cleveland Park | 216 | . | . | 14 | . | . |
| Deanwood | 99 | . | −50 | . | . | . |
| Dupont Circle | 6,120 | . | −29 | . | . | . |
| Eastern Market | 651 | . | . | . | 35 | . |
| Farragut West | 8,108 | . | . | . | 34 | . |
| Federal Center SW | 4,529 | . | −68 | . | . | . |
| Federal Triangle | 6,976 | . | . | 11 | . | . |
| Foggy Bottom | 7,358 | . | . | −22 | . | . |
| Fort Totten | 67 | . | . | −10 | . | . |
| Friendship Heights | 3,292 | . | . | −13 | . | . |
| Gallery Place | 6,969 | . | . | 16 | . | . |
| Judiciary Square | 1,802 | . | . | . | 34 | . |
| L'Enfant Plaza | 825 | . | −41 | . | . | . |
| McPherson Square | 16,488 | . | . | . | 32 | . |
| Metro Center | 12,093 | . | . | . | . | 180 |
| Minnesota Avenue | 558 | . | −61 | . | . | . |
| Potomac Avenue | 626 | . | . | . | 89 | . |
| Rhode Island Avenue | 441 | . | −31 | . | . | . |
| Smithsonian | 85 | . | . | . | 69 | . |
| Tenleytown | 1,028 | . | . | −4 | . | . |
| Union Station | 1,336 | . | −52 | . | . | . |
| Van Ness | 2,019 | . | . | −14 | . | . |
| Woodley Park | 1,859 | . | −43 | . | . | . |
| **Montgomery County** | | | | | | |
| Bethesda | 26,139 | . | −81 | . | . | . |
| Rockville | 1,363 | . | −68 | . | . | . |
| Shady Grove | 48 | . | . | . | . | 931 |
| Silver Spring | 2,561 | . | . | . | 93 | . |
| Takoma Park | 371 | . | −54 | . | . | . |
| Twinbrook | 1,983 | . | −81 | . | . | . |
| White Flint | 1,919 | . | . | 2 | . | . |

*(continued)*

Table 5.12 *(continued)*

| Station name | Commercial floor space (in thousands) | Very low | Low | Good | High | Very high |
|---|---|---|---|---|---|---|
| **Prince George's County** | | | | | | |
| Addison Road | 65 | . | . | . | 26 | . |
| Cheverly | 10 | . | . | . | 63 | . |
| Landover | 6 | . | . | . | . | 899 |
| **Arlington County** | | | | | | |
| Ballston | 3,022 | . | . | −14 | . | . |
| Clarendon | 913 | . | . | . | 82 | . |
| Courthouse | 2,379 | . | −37 | . | . | . |
| Crystal City | 1,438 | . | −43 | . | . | . |
| Rosslyn | 5,617 | . | −70 | . | . | . |
| Virginia Square | 614 | . | . | . | 63 | . |
| **Alexandria** | | | | | | |
| Braddock Road | 210 | . | . | . | 26 | . |
| Eisenhower Avenue | 1,250 | . | −30 | . | . | . |
| King Street | 130 | . | . | . | . | 627 |
| **Fairfax County** | | | | | | |
| Huntington | 72 | . | . | . | 63 | . |

levels among station areas in the region. LOCDEV is statistically strong compared to other such models, as described in Chapter 2. LOCDEV achieves this strength without resorting to categorical independent variables (dummy variables used to separate out categories of the sample whose differences cannot be captured with relatively continuous data), which suggests that station areas are reasonably comparable with each other.

The specified independent variables almost all turn out to be significant, often at very high levels of probability as measured by the *t*-test. Such significance is a prerequisite for the modeling work to have any policy implications.

The aggregate residual analysis suggests that the model is generally unbiased. However, individual residuals are often large, with high residual-to-dependent variable ratios. Downtown District of Columbia stations tended to be predicted best, Montgomery County stations to be overestimated, and Prince George's County stations to be somewhat underestimated. This may well be due to the absence of variables in the model that would reflect particular, nonmarket, institutional barriers to development at particular station sites. Thus, the residuals in the model may actually alert policy makers both to market-based prospects for development at locations currently encumbered by institutional impediments to development, and to situations where market conditions do not warrant high expectations of development even with assistance from the public sector.

The model implies that some policies will work better than others in stimulating development based on which of the independent variables they affect. Travel times to station areas (including both public and private modes) figure heavily in all three models. Total and median income levels of zones of origin proved to be the crucial variables used to weight these interzonal impedances, suggesting that the accessibility of effective demand, rather than of population or of employed workers, is the major factor to consider in estimating future development prospects in station areas. Policies that would speed effective demand to station areas by either public or private modes of transportation would therefore be likely to increase development possibilities in terms of commercial floor space, retail sales, and aggregate employment. Travel time reductions for private vehicles can be achieved through additional roads, widening existing roads, establishing HOV lanes, and providing adequate parking facilities at or close to Metrorail stations. Travel time reductions (especially reductions in waiting time) for bus transportation can be achieved by route alterations, shorter headways, and exclusive bus lanes. Travel time reductions for rail transportation can be achieved by shorter headways (reducing waiting times), higher speed limits where distances between stations allow it, express trains between specific stations (although this can lengthen waiting times in stations not served by them), and improved pedestrian access to stations, as well as through the completion of the Metrorail system. The development of separate light-rail and commuter lines and the upgrading of already existing ones (the MARC lines) would also improve rail transit trip times.

The policymaker can do little to directly affect land or building values or the share of a station area that is already commercial. However, LOCDEV shows that high land and office prices typically are associated with high-density development. Developers apparently strongly desire to build high-rise commercial developments in areas with high land prices; the strength of this interest should be considered by planners in their negotiations with developers. Similarly, the model suggests that, for floor space and sales, the overall character of a station area plays a crucial role in the promotion of further development. Areas with large and/or influential residential populations and small commercial shares of land use are difficult to develop. If planners wish to stimulate development at such sites, they would need to ease the zoning restrictions typically associated with such areas, facilitate lot assembly where possible, and support developers' efforts to facilitate the movement of current residents from the area. Such approaches may not be generally desirable, let alone politically feasible; in fact, an equally valid implication is that large-scale, high-density development should not be encouraged in such areas in the first place. In any case, the importance of the overall character of the station area to the development process is one of the strongest implications of these models.

The most important factor affecting development in the long run, however, is accessibility. Impedance reduction has the most profound effect on development, at least over a substantial time period. This is something that local governments can affect through their concrete planning operations. Thus, LOCDEV points here to the usefulness of public initiatives that can improve regional access to the station areas and create a better climate for development.

The LOCDEV estimates lead to implications for public policy, since they indicate certain areas where planners can intervene with incentives (or at least sensitivity) responding to the revealed needs of private developers in the process of local development. While the political process may dictate the contours of acceptable development at a given station area, the estimates from LOCDEV can help the planner decide which acceptable goals are also feasible and likely to be achieved. They also suggest that access improvements head the list of public policies that would stimulate private development around stations.

### Modeling Small Areas

The LOCDEV estimations indicate that station area development can be successfully modeled on a cross-sectional basis. This is an important result in and of itself, given the historic difficulties experienced in small-area studies. LOCDEV is quite accurate for downtown stations in the District of Columbia that are already well developed, and for certain other moderately well developed areas. It loses some of its accuracy in suburban locations where development is at a lower level, perhaps due to the recency of station openings. There is a virtue in this weakness, however; stations that are overestimated by the model are often ones that have objective qualities conducive to development but face institutional barriers to achieving high levels of it. Similarly, underestimated areas are not especially attractive to developers in the first place.

It is also important to recall the limitations of a LOCDEV-style model. Local areas are subject to inherently unmodelable influences. This is more serious the smaller the area involved; random variations that tend to even out in a large zone may dominate in a small area. Nevertheless, many plausible inferences about development trends and policy effects can be drawn from such models, and their creation and use are reasonable ways of studying, evaluating, and planning both the public and private sides of local development activity.

# Appendix 5.1

# Calculating Elasticities of Development Variables with Respect to Impedance Changes

The response of development to changes in impedance (trip times) presents a serious calculation problem because of the complexity of the relative accessibility index. This index multiplies activity levels at origin zones by a nonlinear function of travel times between origin and station destination zones, and uses a calibration parameter. Computing an elasticity value requires three steps: first, computing the response of the relative accessibility index to changes in impedance; second, computing the response of the dependent variable to changes in the relative accessibility index; and third, multiplying these two elasticities together.

## Response of the Relative Accessibility
## Index to Impedance Changes

The response to impedance changes cannot be calculated in general. It can only be calculated for each station area. Also, because the relationship is nonlinear, it can only be calculated for a specific change in impedance. To compute the elasticity of the index with respect to impedance for a given zone, it is assumed that trip times from all 181 other zones to it are reduced by a specific percentage. The access index is then recalculated. The elasticity of the access index with respect to this specific impedance change is then calculated (i.e., the percentage change in the index is divided by the given percentage change in impedance). This value is valid only for one station area and one value of percentage change in impedance.

The second step—calculating the elasticity of the dependent variable with respect to the access index—is carried out by using the midpoint formula for the aggregate and retail employment equations, and by taking the coefficient of the relative accessibility index for the commercial floor space equation.

In the third step, the two elasticities are multiplied together, yielding the elasticity of the dependent variable with respect to changes in impedance *only* for a specific percentage change and only for that specific station. Since it is desirable to estimate a representative elasticity, steps one through three are repeated for each station area, and the mean elasticity is taken to be representative of the relationship between impedance changes and changes in the dependent variable *for that specific percentage change in impedance*. Several alternative values for percentage change in impedance are used to assess the effect of the nonlinearity in the relative accessibility index. These mean values are reported for five such alternative percentage changes in Table A5.1. The value for a 1 percent change in impedance is selected for inclusion in the general elasticity table (Table 5.3).

### Evaluation of the Elasticity Values

The elasticities computed here are reasonable in several ways. First, for every specified percentage change in impedance, retail activity is the most responsive, followed in order by aggregate employment and commercial floor space. This makes sense; retail activity would respond the most to general regional access of customers' aggregate demand, represented by median or total income variables used as the activity weight in the relative accessibility index. Aggregate employment would logically react less since basic, government, and even most service employment is less attuned to the needs of consumers, but it would still be more flexible than commercial floor space. Second, as the percentage change in impedance rises from 1 to 20 percent, the induced

Table A5.1

**LOCDEV Structural Equations: Responsiveness of Commercial Floor Space, Aggregate Employment, and Retail Employment to Changes in Impedance—Selected Percentage Changes in Impedance**

| Percentage reduction in impedance | Elasticities with respect to impedance for | | |
|---|---|---|---|
| | Commercial floor space | Aggregate employment | Retail employment |
| 1 | −0.07 | −1.98 | −8.57 |
| 2 | −0.07 | −1.98 | −8.63 |
| 5 | −0.08 | −1.99 | −8.79 |
| 10 | −0.10 | −2.00 | −9.05 |
| 20 | −0.16 | −2.01 | −9.51 |

*Note:* Elasticity is the ratio of the percentage change in a dependent variable (commercial floor space, aggregate employment, and retail employment here) to that in an independent variable (impedance in this case). The first −0.07 entry means that, for a one percent reduction in impedance (a negative value), there would be 7/100 of a percent increase (a positive value) in commercial floor space. The elasticity values in the table are the product of the elasticity of the dependent variable with respect to the relative accessibility index, and the elasticity of the relative accessibility index with respect to impedance.

percentage changes in the development variables rise faster. Since the simulated change in impedance represents an improvement in access from all zones in the region to the given station area relative to all other possible trips, it is not surprising that larger changes stimulate proportionately larger responses, even for the sticky floor space variable, since all other station areas stay at their original level of accessibility.

The magnitude of the retail employment elasticity is unrealistically high, however; even that for aggregate employment seems high. Nevertheless, for cross-sectional equations modeling long-run adjustments, such high values are reasonable indicators of the importance of accessibility in the pattern of urban development even if their precise values exaggerate this pattern. The compactness of the equations contributes to this finding, because many variables that explain variation between station-area development levels are omitted and their effects therefore are erroneously captured in the access effect. Also, the large size of the values is partly due to the exclusively cross-sectional nature of the data. Location differences can, over a long period of time, lead to substantial differences in development at such sites because of many historical and structural factors. Few of these are explicitly modeled here, but all of them have effects that are captured in the variations among station areas. Thus, the elasticities calculated here are strictly long-run elasticities reflecting complete adjustments over many years, and even so tend to be overstated because of omitted-variable bias. Hence it would be incorrect to say, for example, that a 10 percent reduction in impedance in 1990 would lead to a 93 percent increase in retail sales by 1993 in the Friendship Heights station area, as a casual inspection of the elasticity table might imply. It would be correct, however, to say that sales at Friendship Heights would respond much more elastically to impedance reductions than to increases in commercial floor space in the station area.

In chapter 6, where LOCDEV is modified to become a forecasting equation including time-series information, the impedance elasticities are much more realistic for midrange analysis than the ones estimated here. (See Table 6.3.)

*Six*

# The Local Development Model (LOCDEV): Specification and Estimation of the Forecasting Version for the Washington, D.C., Region

The LOCDEV model described in chapter 5 yielded significant information about the relative importance of certain variables in creating positive or negative development conditions at station areas. Is it possible to go further and use (or modify) LOCDEV to provide reasonable indicators of the future course of development in station areas? In short, can the structural version of LOCDEV be transformed into a midrange forecasting model?

The structural equations developed in chapter 5 offer promise in this regard because of their high statistical quality for cross-sectional studies. For forecasting purposes, an even greater level of explanatory power would be preferred. The LOCDEV equations are modified here to include lagged dependent variables. This improves their statistical fit, and therefore their usefulness as forecasting tools, at the cost of some loss in theoretical rigor. For instance, because of the combination of cross-sectional and time-series information in the forecasting version of the model, the response time of dependent variables to independent variables is ambiguous.[1] Nevertheless, by assuming that the length of the lag in the lagged term is the response time, it is possible

---

[1]Pure cross-sectional studies produce long-run elasticities. Pure time-series studies produce elasticities that correspond to the time period between observations. Any kind of pooling of time-series and cross-sectional variables and observations renders the impact time ambiguous. In general, it is expected that the elasticities produced by the pooled model would be lower than those in the structural or pure cross-sectional model, but it is impossible rigorously to specify a reaction period.

Figure 6.1. **Forecasting Versions of LOCDEV (residuals term included)**

Aggregate employment equation

$$E_i = a_1 + b_1A_{1i} + c_1E_{-1i} + d_1V_i + R_{1i}$$

where

| | |
|---|---|
| $E$ | = aggregate employment in the forecast period; |
| $A_1$ | = accessibility index (median income weights); |
| $E_{-1}$ | = lagged aggregate employment; |
| $V$ | = average value of commercial floor space; |
| $R_1$ | = residual from calibration experiment (optional); and |
| $i$ | = small area of interest. |

Retail employment equation

$$T = a_2 + b_2A_{2i} + c_2F_i + d_2B_{-1i} + e_2P_i + f_2S_i + R_{2i}$$

where

| | |
|---|---|
| $T$ | = retail employment in the forecast period; |
| $A_2$ | = accessibility index (total income weights); |
| $F$ | = commercial floor space level; |
| $B_{-1}$ | = lagged basic employment; |
| $P$ | = population; |
| $C$ | = commercial share of land uses; |
| $R_2$ | = residual from calibration experiment (optional); and |
| $i$ | = small area of interest. |

Commercial floor space equation

$$LF = a_3 + b_3LA_{1i} + c_3LN_{-1i} + d_3LD_i + e_3LO_i + f_3LC_i + R_{3i}$$

where

| | |
|---|---|
| $L$ | = logarithm of variable; |
| $F$ | = commercial floor space in the forecast period; |
| $A_i$ | = accessibility index (median income weight); |
| $N_{-1}$ | = lagged nonbasic employment (retail, wholesale, and service); |
| $D$ | = average land value; |
| $O$ | = average value of office space; |
| $C$ | = commercial share of land use; |
| $R_3$ | = residual from calibration (optional); and |
| $i$ | = small area of interest. |

to calibrate and then use a forecasting version of LOCDEV.

## The Forecasting Version of the LOCDEV Model

The LOCDEV forecasting model differs in principle from its structural counterpart because its equations use lagged variables, including lagged dependent variables. This leads to improved levels of explanation (higher $R^2$s) because development tends not to change dramatically over the moderate periods reflected in the lagged variables; for example, the largest areas in 1976 were still the largest in 1980. One negative statistical effect associated with the use of lagged dependent variables is their tendency to overshadow the effects of other variables, in some cases even rendering otherwise important independent variables insignificant (usually because of high degrees of collinearity between the independent variables and the lagged dependent variable). Respecification of the LOCDEV equations for forecasting must therefore be carried out carefully to make sure that many of the variables proven to be crucial in the structural equations remain important in the forecasting version (see Figure 6.1).

### *The Model Specifications*

The three equations of the cross-sectional model are here respecified for the forecasting version.

### *Aggregate Employment Equation*

The forecasting version of the aggregate employment equation for each station area is:

$$E_i = a_1 + b_1 A_{1i} + c_1 E_{-1i} + d_1 V_{bi},$$

where

$E$    = aggregate employment in the forecast period;
$A_1$  = accessibility index (median income weights);
$E_{-1}$ = lagged aggregate employment;
$V_b$  = average value of commercial floor space;
$a_1$   = intercept;

Table 6.1

## Local Development (LOCDEV) Model: Estimated Forecasting Equations

**Total employment** (adj $R^2$ = 0.9738; α = 0.38[c])

| Dependent variable | Intercept | Access[a] | Lagged employment[b] | Commercial bldg. value | Commercial share of land uses |
|---|---|---|---|---|---|
| | -2560.36† | 358952.20† | 1.041179† | 25.86781† | 17.8902† |
| | (-2.390)[d] | (1.691) | (45.52) | (1.909) | (2.345) |
| | (0.0253)[e] | (0.0973) | (0.0001) | (0.0622) | (0.0234) |

**Sales (Retail employment)** (adj $R^2$ = 0.4846; α = 0.3)

| Dependent variable | Intercept | Access[f] | Commercial floor space (1980) | Lagged[b] basic employment | Population |
|---|---|---|---|---|---|
| | -1196.72† | 127500.87 | 0.000080779† | 0.041969† | -0.01919 |
| | (-1.676) | (1.452) | (2.186) | (2.112) | (-0.179) |
| | (0.1005) | (0.1533) | (0.0339) | (0.0402) | (0.8589) |

**Floor space (log)** (adj $R^2$ = 0.7969; α = 2.0)

| Dependent variable | Intercept | Log access[a] | Log lagged non-basic employment | Log land value | Log office floor space value | Log commercial share of land uses |
|---|---|---|---|---|---|---|
| | 4.95923† | 52.1776† | 0.295881† | 0.528268† | 0.251371 | 1.120737† |
| | (4.635) | (1.699) | (1.653) | (3.091) | (0.937) | (5.432) |
| | (0.001) | (0.0972) | (0.1061) | (0.0036) | (0.3546) | (0.0001) |

[a]Weight is median income.
[b]Lag is 4 years.
[c]Calibration parameter in access index.
[d]$t$-statistic.
[e]Significance level.
[f]Weight is total district income.
†Significant at 0.10 level, two-tailed test.

$b_1$–$d_1$    = coefficients; and
$i$        = station area.

This equation is slimmer than its counterpart in the structural model, with land value, commercial share of land uses, monthly mortgage, and population variables all dropped and lagged employment added. Nevertheless, the access index (weighted by median income) and the price of commercial floor space term, both key variables in the structural model of chapter 5, have been retained.

The empirical estimation of the equation, presented in more detail in Table 6.1, is:

$$E_i = -2560 + 35895A_{1i} + 1.04E_{-1i} + 25.87V_{bi}.$$

This equation fits the data extremely well, with an adjusted $R^2$ of 0.9738. The signs correspond to intuition, and each of the three independent variables is significant at the 0.10 level (two-tailed $t$-test).

### Retail Employment Equation

The insertion of a lagged dependent variable into the structural version of the retail employment equation renders the entire equation unusable; only the lagged term remains significant. Therefore, rather than use lagged retail employment, lagged basic employment is used as the lagged dynamic variable in the equation. Here "basic" is expanded from its usual definition of manufacturing, mining, etc. (SIC01) to include government activity, because in the Washington area federal government employment functions in much the same way that manufacturing employment does in other urban regions (at least from the standpoint of location theory, which suggests that retail activity logically comes after the establishment of basic employment in a particular site as a response to demand from basic-sector firms and workers). This equation is:

$$T_i = a_2 + b_2A_{2i} + c_2F_i + d_2B_{-1i} + e_2P_i + f_2S_i,$$

where

$T$    = retail employment in the forecast period;
$A_2$    = accessibility index (total income weights);

$F$       = commercial floor space level;
$B_{-1}$   = lagged basic employment;
$P$       = population;
$S$       = commercial share of land uses;
$a_2$     = intercept;
$b_2$–$f_2$  = coefficients; and
$i$       = station area.

This equation differs from the structural version of the model only in that the lagged basic employment variable is added. The estimated version of the model, which appears in more statistical detail in Table 6.1, is:

$$T_i = -1197 + 127501A_{2i} + 0.000081F_i + 0.04B_{-1i} - 0.02P_i + 17.89S_i.$$

In the estimation of the respecified equation, the significance of the access term drops somewhat, while that of population falls precipitously. The commercial floor space, lagged basic employment, and commercial share of land use variables all perform well. The adjusted $R^2$ is 0.4964, only a bit higher than that for the structural model. This level of explanation is suitable only for indicative forecasting purposes.

### The Commercial Floor Space Equation

To convert the structural equation into a forecasting version, lagged nonbasic employment is inserted as a proxy for lagged commercial floor space since data are not available for the latter. This is reasonable since nonbasic employment, which includes retail, wholesale, warehouse, and service categories, moves closely with commercial floor space. The forecasting equation is specified:

$$LF_i = a_3 + b_3LA_{1i} + c_3LN_{-1i} + d_3LD_i + e_3LO_i + f_3LC_i,$$

where

$L$    = logarithm of variable;
$F$    = commercial floor space in the forecast period;
$A_1$   = accessibility index (median income weight);

$N_{-1}$ = lagged nonbasic employment (retail, wholesale, and service);
$D$ = average land value;
$O$ = average value of office space;
$C$ = commercial share of land use;
$a_3$ = intercept;
$b_3$–$f_3$ = coefficients; and
$i$ = station area.

The estimated version of the model, which appears in more statistical detail in Table 6.1, is:

$$LF_i = 4.96 + 52.18LA_{1i} + 0.30LN_{-1i} + 0.53LD_i + 0.25LO_i + 1.12LC_i.$$

The forecasting version of the model does not substantially alter the relations among variables estimated in the structural version of the model. The adjusted $R^2$ of the floor space model is 0.7969, slightly larger than that for the structural version. The variables are significant except for the value of office floor space. This equation, like the retail employment one, is satisfactory only for indicative forecasting purposes and will not produce as accurate a forecast as the employment equation because of its lower $R^2$.

**Responsiveness of the Forecasting Model Variables**

Elasticities of the development variables with respect to the independent variables are calculated in the same manner as in chapter 5 and are reported in Table 6.2 alongside their structural counterparts (where appropriate). The detailed elasticity table for the access term, paralleling that in Table A5.1 (in the appendix to chapter 5), appears in Table 6.3.

The elasticity of employment with respect to lagged employment approaches unity, which is not surprising given the continuity in the region in development levels over the historical period. The elasticity of employment with respect to the price of commercial buildings is 0.09 (meaning that a 10 percent increase in the price of commercial floor space would lead to a slightly less than 1 percent increase in employment), only one-fifth the corresponding level in the structural equation. The lower value reflects both the muting effect of lagged dependent variables on some of the variables in the equation, and the shorter-term character of elasticity based on pooled models compared

Table 6.2

**LOCDEV Forecasting Equations: Elasticities of Development Variables with Respect to Independent Variables**

|  | Aggregate employment | Retail employment | Commercial floorspace |
|---|---|---|---|
| Land value | — | — | 0.53 (0.75)[b] |
| Commercial building value | 0.10 (0.46) | — | — |
| Office building value | — | — | 0.25 (0.45) |
| Commercial floor space | — | 0.21 (0.31) | — |
| Commercial share of land uses | — | 0.87 (0.70) | 1.12 (1.25) |
| Population | — | 0.03 (−0.30) | — |
| Relative[a] accessibility | −0.16 (−1.98) | −0.68 (−8.57) | −0.07 (−0.07) |

[a]For more details about the computation of these values, see Appendix 5.1.
[b]Values in parentheses are elasticities for corresponding variables in the structural version.

Table 6.3

**LOCDEV Forecasting Equations: Responsiveness of Commercial Floor Space, Aggregate Employment, and Retail Employment to Changes in Impedance—Selected Percentage Changes in Impedance**

| Percentage reduction in impedance | Elasticities with respect to impedance for | | |
|---|---|---|---|
|  | Commercial floor space | Aggregate employment | Retail employment |
| 1 | −0.07 | −0.16 | −0.68 |
| 2 | −0.07 | −0.17 | −0.69 |
| 5 | −0.08 | −0.17 | −0.72 |
| 10 | −0.10 | −0.19 | −0.77 |
| 20 | −0.15 | −0.22 | −0.87 |

*Note:* See the text in Appendix 5.1 for discussion of the methodology used here.

to the long-run character of that based on purely cross-sectional models. The response of aggregate employment to reductions in impedance is also much less (and within a more credible range) in the forecasting model than in the structural version.

The elasticity of retail employment with respect to floor space similarly drops by half to 0.21 while that with respect to the commercial share of land uses increases by a third to 0.87. Lagged basic employment has an elasticity of 0.32, which suggests that the changes noted above are within reason. An important improvement is that the response to impedance changes is much more credible while still larger than the response of the other dependent variables to this variable, as expected (see Table 6.3).

A similar finding emerges with the commercial floor space equation. The elasticity of land price changes to 0.53 in the forecasting version from 0.75 in its structural counterpart, that of the value of office building prices falls to 0.25 from 0.45, while that of the commercial share of land uses nudges downward to 1.12 from 1.25. The elasticity of lagged basic employment is a reasonable 0.30. The response to impedance improvements remains almost identical between the two versions of the model. Thus, the general trends in responsiveness in the two equations are quite similar, although the shorter-run elasticities in the forecasting equation are usually (as expected) smaller than the long-run elasticities in the structural model.

## Model Accuracy: Residual Analysis

Residual analysis at both the aggregate and the observation level can help identify general and specific strengths and weaknesses in the model.

### Aggregate Residuals

The mean percent error (AME-based) is much lower in general for the forecasting model than for the structural model (see Tables 5.5 and 6.4). This is expected given the higher level of explanation achieved in the forecasting model. Employment is especially accurate, with a mean percent error (AME-based) of only 13.5. The retail employment equation and the floor space equation, however, have mean percent errors (AME-based) between 60 and 70 (the RMSE-based values are also

Table 6.4

**Aggregate Residuals for LOCDEV Forecasting Model**

|  | Equation | | |
|---|---|---|---|
|  | Aggregate employment | Retail employment | Commercial floor space (in thousands)[a] |
| Adj $R^2$ | 0.98 | 0.49 | 0.80 |
| Mean of dependent variable (MDV) | 8,350 | 829 | 2,997 |
| Root mean square error (RMSE) | 1,910 | 876 | 4,932 |
| Absolute mean error (AME) | 1,126 | 579 | 1,947 |
| Mean percent error (RMSE/MDV) | 23 | 106 | 164 |
| Mean percent error (AME/MDV) | 14 | 70 | 65 |

[a]Values converted to linear form for this analysis.

Table 6.5

**Correlations of Residuals with Dependent Variables: LOCDEV Forecasting Model**

|  | Residuals | Residuals/dependent variable |
|---|---|---|
| Aggregate employment | 0.16 | −0.11 |
|  | (0.26)[a] | (0.44) |
| Retail employment | 0.63 | 0.17 |
|  | (0.00) | (0.23) |
| Commercial floor space | 0.43 | 0.31 |
|  | (0.00) | (0.04) |

*Note:* The correlation between the residuals and the independent variables was 0.00 in all cases.
[a]Probability of no significance.

very large, suggesting some outliers in the sample). These values are too high for these two LOCDEV equations to be precise forecasting tools but satisfactory for them to serve as indicative instruments.

## *Residual Correlations with Variables*

The independent variables in all of the equations are uncorrelated with

Table 6.6

## Aggregate Employment Equation: Residuals as Percentage of Aggregate Employment in 1980, Selected Stations by Jurisdiction

| Station name | Employment in 1980 | Very low | Low | Good | High | Very high |
|---|---|---|---|---|---|---|
| **District of Columbia** | | | | | | |
| Archives | 20,683 | . | . | 20 | . | . |
| Benning Road | 248 | . | −72 | . | . | . |
| Brookland | 881 | . | . | 19 | . | . |
| Capitol South | 13,658 | . | . | − 5 | . | . |
| Cleveland Park | 781 | . | . | . | 31 | . |
| Deanwood | 105 | −1049 | . | . | . | . |
| Dupont Circle | 18,041 | . | . | − 9 | . | . |
| Eastern Market | 1,679 | . | . | 9 | . | . |
| Farragut West | 55,969 | . | . | −15 | . | . |
| Federal Center SW | 17,418 | . | . | 2 | . | . |
| Federal Triangle | 27,366 | . | . | 8 | . | . |
| Foggy Bottom | 15,773 | . | . | − 1 | . | . |
| Fort Totten | 209 | − 334 | . | . | . | . |
| Friendship Heights | 4,268 | . | . | 6 | . | . |
| Gallery Place | 17,290 | . | . | 4 | . | . |
| Judiciary Square | 21,948 | . | . | 24 | . | . |
| L'Enfant Plaza | 33,992 | . | . | − 5 | . | . |
| McPherson Square | 42,874 | . | . | 1 | . | . |
| Metro Center | 32,424 | . | . | 13 | . | . |
| Minnesota Avenue | 442 | − 265 | . | . | . | . |
| Potomac Avenue | 326 | . | . | . | 39 | . |
| Rhode Island Avenue | 380 | . | . | 2 | . | . |
| Smithsonian | 15,930 | . | . | 11 | . | . |
| Stadium-Armory | 2,414 | . | −49 | . | . | . |
| Tenleytown | 1,131 | . | . | . | 60 | . |
| Union Station | 12,479 | . | . | 1 | . | . |
| Van Ness | 1,764 | . | . | . | 65 | . |
| Woodley Park | 1,092 | . | . | . | 48 | . |
| **Montgomery County** | | | | | | |
| Bethesda | 7,536 | . | . | − 2 | . | . |
| Grosvenor | 147 | . | . | . | . | 478 |
| Rockville | 2,741 | . | . | 2 | . | . |
| Shady Grove | 303 | . | −57 | . | . | . |
| Silver Spring | 7,951 | . | . | − 4 | . | . |
| Takoma Park | 636 | . | . | 10 | . | . |
| Twinbrook | 1,448 | . | −27 | . | . | . |
| White Flint | 3,061 | . | . | −18 | . | . |

(continued)

Table 6.6 *(continued)*

| Station name | Employment in 1980 | Very low | Low | Good | High | Very high |
|---|---|---|---|---|---|---|
| **Prince George's County** | | | | | | |
| Addison Road | 216 | . | . | . | . | 141 |
| Capitol Heights | 234 | −337 | . | . | . | . |
| Cheverly | 396 | −198 | . | . | . | . |
| Landover | 570 | −107 | . | . | . | . |
| **Arlington County** | | | | | | |
| Ballston | 4,027 | . | . | . | 49 | . |
| Clarendon | 2,102 | . | −31 | .. | . | . |
| Courthouse | 2,584 | . | . | 25 | . | . |
| Crystal City | 20,090 | . | . | −14 | . | . |
| Pentagon City | 1,252 | . | . | − 6 | . | . |
| Rosslyn | 8,381 | . | . | − 2 | . | . |
| Virginia Square | 2,169 | . | . | − 4 | . | . |
| **Alexandria** | | | | | | |
| Braddock Road | 1,000 | . | . | . | 31 | . |
| Eisenhower Avenue | 3,622 | . | −75 | . | . | . |
| King Street | 937 | . | . | . | 27 | . |
| **Fairfax County** | | | | | | |
| Dunn Loring | 769 | . | . | . | . | 356 |
| Huntington | 438 | −383 | . | . | . | . |

the residuals. While the dependent variables do have some degree of correlation with the residuals, the correlation between the residual as a percentage of the dependent variable with the dependent variable is not very significant (see Table 6.5). The bias associated with such problems is therefore not of great concern.

### Individual Residuals

The employment model predicts twenty-five of the fifty-two stations in the sample quite well (all twenty-five within 25 percent, twenty within 10 percent of the actual). While most of these are downtown D.C. stations, the model does quite well for Friendship Heights, Bethesda, White Flint, and Rockville on the western portion of the Montgomery County Red Line, for Silver Spring and Takoma Park on the eastern portion of the same line, for Rosslyn, Crystal City, and Pentagon City

Table 6.7

**Retail Employment Equation: Residuals as Percentage of Retail Employment in 1980, Selected Station Areas by Jurisdiction**

| Station name | Retail employment in 1980 | Very low | Low | Good | High | Very high |
|---|---|---|---|---|---|---|
| District of Columbia | | | | | | |
| Archives | 1,019 | . | . | . | 89 | . |
| Benning Road | 53 | −628 | . | . | . | . |
| Brookland | 146 | . | . | . | . | 207 |
| Capitol South | 805 | . | −93 | . | . | . |
| Cleveland Park | 215 | . | . | . | 93 | . |
| Deanwood | 17 | . | . | 16 | . | . |
| Dupont Circle | 2,471 | . | −58 | . | . | . |
| Eastern Market | 495 | . | . | −16 | . | . |
| Farragut West | 4,597 | . | −46 | . | . | . |
| Federal Center SW | 408 | . | . | . | . | 171 |
| Federal Triangle | 950 | . | . | . | . | 159 |
| Foggy Bottom | 1,331 | . | . | 14 | . | . |
| Fort Totten | 61 | −362 | . | . | . | . |
| Friendship Heights | 1,417 | . | −28 | . | . | . |
| Gallery Place | 4,414 | . | −55 | . | . | . |
| Judiciary Square | 1,521 | . | . | 6 | . | . |
| L'Enfant Plaza | 672 | . | . | . | 84 | . |
| McPherson Square | 2,470 | . | . | . | 50 | . |
| Metro Center | 6,878 | . | −49 | . | . | . |
| Minnesota Avenue | 41 | . | . | . | . | 1,137 |
| Potomac Avenue | 125 | . | . | . | . | 277 |
| Rhode Island Avenue | 33 | . | . | . | . | 1,427 |
| Smithsonian | 517 | . | . | 4 | . | . |
| Stadium–Armory | 6 | . | . | . | . | 1,380 |
| Tenleytown | 252 | . | . | . | . | 211 |
| Union Station | 314 | . | . | . | . | 407 |
| Van Ness | 314 | . | . | . | . | 216 |
| Woodley Park | 255 | . | . | . | 31 | . |
| Montgomery County | | | | | | |
| Bethesda | 1,702 | . | . | . | 88 | . |
| Grosvenor | 17 | . | . | . | . | 651 |
| Rockville | 412 | . | −42 | . | . | . |
| Shady Grove | 130 | . | . | . | . | 677 |
| Silver Spring | 1,852 | . | . | − 5 | . | . |
| Takoma Park | 210 | . | . | 20 | . | . |
| Twinbrook | 405 | . | . | . | 75 | . |
| White Flint | 1,280 | . | −28 | . | . | . |

*(continued)*

Table 6.7 *(continued)*

| Station name | Retail employment in 1980 | Very low | Low | Good | High | Very high |
|---|---|---|---|---|---|---|
| **Prince George's County** | | | | | | |
| Addison Road | 10 | . | . | . | . | 2,543 |
| Capitol Heights | 37 | −1,049 | . | . | . | . |
| Cheverly | 224 | −194 | . | . | . | . |
| Landover | 389 | −143 | . | . | . | . |
| **Arlington County** | | | | | | |
| Ballston | 385 | . | . | . | . | 184 |
| Clarendon | 783 | . | . | . | 26 | . |
| Courthouse | 238 | . | . | . | . | 140 |
| Crystal City | 870 | . | . | −14 | . | . |
| Pentagon City | 92 | −674 | . | . | . | . |
| Rosslyn | 817 | . | −26 | . | . | . |
| Virginia Square | 441 | . | . | . | 60 | . |
| **Alexandria** | | | | | | |
| Braddock Road | 278 | −143 | . | . | . | . |
| Eisenhower Avenue | 82 | . | . | . | . | 821 |
| King Street | 461 | . | . | −22 | . | . |
| **Fairfax County** | | | | | | |
| Dunn Loring | 112 | . | . | 15 | . | . |
| Huntington | 97 | −292 | .. | . | . | . |

on the Blue Line in Virginia, and for Courthouse on the Orange Line in Arlington, Virginia. The model seriously underestimates the Prince George's County Orange and Blue Line stations, and misses badly on Dunn Loring (in Fairfax County) and Grosvenor (in Montgomery County) as well. See Table 6.6 for the percentage deviations of predicted from actual values by station area.

The retail employment equation predicts twelve stations well (all within 25 percent of the actual value, three of these within 10 percent of the actual value). Five of the twelve are D.C. stations. The equation predicts well for Silver Spring and Takoma Park on the eastern portion of the Montgomery County Red Line, Rosslyn and Crystal City on the Blue Line in Virginia, King Street on the Yellow Line in Alexandria, Clarendon on the Orange Line in Arlington, and Dunn Loring on the Orange Line in Fairfax County. It performs rather poorly for stations

Table 6.8

**Commercial Floor Space Equation: Residuals as a Percentage of Commercial Floor Space in 1985, Selected Station Areas by Jurisdiction**

| Station Name | Commercial floor space (in thousands) | Very low | Low | Good | High | Very high |
|---|---|---|---|---|---|---|
| **District of Columbia** | | | | | | |
| Archives | 3,608 | . | . | . | 51 | . |
| Benning Road | 30 | . | . | 0 | . | . |
| Capitol South | 569 | . | −27 | . | . | . |
| Cleveland Park | 216 | . | . | 12 | . | . |
| Deanwood | 99 | . | −59 | . | . | . |
| Dupont Circle | 6,120 | . | . | −7 | . | . |
| Eastern Market | 651 | . | . | . | 25 | . |
| Farragut West | 8,108 | . | . | . | . | 104 |
| Federal Center SW | 4,529 | . | −74 | . | . | . |
| Federal Triangle | 6,976 | . | . | −16 | . | . |
| Foggy Bottom | 7,358 | . | . | −4 | . | . |
| Fort Totten | 67 | . | . | 9 | . | . |
| Friendship Heights | 3,292 | . | . | −3 | . | . |
| Gallery Place | 6,969 | . | . | . | 26 | . |
| Judiciary Square | 1,802 | . | . | . | 26 | . |
| L'Enfant Plaza | 825 | . | −30 | . | . | . |
| McPherson Square | 16,488 | . | . | . | 68 | . |
| Metro Center | 12,093 | . | . | . | . | 180 |
| Minnesota Avenue | 558 | . | −65 | . | . | . |
| Potomac Avenue | 626 | . | . | 15 | . | . |
| Rhode Island Avenue | 441 | . | −39 | . | . | . |
| Smithsonian | 85 | . | . | . | 58 | . |
| Tenleytown | 1,028 | . | . | −5 | . | . |
| Union Station | 1,336 | . | −34 | . | . | . |
| Van Ness | 2,019 | . | . | −20 | . | . |
| Woodley Park | 1,859 | . | −49 | . | . | . |
| **Montgomery County** | | | | | | |
| Bethesda | 26,139 | . | −76 | . | . | . |
| Rockville | 1,363 | . | −63 | . | . | . |
| Shady Grove | 48 | . | . | . | . | 668 |
| Silver Spring | 2,561 | . | . | . | . | 135 |
| Takoma Park | 371 | . | −49 | . | . | . |
| Twinbrook | 1,983 | . | −75 | . | . | . |
| White Flint | 1,919 | . | . | −12 | . | . |

*(continued)*

Table 6.8 *(continued)*

| Station Name | Commercial floorspace (in thousands) | Very low | Low | Good | High | Very high |
|---|---|---|---|---|---|---|
| **Prince George's County** | | | | | | |
| Addison Road | 65 | . | . | 6 | . | . |
| Cheverly | 10 | . | . | . | . | 147 |
| Landover | 6 | . | . | . | . | 913 |
| **Arlington County** | | | | | | |
| Ballston | 3,022 | . | −32 | . | . | . |
| Clarendon | 913 | . | . | . | 94 | . |
| Courthouse | 2,379 | . | −44 | . | . | . |
| Crystal City | 1,438 | . | −31 | . | . | . |
| Rosslyn | 5,617 | . | −69 | . | . | . |
| Virginia Square | 614 | . | . | . | 78 | . |
| **Alexandria** | | | | | | |
| Braddock Road | 210 | . | . | 15 | . | . |
| Eisenhower Avenue | 1,250 | . | −57 | . | . | . |
| King Street | 130 | . | . | . | . | 509 |
| **Fairfax County** | | | | | | |
| Huntington | 72 | . | . | . | 71 | |

on the Orange Line in Prince George's County, generally seriously underestimating them, while it greatly overestimates several stations in the District of Columbia. See Table 6.7 for the percentage deviations of predicted from actual values by station area.

The floor space equation predicts twenty-three stations well; seventeen of these are in the District of Columbia. The model also predicts well for Friendship Heights and White Flint in the western segment of the Montgomery County Red Line, Crystal City for the Arlington Blue Line, Ballston for the Arlington Orange Line, and Braddock Road for the Alexandria Yellow Line. It does poorly on the Prince George's County Orange Line, seriously overestimating Landover and Cheverly while substantially underestimating nearby Deanwood and Minnesota Avenue stations. See Table 6.8 for the deviations of predicted from actual values by station area.

**Can Small Areas Realistically Be Forecasted?**

The differences in development among station areas are often brought about by discrete decisions of particular actors (such as developers, government agencies, or community activists) and individual decisions cannot be accurately predicted. However, a forecasting version of LOCDEV can indicate which stations are the most likely to be the focus of discrete development-related decisions and actions inasmuch as accessibility, site characteristics, and past development activity in the station area—all measured in the LOCDEV forecasting equations—are well-known determinants of development. A systematic study of these factors in a modeling framework can assist developers and/or planners in their preliminary assessment of policy with regard to development in various station areas. Forecasts made with LOCDEV are necessarily highly conditional because of the small size of the forecasted area. In principle, the caprice of a single major actor (public or private) could swamp the underlying trends assessed by LOCDEV and render a forecast obsolete. Even such less dramatic factors as a persistent and especially forthcoming public sector could greatly alter the incentives in a particular station area in ways not directly captured by LOCDEV. LOCDEV nevertheless can provide important information to planners and developers by forecasting the levels of private development to be expected in the absence of unusual public sector initiatives (or other institutional factors), thereby giving some indication of the degree of support from the government side that might realistically be required for development to take off in particular station areas.

All three forecasting equations are more accurate than their counterparts in the structural equation in terms of this residual analysis. The aggregate employment forecasting equation is especially superior to its structural version. Nevertheless, the same tendencies toward over- and underestimation that show up in the structural model also appear in these findings. Since the models have been transformed into forecasting equations, such errors must be taken into account in making forecasts to avoid serious over- and underprediction. Including the residuals computed during the ordinary least squares estimation procedure in the final forecasting version turned out to the best way of handling this problem (see chapters 7 and 8). The next task is to make forecasts with these equations and evaluate their quality.

*Seven*

# An Indicative Forecast of Station Area Development in the Washington, D.C., Region

LOCDEV's estimated equations, their residuals, and constraints and forecasts of independent variables drawn from the ITLUP model were used to forecast 1990 development levels around station areas. The forecast is presented here, followed by discussions of the independent variables, the constraining process, and the overall quality of the LOCDEV forecast; for a step-by-step guide to the LOCDEV forecasting procedure, see chapter 8.

**The LOCDEV Forecasts**

The station areas are grouped by jurisdiction (and some are further classified as downtown or non-downtown) for this discussion.

*The District of Columbia*

The District of Columbia contains the major central business district (CBD) of its Standard Metropolitan Statistical Area (SMSA). The office development in and near this CBD has been pronounced for the last decade, although the shopping district continues to languish. Much of the rest of the city consists of black residential areas, often poor, that have over the last three decades experienced little development other than some well-publicized instances of gentrification.

Some kinds of development in the District are impeded by height restrictions, the most permissive of which limit buildings to fourteen or fifteen stories. This limitation reduces the potential profitability of office building construction since the marginal cost of additional stories falls as the number of stories increases, while the marginal revenue remains constant. These restrictions have been partly responsible for the mushrooming growth in the sections of suburban jurisdictions that adjoin the District (and that have much more permissive height restrictions).

*General Forecast*

For the District as a whole, only five stations are forecasted to lose workers (some of these losses are very slight), while twenty-two others are forecasted to gain workers, some quite strongly (see Table 7.1). The pattern of steady, low growth rates that has led to absolute increases in District employment over the last two decades (despite a relative decrease in regional share of employment) is forecasted to continue. Retail employment forecasts follow the same pattern. Commercial floor space, however, is forecasted to grow much more rapidly than employment. This finding is consistent with the existing moderate private economic growth coupled with a very slow rate of growth of government employment that has been the pattern in the District in the recent past and is expected to continue for some time.

Retail employment in the District's station areas is forecasted to increase by 32 percent, or about 4,700 workers, from 1980 to 1990, coincidentally accounting for 32 percent of all retail jobs in station area zones in the District. Despite the marked suburbanization of retail activity, retail employment is expected to increase its share of aggregate jobs in the District because of the stagnation in government employment there.

*Downtown Commercial Stations*

In the high-employment, downtown stations, further increases in employment—occasionally at quite high rates—are forecasted to occur (see Table 7.2). LOCDEV suggests that Foggy Bottom will grow by 20 percent to about 19,000 workers, Farragut West by 19 percent to over 66,000 workers, and Dupont Circle by 18 percent to over 21,000 workers. LOCDEV forecasts that some downtown stations will grow at a more modest pace; Union Station is forecasted to grow 10 percent (1,240 workers) and McPherson Square only 2 percent (under 1,000). Metro Center is forecasted to gain even fewer workers for less than a 2 percent increase over the ten-year period. Some downtown stations are

Table 7.1

**Development Variables in Twenty-seven Station Areas in the District of Columbia**

|  | 1980 | 1990 | Change | Percentage change |
|---|---|---|---|---|
| Employment ($\times 10^3$) | 357 | 382 | 25 | 7 |
| Retail employment ($\times 10^3$) | 30 | 35 | 5 | 15 |
| Commercial floor space ($\times 10^6$) | 85 | 106 | 31 | 37 |

actually forecasted to lose employment: Judiciary Square and Archives are each forecasted to lose about 400 jobs, while Smithsonian is forecasted to lose over 1,000. The forecasted employment losers among the downtown stations are those that have relatively little commercial activity around them, and mainly serve government office centers.

The commercial floor space forecasts are generally consistent with the employment projections. LOCDEV indicates that the major downtown station areas will add substantial floor space by 1990. Gallery Place is forecasted to add three million square feet (a 37 percent increase), Farragut West over two million square feet (a 37 percent increase), Foggy Bottom about two million square feet (a 26 percent increase), and Union Station over one million square feet (a 79 percent increase). Dupont Circle is forecasted to add only half a million square feet, a modest 9 percent growth rate. The downtown stations that are forecasted to lose employment also are not expected to experience major increases in floor space. Smithsonian is forecasted to gain only 70,000 square feet, and L'Enfant Plaza 160,000. Judiciary Square is forecasted to gain about a half-million square feet of commercial floor space, despite its forecasted drop of 2 percent in employment.

Significant increases in retail employment are also forecasted to occur at the major downtown stations, but at different rates from the increases in aggregate employment. LOCDEV forecasts that Dupont Circle and Farragut West will add retail workers at a pace only slightly lower than that of aggregate employment, but Foggy Bottom is forecasted to lose 1.5 percent of its retail employment in contrast to its forecasted gain of 20 percent in aggregate employment. LOCDEV forecasts that Union Station will add retail workers at a 13 percent rate, rising to 356 retail workers, compared to a 10 percent increase in total

Table 7.2

**Development Variables in Fifteen Selected Downtown Station Areas in the District of Columbia**

|  | 1980 | 1990 | Change | Percentage change |
|---|---|---|---|---|
| Employment (×10³) | 348 | 369 | 22 | 6 |
| Retail employment (×10³) | 29 | 32 | 3 | 11 |
| Commercial floor space (×10⁶) | 79 | 98 | 19 | 24 |

employment. Metro Center's retail employment is also forecasted to grow by 7 percent to well over 7,000 retail workers despite its modest growth (2 percent) in total employment.

*Non-Downtown Stations*

LOCDEV indicates that most station areas in the District that are not in the downtown area will fare poorly in terms of employment increases (see Table 7.3). (Several stations in high-income residential neighborhoods are exceptions to this pattern and are discussed separately below.) Benning Road looks brightest, with a forecasted increase of 444 workers (a 179 percent increase over its low 1980 value). Brookland is forecasted to add 241 workers, and Eastern Market 378 workers. However, most of the non-downtown station areas are forecasted to add few workers: LOCDEV predicts that Rhode Island Avenue will gain only 100, Minnesota Avenue 79, Fort Totten 71, and Deanwood 25.

The forecast for gains in commercial floor space in these stations is not sanguine either. LOCDEV indicates that Benning Road will gain only 7,000 square feet of commercial floor space, Minnesota Avenue 130,000, Deanwood 27,000, and Rhode Island Avenue 160,000. Eastern Market is forecasted to gain a quarter of a million square feet, an amount substantially more than that to be gained by the other non-downtown District station areas, but in line with its forecasted 22 percent employment gain.

These stations are all projected to have extremely modest increases in retail employment. No station stands out here as an exception. Brookland (the biggest increase) is forecasted to add only about 30 jobs.

Table 7.3

**Develpment Variables in Eight Selected Non-Downtown Station Areas in the District of Columbia**

|  | 1980 | 1990 | Change | Percentage change |
|---|---|---|---|---|
| Employment ($\times 10^3$) | 7 | 8 | 2 | 25 |
| Retail employment ($\times 10^3$) | 1 (–) | 1 (+) | 0 (+) | 28 |
| Commercial floor space ($\times 10^6$) | 3 | 4 | 1 (–) | 30 |

Based on the LOCDEV forecasts for the three development variables, it is reasonable to conclude that this set of stations will not have sustained a major development effect from Metrorail by 1990 despite their location in the District of Columbia.

*High-income Residential Stations*

Three Connecticut Avenue stations that are in well-established high-income residential neighborhoods are forecasted to develop commercially at a significantly faster pace than the other non-downtown station areas (see Table 7.4). LOCDEV's indicative findings do not take into account the substantial and effective resident resistance to development that has emerged during the 1980s at these station areas, and so its forecasts represent the impact only of selected economic factors in making these locations desirable for developers. Their substantial values indicate, however, that there may well be persistent efforts to develop these areas despite the preferences of the current residents.

Woodley Park is forecasted to add just under 400 workers for a 35 percent increase, Cleveland Park 295 for a 38 percent increase, and Tenleytown 459 for a 41 percent increase. Almost all of this new employment is forecasted to be in the retail sector. LOCDEV also predicts some new commercial floor space (with retail uses) in these station areas: Cleveland Park is forecasted to grow by 66 percent (140,000 square feet), Tenleytown by 51 percent (520,000 square feet), and Woodley Park by 500,000 square feet. These increases are quite substantial, especially given the limited availability of developable space in these station areas.

Table 7.4

**Development Variables in Three Selected High-income Residential Station Areas in the District of Columbia**

|  | 1980 | 1990 | Change | Percent change |
|---|---|---|---|---|
| Employment (×10³) | 3 | 4 | 1 (+) | 38 |
| Retail employment (×10³) | 1 (−) | 2 (−) | 1 (+) | 157 |
| Commercial floor space (×10⁶) | 3 | 4 | 1 (+) | 37 |

*Summary*

In general the forecasts for District station areas are reasonable in that they seem to portray the extent of economic forces that are working to make station areas desirable centers for development. The downtown stations most likely will grow, along the lines forecasted by LOCDEV, and the non-downtown station areas will continue to languish. The high-income residential stations will be an interesting battleground between those economic and transportation forces (reflected in LOCDEV) that tend to encourage development at the sites and those unmodelable forces that may impede development there. There are many factors not modeled in LOCDEV, however, so that the forecasts are most appropriately used as indicators of development potential rather than as point forecasts of "what will be."

*Montgomery County*

Montgomery County has experienced a great deal of economic growth in the last two decades. It is considered to have, at the same time, the most rigorous development controls in the region. While it has no overall height limitations like the District of Columbia, it has succeeded in limiting development in many parts of the county, and is encouraging it along the Rockville Pike corridor (parallel to and occasionally crossed by the Shady Grove–Friendship Heights Red Line segment); this has been accomplished with, among other things, what is perhaps the only successful Transferable Development Rights program in the country.

The county is considered a desirable location for office-related economic activity because of the high socioeconomic status of its residents, its direct border with the District (there is no river to cross), its substantial level of federal government activity, and its sound transportation network. ⁻

LOCDEV forecasts that Montgomery County station areas will sustain strong employment and floor space growth (see Table 7.5). Employment is forecasted to rise in all stations, at rates from 11 percent (Twinbrook) to just under 800 percent (Shady Grove). Five of the nine stations (Bethesda, Rockville, White Flint, Shady Grove, and Silver Spring) are each forecasted to gain between 2,000 and 3,000 workers; Friendship Heights is forecasted to gain about 1,300 workers, Grosvenor 700, and Takoma Park, only 200.

The floor space forecasts are similar. Bethesda stands out with a forecast of almost 11 million square feet of new commercial floor space by 1990 (a 42 percent increase from 1985). Three other stations with large forecasted increases are White Flint, about two million, Twinbrook, about one million, and Friendship Heights, about 700,000. Silver Spring is forecasted to gain over 300,000 square feet of commercial floor space.

Retail forecasts for the Montgomery County station areas are large, consistent with the strong development thrust indicated by the employment and floor space forecasts. Overall, station areas are forecasted to experience a 42 percent increase in retail employment from 1980 to 1990. LOCDEV forecasts for Bethesda (an increase of 850 jobs) and Silver Spring (650) stand out, but forecasts for other areas indicate swift growth as well. White Flint (550), Twinbrook (550), and Takoma Park (350, including the District side) are all projected to be big gainers in retail activity. Grosvenor is projected to remain the same, consistent with its residential character, while LOCDEV indicates that Rockville will add only a few retail jobs.

These retail employment forecasts follow the same pattern as the aggregate employment forecasts. According to LOCDEV, Takoma Park is likely to experience most of its employment gains in the retail sector, while the other station areas will have a broader mix of types of new employment and commercial floor space.

These forecasts are reasonable, although there are a few incongruities. The forecast for Grosvenor, while modest in absolute terms, may still be too large given the heavily residential character of that station area. Also, the physical difficulty of gaining access to the station itself

Table 7.5

**Development Variables in Nine Station Areas in Montgomery County**

|  | 1980 | 1990 | Change | Percentage change |
|---|---|---|---|---|
| Employment ($\times 10^3$) | 28 | 43 | 15 | 52 |
| Retail employment ($\times 10^3$) | 7 | 11 | 3 | 42 |
| Commercial floor space ($\times 10^6$) | 38 | 53 | 15 | 40 |

and of building nearby (factors that cannot be captured by LOCDEV) militate against such development. The high-income local residents provide little specific market for station area development, since White Flint Mall and other shopping centers are within two miles, an easy drive. LOCDEV forecasts for Silver Spring, by contrast, seem to be too low in light of the major plans for development under way there. It may be that LOCDEV's low forecast (compared to the bold plans for development) should be read as a caution to the development process there. The high vacancy rate in new office buildings there, while perhaps temporary, may offer the same caution. Alternatively, it may well be that certain factors not accounted for by LOCDEV have led the model to underforecast the development potential of the area. Improvements to transportation networks, other infrastructural support, and political support for focusing development there (all of which cannot be modeled by LOCDEV) may work to enable large-scale development to succeed at this site. Clearly, LOCDEV cannot provide a conclusive forecast to "settle the issue" because of its limited set of explanatory variables.

## Prince George's County

Prince George's County has for decades been considered the blue-collar suburb of Washington, D.C. The socioeconomic status of its residents is on the average substantially lower than that in the other suburban jurisdictions. In the last decade, however, this image has begun to change; some important upscale office parks have been established there, and several innovative development projects have been undertaken (e.g., PortAmerica). Development restrictions are few in number, and the county government's enthusiasm for new developers

Table 7.6

**Development Variables in Four Station Areas in Prince George's County**

|  | 1980 | 1990 | Change | Percentage change |
|---|---|---|---|---|
| Employment ($\times10^3$) | 1 | 4 | 2 | 157 |
| Retail employment ($\times10^3$) | 1 (–) | 1 (+) | 1 (–) | 17 |
| Commercial floor space ($\times10^6$) | 0 | 0 | 0 | 101 |

has created a very positive development climate in the county. Although, like neighboring Montgomery County, it has direct access to the District, its transportation network is not as well developed for peak-hour traffic flows.

LOCDEV's forecasts for the four stations considered here all include large employment gains (see Table 7.6); Addison Road is expected to grow to over 900 workers from its 1980 level of 66, while adjacent Capitol Heights is expected to reach over 500. On the Orange Line, LOCDEV projects substantial growth, with Cheverly reaching 711 workers, an 80 percent increase over its 1980 level, and Landover swelling by 900 workers to over 1,500 by 1990. LOCDEV forecasts that commercial floor space around Addison Road will double to a modest 140,000 square feet, while Cheverly and Landover remain virtually constant. LOCDEV projects retail employment to grow around Landover, Cheverly, and Addison Road, with 100 to 200 new retail jobs in each station area. Capitol Heights is forecasted to remain stable in retail employment, despite its substantial expected growth in aggregate employment, which therefore will be most likely to occur in service-related activity.

### *Arlington County*

Arlington County is just across the Potomac River from the District of Columbia. A major section of the county is part of the economic core of the region, despite its suburban status. Office densities are quite high in the northeastern portion of the county owing to its quick access to the District and the relatively lenient height limitations on office construction. Western portions of the county remain residential, with a mixture of traditional low-density single-family dwellings and high-

Table 7.7

**Development Variables in Seven Station Areas in Arlington County**

|  | 1980 | 1990 | Change | Percentage change |
|---|---|---|---|---|
| Employment ($\times 10^3$) | 41 | 49 | 8 | 21 |
| Retail employment ($\times 10^3$) | 4 (−) | 4 (+) | 1 (−) | 16 |
| Commercial floor space ($\times 10^6$) | 62 | 79 | 17 | 39 |

rise condominiums and apartment complexes. Several of the older shopping centers along the Lee Highway corridor (parallel to and crossed by the Orange Line) are undergoing redevelopment, with enthusiastic encouragement from county planners.

Rosslyn, the major development center of the Metro lines in Arlington County, is expected according to LOCDEV to sustain large employment gains (over 3,000 new workers by 1990), and large amounts of new floor space (over 3 million square feet) (see Table 7.7). Given low forecasts of retail employment there, it is likely that these new jobs will be in service-related activity. Most Orange Line stations are forecasted to grow as well, but more modestly. Their employment levels are projected to grow by 300 new jobs at Virginia Square, by over 1,500 new jobs at Courthouse, and by intermediate figures at Clarendon and Ballston. Ballston is forecasted to gain over 2 million square feet of floor space, about the same as Clarendon, Courthouse, and Virginia Square combined.

LOCDEV forecasts indicate that Arlington's Orange Line stations will grow modestly in retail activity. Ballston looks to be the biggest gainer, with a forecast of a 50 percent increase in retail (reaching almost 600 jobs) while increases projected for the other Orange Line stations hover around 10 percent.

LOCDEV's forecast for Crystal City shows only modest growth, on a par with the Orange Line stations. Much of its employment growth is forecasted to be in the retail sector. Interestingly, however, the unconstrained LOCDEV forecast included huge gains in both employment and floor space for this station area; perhaps Crystal City, one of the major development centers in the region, will end up resembling the unconstrained forecast more than the constrained version. In this case, the ITLUP contextual forecast may be misleading for the small-area

Table 7.8

**Development Variables in Three Station Areas in Alexandria**

|  | 1980 | 1990 | Change | Percentage change |
|---|---|---|---|---|
| Employment ($\times 10^3$) | 6 | 8 | 3 (–) | 45 |
| Retail employment ($\times 10^3$) | 1 | 2 | 1 (–) | 66 |
| Commercial floor space ($\times 10^6$) | 2 | 2 | 1 (–) | 46 |

forecast, since outside the immediate Crystal City environs the zone containing this station area has largely low-density residential uses.

## Alexandria

The city of Alexandria is densely settled, with substantial office development within its boundaries. It too is considered a part of the core of the region, although not part of the region's central business district. High levels of traffic congestion in the main corridors of Alexandria have led to significant development constraints there, while in the southern and western portions of the city substantial incentives have been provided to developers to proceed with a wide range of economic activity.

In Alexandria, LOCDEV gives a very mixed forecast for the three station areas considered (see Table 7.8). Eisenhower station has the most sanguine forecast; it is expected to gain almost 700,000 square feet of commercial floor space and almost 2,000 workers by 1990, a fifth of whom will be working in the retail sector. Given the recent flurry of activity around this station area, such forecasts are reasonable, although 1990 may be a bit too early for their realization. LOCDEV forecasts King Street to gain under 400 workers, almost all of them in the retail sector, and about 70,000 square feet of commercial floor space, representing a 39 and 57 percent increase respectively over the 1980 values. The Braddock Road station is expected to remain stable, gaining 250 workers (40 of them in the retail sector) and no significant level of new commercial floor space.

## Fairfax County

Fairfax County has experienced rapid economic and population growth, leading to serious problems of traffic congestion along its

Table 7.9

**Development Variables in Two Station Areas in Fairfax County**

|  | 1980 | 1990 | Change | Percentage change |
|---|---|---|---|---|
| Employment ($\times 10^3$) | 1 | 3 | 2 | 177 |
| Retail employment ($\times 10^3$) | 0 | 0 | 0 | 6 |
| Commercial floor space ($\times 10^6$) | 0 | 0 | 0 | 8 |

major arteries. Development has been of a dispersed, patchwork variety, with several major centers (much larger than office parks) emerging in such locations as Tysons Corner and Fair Oaks, and many smaller ones scattered throughout the county. The county was led for many years by strongly prodevelopment political figures who put few obstacles in the way of economic development, a situation that seems to be continuing despite a change in leadership. Only two Fairfax County stations were included in the present study: Dunn Loring and Huntington. Dunn Loring is forecasted to gain almost 2,000 workers (of which less than 5 percent will be engaged in retail activity), a large gain over its 800 workers in 1980. Huntington is forecasted to gain 57 percent more workers (or 250, almost none in retail), while experiencing essential stability in commercial floor space (see table 7.9).

The LOCDEV forecast for Dunn Loring is almost certainly too large given the weak development efforts going on there. Nevertheless, LOCDEV suggests that there is a basis for developers to take a serious look at Dunn Loring. The forecast for Huntington is reasonable, given the modest and growing development opportunities there, which have already been observed and acted on by some developers in the county. Most development in Fairfax County, however, will certainly occur outside of the few rapid transit-station areas in the county.

*Conclusion*

LOCDEV has proven to be a useful indicator of development potential stemming from economic forces in station areas, especially when used in conjunction with a regional model (ITLUP). Many forecasts are reasonably close to actual developments, while in other instances they do not coincide with what is "on the ground." This unevenness is to be expected, given the indicative character of LOCDEV. It uses a small number of variables to forecast potential development outcomes in small areas; many variables that strongly enhance or impede development in small areas cannot be modeled.

Its forecasts for 1990 indicate that overall station area development will proceed at a pace that ensures that many station areas will remain important centers of economic activity. Many of the projected gainers are already major centers of activity. This includes some of the major downtown stations, several of the Montgomery County stations, and Rosslyn and Crystal City in Arlington.

LOCDEV forecasts steady growth and expansion along the Red Line in Montgomery County, the Orange Line in Arlington, and the Blue Line in Prince George's County, although different institutional settings may affect the realization of such development potential. For instance, Montgomery County has targeted Rockville Pike (which runs adjacent to the Red Line from Shady Grove to Friendship Heights) as a countywide corridor of development, and is actively encouraging developers to place their activities there instead of in other parts of the county. The other branch of the Red Line in Montgomery County includes Silver Spring, over which a vigorous battle has occurred between pro- and anti-development forces, with the pro-development forces apparently holding the upper hand politically at the moment. Arlington planners are enthusiastic about rebuilding Ballston and several other areas on the Orange Line corridor. The Prince George's County government has developed a pro-development attitude in recent years, but it has not specifically targeted the Blue Line for attention. In summary, the specific outcomes around the three lines that LOCDEV favors are difficult to predict because of institutional, political, and local factors that cannot be readily modeled. LOCDEV does indicate, however, that there is substantial development potential in all three of these lines; all deserve a close look by planners and developers.

LOCDEV forecasts uneven growth in the Orange Line in Prince George's County, the Blue and Yellow Lines in Alexandria/Fairfax, and along the Orange Line in Fairfax County. Certain stations—especially Eisenhower and Dunn Loring—are identified by LOCDEV as having many desirable economic qualities about them. These stations should be closely studied by developers and planners for future development purposes.

LOCDEV forecasts little growth in the non-downtown District stations based on low level of economic attractiveness of these areas. If planners wish to stimulate development at these sites, they will need to take into account these difficulties identified by LOCDEV.

LOCDEV forecasts a considerable amount of development in several high-income residential area stations (Woodley Park, Cleveland Park, and Tenleytown), especially in retail activity. Interestingly, Grosvenor, another high-income residential station area (although in Montgomery County) is also forecasted to experience significant commercial expansion, but not in the retail sector. The LOCDEV forecasts therefore indicate that strong economic pressures for development are present despite the historically residential character of these areas. This indicative forecast means that anti-development residents in those station areas will have an uphill battle ahead of them to limit commercial development there.

### Forecasting Independent Variables for Station Areas

Forecasting the independent variables for the Washington region requires using values of several variables that have been forecasted by the regional modeling system ITLUP. This, calibrated for a 182-zone partition of the region, provides quinquennial forecasts to the year 2010 (see Table 5.1 for the variable list). Various operations with and transformations of the forecasted values at the large ITLUP zone level allow LOCDEV-level variables to be forecasted as well. These transformations and operations are described below.

#### *Relative Accessibility*

Each of the LOCDEV forecasting equations includes an access index made up of combinations of off-peak interzonal trip times (impedances) and median or total zonal income (weights).[1] To forecast the relative accessibility indices for 1990:

1. Calculate the percentage change in peak travel times from 1980 to 1990 for each *ij* member of the trip time matrix from the ITLUP base and forecast year estimates;

2. Multiply both transit and auto off-peak travel times by one plus the corresponding percentage change computed in step 1 (see note 1 as well);

3. Substitute the resulting adjusted off-peak travel time matrices for the original ones;

4. Estimate the regional increase in real median income from 1980 to 1990 (this was 19 percent over ten years, based on extrapolation of the 1980–85 rate of change);

5. Estimate the break points between octiles (eighths) of the regional household income distribution;

6. Multiply each break point by the percentage increase in the region in real median income (this procedure assumes that the income distribution shifts outward uniformly);

7. Using the four new odd octile break points as median values for the corresponding quartiles, compute the aggregate income for each zone according to the formula:

$$\text{INC}_j = \sum_{i=1,4} (H_{ij} * M_i) \,,$$

where

$H_{ij}$ = number of households in quartile $i$ in zone $j$; and

$M_i$ = median income of quartile $i$.

For those access indices that use median income, divide $\text{INC}_j$ by the sum of the households:

$$\text{MED}_j = \text{INC}_j / \sum_{i=1,4} H_{ij} \,;$$

8. Substitute these 1990 forecasts for total and median income into the equation for the relative accessibility index; and

9. Calculate the new relative accessibility indices using the 1990 trip times and the 1990 income weights.

### Employment Variables as Independent Variables

Each of the three LOCDEV equations uses a lagged value of employment as an independent variable. Specifically, aggregate employment, nonbasic employment, and basic employment are used in the employment, commercial floor space, and retail employment equations respectively. These variables must be forecasted to 1985 to serve as lagged inputs for the 1990 forecasts.

The rate of change from 1980 to 1985 in each employment measure for each of the 182 zones in the regional system is calculated from ITLUP forecasts. The employment values for 1985 for each LOCDEV station area are then estimated by multiplying the base-year station area values by the rates of change in the corresponding variables for the entire ITLUP zone in which the station area is located (such zones will hereafter be called "station area zones").[2]

### *Commercial Share of Land Uses*

The share of land used commercially in a station area is forecasted in much the same way as employment, above. The base-year share of land used commercially is calculated by summing parcel-level land-use data for the station area. This sum is then multiplied by the percentage change in commercial share forecasted by ITLUP for the station area zone, yielding an estimated 1990 value.

### *Population*

The 1990 value of population is forecasted for each station area by calculating the percentage change in the number of households in the station area zone from 1980 to 1990 (based on ITLUP forecasts) and applying it to the 1980 value for population in the station area.[3]

### *Floor Space and Price Variables*

Both geographically disaggregated data and credible regional forecasts of these variables are lacking at this time. Hence, the prices of land, office floor space, and commercial floor space are simply assumed to increase by 25 percent, 50 percent, and 50 percent, respectively, from 1980 to 1990. Similarly, it is assumed that commercial floor space increases by 10 percent from 1985 to 1990 in each station area.[4] These percentage increases are applied across all station areas uniformly.

### **Constraints on LOCDEV Forecasts**

LOCDEV forecasts values for each station separately; there is no control total for the universe under study. There is therefore a tendency for such forecasts to exaggerate or understate real world trends.

It is desirable to rein in such tendencies through the judicious use of constraint procedures.

Three constraints are used, all derived from ITLUP. Each requires some discussion.

## Level Constraint

The change in a station area is constrained not to exceed the change in the zone containing it. Note that the constraint is the absolute change at the zone level, not the percentage change. Since station area zones are, on the average, fifteen times larger geographically than station areas, this is usually a loose constraint. A station area tends to capture a disproportionately large share of the aggregate employment, commercial floor space, and retail employment locating in its zone (relative to its geographical share), but it would be extremely unusual (although not impossible[5]) for one to capture over 100 percent of the additions to the development variables in the station area zone. Similarly, it would be remarkable if the net loss in development variables in a station area zone occurred entirely within the station area. Therefore, the net change in the station area zone serves as an upper (lower) limit for development variables in each station area that grows (declines).[6]

## Sign Constraint

Changes in development variables in a station area are constrained to be in the same direction as those that occur in its station area zone. If, for example, employment in a station area zone increases (according to ITLUP) but falls in the station area (according to LOCDEV), the LOCDEV forecast is dropped. It is replaced by a value equal to the station area's base-year value multiplied by the rate of change of that variable in the station area's zone. The new LOCDEV forecast therefore corresponds closely to the ITLUP forecast when the sign constraint is implemented.

Use of this constraint is more controversial than that of the size limit constraint since there are reasonable situations in which the station area and its zone can change in opposite directions, especially when the changes are small. The most questionable use of the sign constraint might be in the case when ITLUP forecasts that the zone will shrink while LOCDEV forecasts that the station area will grow. Metrorail's impact might well suffice to offset locally a geographically broader trend of reduction. As a practical matter, however, in only 1 out of 150 forecasts was the sign constraint used when the unconstrained change was positive in the station area and negative in the zone, while it was used thirty-nine times for the reverse situation, where it is highly appropriate. ITLUP's forecasts, unlike LOCDEV's, are based on broad regional trends so that it is reasonable to let the former bind the direction of the latter, while allowing for wide differences in rates of changes between the two levels of aggregation when the signs do not conflict.

### *Control Totals*

For retail employment, an additional constraint was needed due to LOCDEV's gross underestimate across the board for this variable.[7] The goal here was to preserve the distribution of forecasts of retail activity for the various station areas, since this information was credible, but to scale up each forecast in a consistent way so that their sum equaled the sum of the ITLUP-based station area forecasts. This was accomplished using the following steps:

1. Calculate an ITLUP-based control total of station area forecasts for the universe of fifty-two station areas by incrementing the base-year value of retail employment in each station area by the percentage change in retail employment forecasted by ITLUP for the station area zone containing it. The sum of these incremented values is the control total for retail employment for the fifty-two stations.

2. The retail employment values forecasted by LOCDEV are then constrained to sum to this control total by scaling up all values proportionately. These values are then subjected to the other constraints, and once again constrained to sum to the control total.

Similar procedures could, in principle, be used for the other development variables as well, but this was not done because of the reasonableness of their results without such constraints.

### *The Use of the Constraints*

The ITLUP-derived constraints are boundaries between the reasonable and the unreasonable. If the constraints were used too frequently, doubt would be cast on LOCDEV's "stand-alone" forecast accuracy,

Table 7.10

**Frequency of Implementation of Constraint**

| Equation | Forecasts | Level | Sign |
|---|---|---|---|
| Employment | 52 | 12 | 9 |
| Commercial floor space | 46 | 8 | 4 |
| Retail employment | 52 | 12 | 26 |

even if the adjusted values were reasonable. Table 7.10 indicates these frequencies; for each equation, the number of station-site forecasts is followed by the numbers constrained by level and by sign.

The level constraint was used mainly for the large downtown District stations such as Dupont Circle, Farragut West, Judiciary Square, and McPherson Square. In Arlington, forecasts of the development variables for the two biggest stations—Crystal City and Rosslyn—similarly overshot the ITLUP constraints. Unconstrained LOCDEV forecasts therefore have a tendency to exaggerate levels of development variables in stations that already have extremely large employment levels.

The sign constraint was used most frequently in the retail equation. It was used for sixteen of the twenty-seven District stations (60 percent) and ten of the twenty-five suburban stations (40 percent). The high frequency in the District of Columbia reflects the tendency for the unconstrained LOCDEV equation, even when scaled thro ugn the use of an ITLUP-based control total, to predict a major decline in retail activity in the District. Given the decline of the District's share of the region's commercial activity, these forecasts are exaggerations of a trend rather than misdirected. Use of the ITLUP-based estimate reasonably adjusts such exaggerated values.

LOCDEV's unconstrained forecasts are credible indicators even though they tend to exaggerate certain trends. With the ITLUP constraints, the forecasts are even more reasonable.

**Evaluating the LOCDEV Forecasts**

How good are the constrained LOCDEV forecasts? The first criterion is the extent to which the forecasts generally agree with common sense and conventional wisdom about development in each of the station areas; this was considered above in the discussions of the forecasts for each jurisdiction. (A comprehensive comparison between the forecasts and what is "on the ground" is beyond the scope of this work.)

Another way of addressing this issue is to calculate the changes in the station areas' share of activity in the station area zones containing them at both the regional and jurisdictional levels. If the forecasted shifts in share are relatively small, the forecasts are likely also to be reasonable.

LOCDEV's forecasts for all fifty-two areas and their zones taken together indicate great continuity in the station areas' share of their zones (see Table 7.11). Forty-three percent of the new jobs, 40 percent of the new commercial floor space, and 32 percent of the retail employment forecasted for the station area zones by ITLUP are projected by LOCDEV to be located in the station areas themselves. This keeps the previous station area to station-area zone ratios virtually unchanged: the station areas' share of their zones' aggregate employment drops by less than a percentage point (to 43 percent); parallel values for commercial floor space and retail employment increase by one-third of a percentage point and slightly under one percentage point to 30 and 28 percent respectively.

Such levels of concentration are reasonable even though the station areas account for only 6.8 percent of the area of the station area zones, since many stations were planned to serve existing or future activity centers. Continuity in this level of concentration, as forecasted in the aggregate by LOCDEV, is a reasonable finding, and supports the overall reliability of the modeling results.

At the jurisdiction level of analysis, an important difference in trends of shares emerges between the District of Columbia and the inner suburbs (Montgomery, Prince George's, Arlington, and Fairfax Counties and the city of Alexandria) as a whole.[8] The station areas' share of aggregate employment, commercial floor space, and retail employment fall in the District but rise, in some cases quite significantly, in the inner suburbs.

There is substantial variation among the inner suburban areas as well, but all within a general trend of increasing share. Arlington is forecasted to increase its share of employment by two percentage points, Fairfax by six, and each of the other three jurisdictions by four. A somewhat more modest pattern of increases is forecasted to occur for commercial floor space, with a two- to three-point increase in

Table 7.11

**Station Areas' Shares of Station-Area Zone Levels: Development Variables, 1980 and 1990**

|  | District of Columbia | | | Inner suburbs | | |
|---|---|---|---|---|---|---|
|  | 1980 | 1990 | Change | 1980 | 1990 | Change |
| Employment | 55 | 54 | −1 | 21 | 25 | +4 |
| Commercial floor space | 37 | 35 | −2 | 15 | 16 | +1 |
| Retail employment | 44 | 42 | −2 | 15 | 17 | +1 |

Montgomery, Prince George's, and Arlington, a one-point increase in Alexandria, and a one-point decrease in Fairfax. LOCDEV forecasts that changes in retail employment shares will vary more dramatically, with an increase of ten points in share in Alexandria, relative constancy in Fairfax and Arlington, a four-point share increase in Montgomery County, and a two-point increase in Prince George's.

The concentration of activity near stations within the station area zones varies among the jurisdictions. There is greater concentration in Arlington, Alexandria, and Montgomery Counties, all densely settled in the areas served by rail, than there is in Prince George's and Fairfax Counties, where activity densities, both residential and commercial, are far lower.[9]

# Appendix 7.1

# Constraining Retail Employment Forecasts

The goal of a constraint in a modeling procedure is to render the projections made by the model more realistic without losing important information offered by the model. In assessing the retail employment model, it was clear that the forecasts were far too low, although the relative patterns of high and low forecasts for various station areas seemed plausible. Thus, a scaling procedure was needed that in turn required a control total to serve as the basis for the adjustment. As noted in the text, ITLUP provided the means to estimate a control total for retail employment for the universe of fifty-two station areas.

The most apparently straightforward method of scaling the forecasts would be to calculate the ratio of the control total to the unconstrained total, and then apply this ratio to each forecast to obtain a reasonable level for the forecasts. However, the presence of many negative values made this procedure incorrect. The alternative procedure used was:

1. Displace the origin to the left of the lowest number (–600).

2. Multiply all values by a scalar to increase their values appropriately (1.4952).

3. Move the origin back by the original value multiplied by the same scalar in step 2.

The sum of the forecasts now equals the control total. Notice that displacing the origin before multiplying the forecasts by the scalar has the effect of increasing the variance of the forecasts; large forecasts will be incremented by more than they would have been without displacement of the origin, while low forecasts will be changed very little. The advantage of the procedure is that it allows the same scalar to be applied to (originally) negative or positive values.

## Notes

1. Ideally, peak trip times are preferred as a measure of impedance, but they were not available at the time of model calibration. Thus, the estimation of future relative accessibilities was more complicated because ITLUP forecasts only peak trip times.

2. This estimation procedure tends to understate the 1985 levels of station area employment since a station area typically grows faster than its zone.

3. The use of the percentage change in households to predict changes in population implicitly assumes the constancy of household size over the ten-year period.

4. A preferable alternative procedure would be to use the commercial floor space equation in LOCDEV to forecast the 1990 value for each station area. Time constraints precluded this.

5. For instance, if the non-station-area portion of a station area zone loses employment, while the station area portion gains, then more than 100 percent of the net gain in employment in this zone would be accounted for by the station area itself.

6. For employment and retail employment, this constraining procedure is straightforward. The zone and station area values can be directly compared since the same variable occurs in both ITLUP and LOCDEV forecasts. However, there is no floor space variable in ITLUP, so one must be constructed to make the limit constraint possible. The first step is to estimate the commercial floor space in station area zones for the base year (1985). Assume that nonbasic employment is directly proportional to floor space. Calculate the floor space-to-nonbasic employment ratio in the station area for 1985. Then apply this ratio to the station area zone's 1985 nonbasic employment level for the station-area-zone to estimate the

zonal floor space value. Next, calculate the percentage change in non-basic employment in the zone from 1985 to 1990. Apply this percentage change to the 1985 estimate for zonal floor space to estimate the 1990 level of zonal floor space. The difference in these estimates of floor space for 1985 and 1990 for the zone then provides the upper bound for changes in floor space in the station area itself.

This estimation technique is reasonable since it is intended to produce an upper bound for floor space; the accuracy of its zonal floor space estimate is difficult to determine since it is based completely on the validity of the assumption of a consistent floor space-to-nonbasic employment ratio.

7. The work with this equation is described in detail in Appendix 7.1.

8. The term "inner suburbs" is meant to exclude from consideration Prince William and Loudoun Counties which, although part of the region that is divided into 182 zones, neither adjoin the District of Columbia nor contain any station areas.

9. Part of the different levels in reported concentration is also due to the structure of the zone system; zones in Fairfax and Prince George's tend to be larger geographically than those in the other three inner suburban jurisdictions and much larger than those in the District.

*Eight*

# A User's Guide to LOCDEV

The Local Development (LOCDEV) model provides forecasts of development in small areas within an urban region. This chapter discusses how users can implement LOCDEV to study urban regions of their choice. A sample use of the model is presented later in the chapter.

**Part 1: Questions and Answers about LOCDEV**

*What Specific Variables Does LOCDEV Forecast?*

LOCDEV makes point estimates for small areas of (1) the level of aggregate employment (i.e., the number of employees whose place of work is located within the small area); (2) the level of retail employment (i.e., the number of retail employees whose place of work is within the small area); and (3) commercial floor space (total number of square feet of commercial floor space located in the small area).

*What Is a Small Area?*

The size of a small area must be defined by the user. All small areas in a particular study should be the same geographical size. Small areas are usually smaller than planning districts, traffic districts, and census tracts.

*How Does LOCDEV Forecast the Development Variables?*

LOCDEV contains one equation for each of the three development variables (see part 2 below, and Figure 8.1, page 224). Each equation is first estimated for the relevant urban region using data from that region. The independent variables (right-hand side) must then be forecast. Next, the coefficients from the estimation and the forecast independent variables are combined and the equation solved, producing the desired forecast value. Residuals may be included in the forecast equation at the option of the user if the small area for which the forecast is made is also one of the small areas used in calibration (see Figure 8.1; for an example, see part 3). Constraints may be placed on the forecast values (see part 5).

### How Are the Equations Estimated?

Data must be gathered for each of the variables for a sample of small areas within the urban region under consideration (see part 2 for the variables used in the equations). A sample size of twenty-five or more small areas should be used in this calibration to achieve sound levels of statistical significance. A cross-sectional estimation using ordinary least squares regression is then performed to estimate the coefficients of the independent variables and the residuals for each small area. See part 3 for a sample calibration.

### How Are the Independent Variables Forecasted?

The user must determine the method for forecasting the independent variables. Often a regional model that provides forecasts for zones that are larger than the small areas is helpful in providing ways of estimating the values for small-area variables. See part 3 for an example of how the independent variables may be forecasted.

### How Are the Equations Solved?

Each equation is solved separately to determine the point estimate for that particular variable. There is no simultaneous interaction among the equations.

### What Variables Are Needed to Estimate or Calibrate Each Equation?

For aggregate employment, a relative accessibility index, lagged aggregate employment, and the average value of commercial floor space are needed. For retail employment, a relative accessibility index, the

**Figure 8.1. LOCDEV Forecasting Equations**

Aggregate Employment Equation

$$E = a_1 + b_1 A_1 + c_1 E_{-1} + d_1 V + R_1$$

where

| | |
|---|---|
| $E$ | = aggregate employment in the forecast period; |
| $A_1$ | = accessibility index (median income weights); |
| $E_{-1}$ | = lagged aggregate employment; |
| $V$ | = average value of commercial floor space; and |
| $R_1$ | = residual from calibration experiment (optional).[a] |

Retail Employment Equation:

$$T = a_2 + b_2 A_2 + c_2 F + d_2 B_{-1} + e_2 P + f_2 S + R_2$$

where

| | |
|---|---|
| $T$ | = retail employment in the forecast period; |
| $A_2$ | = accessibility index (total income weights); |
| $F$ | = commercial floor space level; |
| $B_{-1}$ | = lagged basic employment; |
| $P$ | = population; |
| $S$ | = commercial share of land uses; and |
| $R_2$ | = residual from calibration experiment (optional).[a] |

Commercial floor space equation:

$$LF = a_3 + b_3 LA_3 + c_3 LN_{-1} + d_3 LD + e_3 LO + f_3 LS + R_3$$

where

| | |
|---|---|
| $L$ | = logarithm of variable; |
| $F$ | = commercial floor space in the forecast period; |
| $A_3$ | = accessibility index (median income weight); |
| $N_{-1}$ | = lagged nonbasic employment (retail, wholesale, and service); |
| $D$ | = average land value; |
| $O$ | = average value of office space; |
| $S$ | = commercial share of land use; and |
| $R_3$ | = residual from calibration (optional).[a] |

[a] The user may find that including the residuals from the ordinary least squares procedure used in estimating the coefficients of the model will improve the credibility of the forecast. Use of the residuals is optional. Residuals are available only if a forecast is being made for one of the small areas used in the estimation process.

commercial floor space level, lagged basic employment, population level, and the commercial share of land uses are needed. For commercial floor space, a relative accessibility index, lagged nonbasic employment, average land value, average value of office space, and the commercial share of land uses are needed. A more detailed discussion of these variables is presented in part 2.

### How Can Relative Accessibility Be Measured for a Small Area?

A small area is contained in a larger zone, which is part of a regional partition of an urban area. The trip times between all other zones and the one containing the small area, combined with activity weights in the zones of origin, can provide a good measure of the region's access to a particular zone, which in turn can be used as an estimate for the region's accessibility to the small area. The precise formula for this and further discussion is provided in part 4.

### What Constraints Are Used in LOCDEV?

LOCDEV can produce unconstrained or constrained forecasts. Constraints will generally be peculiar to each study. However, some options for constraints are discussed in part 5.

### Part 2: Data Required for LOCDEV Calibration

### A. Employment

To forecast the level of aggregate employment in a small area, the following independent variables are needed along with aggregate employment:

### 1. Relative Accessibility Index

This variable measures the difficulty of reaching the small area from all points in the region weighted by the level of an activity in the origin zones. The weight used in this equation is median income. See part 4 for the data requirements and methods for calculating this index.

## 2. Lagged Aggregate Employment

This variable is the number of workers whose place of work was located in the small area in the previous period. A five-year lag is recommended.

## 3. Average Value of Commercial Floor Space

This variable is estimated by computing the total value of improvements on all commercially used parcels of land within the small area, then dividing this sum by the total number of square feet of commercial floor space in the small area. This procedure yields a dollar value per square foot of commercial floor space. The user may find that data-collection costs require the use of a sampling technique to estimate this value.

## B. Retail Employment

To forecast the level of retail employment in a small area, the following independent variables are needed along with retail employment:

## 1. Relative Accessibility Index

This variable measures the difficulty of reaching the small area from all points in the region weighted by the level of an activity in the origin zones. The weight used in this equation is total income (number of households in the zone multiplied by median household income). See part 4 for the data requirements and methods for calculating this index.

## 2. Commercial Floor Space Level

This variable is the total number of square feet of floor space used for commercial purposes in the small area. It is calculated by summing the number of square feet of commercial floor space in each parcel in the small area.

## 3. Lagged Basic Employment

This variable is the total number of workers employed in basic activity in the small area in the previous period. Basic activity is usually defined as those activities in SIC code 01. The user may adjust this definition according to the particularities of the urban region under study. A five-year lag is recommended.

## 4. Population

This variable is the number of people who currently live in the small area.

## 5. Commercial Share of Land Uses

This variable is the percentage of the land in the small area comprised of parcels used commercially. It may be calculated by summing the land area of all parcels designated commercial, then dividing the sum by the total land area of the small area, and multiplying by 100.

## C. Commercial Floor Space Equation

To forecast the level of commercial floor space existing in a small area, the following independent variables are needed along with the base-year level of commercial floor space.

## 1. Relative Accessibility Index

This variable measures the difficulty of reaching the small area from all points in the region weighted by the level of an activity in the origin zones. The weight used in this equation is median income. See part 4 for the data requirements and methods for calculating this index.

## 2. Lagged Nonbasic Employment

This variable is the total number of workers employed in the small area in nonbasic activity in the previous period. Nonbasic activity is usually defined as all economic activities other than those contained in SIC code 01. The user may adjust this definition according to the particularities of the urban region under study. A five-year lag is recommended.

## 3. Average Land Value

This variable is the average value of land per square foot in the small area. It is calculated by first summing the land values only (not improvement values) for all parcels in the small area, then summing the land area of these same parcels, and finally dividing the former by the latter. Note that a sampling approach may be used to reduce data-collection costs.

### 4. Average Value of Office Space

This is the average value per square foot of improvements in parcels used for commercial office activity. It is calculated by first summing the improvement values only (not land values) for all parcels designated commercial-office, then summing the building floor spaces for the same parcels, and finally dividing the former by the latter.

### 5. Commercial Share of Land Use

This is the same as defined in section B5, for retail employment.

### Part 3: Sample Calibration and Forecast

In order for the user to gain a better sense of the procedures used in LOCDEV, a very simple example is presented below. A nine-zone system is assumed for an urban region, with the zones numbered 1–9. Seven small areas are defined within the region and designated by the letters A–G. Each small area falls completely within one of the nine zones. (See Figure 8.2.)

The aggregate employment equation is calibrated and then used to make a ten-year forecast of aggregate employment in each of the seven small areas. The same procedures can be applied by the user to calibrate the other two equations and make forecasts with them. This example was done using SAS, but any statistical package or programming language can be used.

In this example, the set of relative accessibility indices provided in the input data set (SAMPLE) is assumed to be optimal. The user will note in part 4 that a separate procedure may be appropriate for determining the optimal set of relative accessibility indices.

### A. Calibration

The historical data used for the calibration of the aggregate employ-

Figure 8.2. **Hypothetical Urban Region**

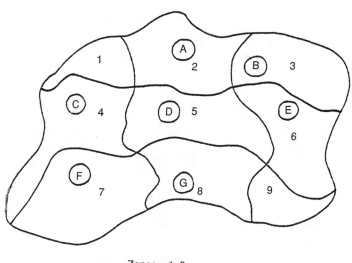

Zones = 1–9
Small areas = A–G

Figure 8.3. **Input Data Set (SAMPLE)**

| | | | | |
|---|---|---|---|---|
| A | 600 | 520 | 20 | .13 |
| B | 400 | 300 | 15 | .08 |
| C | 300 | 125 | 18 | .07 |
| D | 900 | 700 | 30 | .23 |
| E | 400 | 200 | 22 | .07 |
| F | 500 | 450 | 15 | .13 |
| G | 600 | 480 | 19 | .19 |

ment equation of LOCDEV appear in Figure 8.3. A simple SAS program reads in the data and performs the ordinary least squares procedure for calibration (see Figure 8.4). Two permanent SAS data sets are created and stored in the SAS library named LOCDEV: LOCDEV.RESULTS, which contains the original values and the residuals from the calibration experiment, and LOCDEV.COEFF, which contains the values for the intercept and the coefficients of the estimated equation. These data sets appear in Figure 8.5, while the calibration results appear in Figure 8.6.

Figure 8.4. **SAS Program for Calibration of Hypothetical Example**

```
DATA READIN;
*READ IN HISTORICAL DATA FOR CALIBRATION;
  INFILE SAMPLE;
  INPUT SMLAREA $ EMPNOW EMPLAG VCOMFS ACCESS;
*
  VARIABLE DEFINITIONS:
  SMLAREA = SMALL AREA DESIGNATION
  ACCESS = RELATIVE ACCESS VALUE
  EMPNOW = CURRENT EMPLOYMENT
  EMPLAG = EMPLOYMENT LAGGED 5 YEARS
  VCOMFS = VALUE OF COMMERCIAL FLOOR SPACE
;
DATA CALIB;
  SET READIN;
*GENERATE SIMPLE STATISTICS AND CORRELATIONS;
PROC CORR;
*
CALIBRATE FORECASTING EQUATION USING ORDINARY LEAST SQUARES
    REGRESSION, STORING COEFFICIENTS AND INTERCEPT AS A MEMBER
    OF THE PERMANENT SAS LIBRARY REFERENCED BY "LOCDEV".
;
PROC REG OUTEST=LOCDEV.COEFF;
  MODEL EMPNOW = ACCESS EMPLAG VCOMFS / R;
  ID SMLAREA;
*
CREATE OUTPUT DATA SET CONTAINING (1) ORIGINAL VALUES FOR ALL
    VARIABLES AND (2) THE RESIDUALS FOR ALL SMALL AREAS. THIS DATA
    SET IS STORED AS A MEMBER OF THE PERMANENT SAS LIBRARY
    REFERENCED BY "LOCDEV"
;
  OUTPUT OUT=LOCDEV.RESULTS R=RESID;
*PRINT THE CONTENTS OF THE TWO DATA SETS;
DATA PRINT1;
  SET LOCDEV.RESULTS;
PROC PRINT;
DATA PRINT2;
  SET LOCDEV.COEFF;
PROC PRINT;
```

## B. Forecast

A second SAS program (see Figure 8.7) forecasts the independent variables, combines them with the calibration parameters, and makes the ten-year forecast of aggregate employment.

The program first reads in the data from LOCDEV.RESULTS and LOCDEV.COEFF, and then reads in base-year and forecast data for

Figure 8.5. **Output Data Sets**

LOCDEV.RESULTS

| OBS | SMLAREA | EMPNOW | EMPLAG | VCOMFS | ACCESS | RESID |
|---|---|---|---|---|---|---|
| 1 | A | 600 | 520 | 20 | 0.13 | -9.6863 |
| 2 | B | 400 | 300 | 15 | 0.08 | 15.7231 |
| 3 | C | 300 | 125 | 18 | 0.07 | -4.6323 |
| 4 | D | 900 | 700 | 30 | 0.23 | 5.0341 |
| 5 | E | 400 | 200 | 22 | 0.07 | -1.2277 |
| 6 | F | 500 | 450 | 15 | 0.13 | -4.0635 |
| 7 | G | 600 | 480 | 19 | 0.19 | -1.1476 |

LOCDEV.COEFF

| OBS | TYPE | MODEL | DEPVAR | SIGMA | EMPNOW | ACCESS | EMPLAG | VCOMFS | INTERCEP |
|---|---|---|---|---|---|---|---|---|---|
| 1 | OLS | | EMPNOW | 11.6501 | -1 | 485.663 | 0.63669 | 12.2109 | -28.747 |

232

Figure 8.6. **Calibration Results Using SAS Regression Procedure (PROC REG), Sample Problem**

DEP VARIABLE: EMPNOW

ANALYSIS OF VARIANCE

| SOURCE | DF | SUM OF SQUARES | MEAN SQUARE | F VALUE | PROB>F |
|---|---|---|---|---|---|
| MODEL | 3 | 233,878.54 | 77,959.51216 | 574.389 | 0.0001 |
| ERROR | 3 | 407.17780 | 135.72593 | | |
| C TOTAL | 6 | 234,285.71 | | | |

| | | |
|---|---|---|
| ROOT MSE | 11.65015 | R-SQUARE 0.9983 |
| DEP MEAN | 528.5714 | ADJ R-SQ 0.9965 |
| C.V. | 2.204082 | |

PARAMETER ESTIMATES

| VARIABLE | DF | PARAMETER ESTIMATE | STANDARD ERROR | T FOR H0: PARAMETER = 0 | PROB \|T\| |
|---|---|---|---|---|---|
| INTERCEP | 1 | -28.74674672 | 19.14050343 | -1.502 | 0.2301 |
| ACCESS | 1 | 485.66254 | 204.01556 | 2.381 | 0.0976 |
| EMPLAG | 1 | 0.63668980 | 0.05943250 | 10.713 | 0.0017 |
| VCOMFS | 1 | 12.21091193 | 1.18009808 | 10.347 | 0.0019 |

| OBS | ID | ACTUAL | PREDICT VALUE | STD ERR PREDICT | RESIDUAL | STD ERR RESIDUAL | STUDENT RESIDUAL | -2 -1 | 0 1 2 | COOK'S D |
|---|---|---|---|---|---|---|---|---|---|---|
| 1 | A | 600.0 | 609.7 | 8.3577 | -9.6863 | 8.1163 | -1.1934 | ** | | 0.378 |
| 2 | B | 400.0 | 384.3 | 6.8670 | 15.7231 | 9.4111 | 1.6707 | | *** | 0.372 |
| 3 | C | 300.0 | 304.6 | 8.6563 | -4.6323 | 7.7970 | -0.5941 | * | | 0.109 |
| 4 | D | 900.0 | 895.0 | 10.6866 | 5.0341 | 4.6393 | 1.0851 | | ** | 1.562 |
| 5 | E | 400.0 | 401.2 | 8.7576 | -1.2277 | 7.6831 | -0.1598 | | | 0.008 |
| 6 | F | 500.0 | 504.1 | 7.6760 | -4.0635 | 8.7638 | -0.4637 | | | 0.041 |
| 7 | G | 600.0 | 601.1 | 10.0570 | -1.1476 | 5.8808 | -0.1951 | | | 0.028 |

SUM OF RESIDUALS            3.97904E-13
SUM OF SQUARED RESIDUALS    407.1778
PREDICTED RESID SS (PRESS)  2173.433

Figure 8.7. **SAS Program for Forecast of Hypothetical Example**

```
DATA READIN1;
*READ IN ORIGINAL DATA AND THE RESIDUALS FROM CALIBRATION;
 SET LOCDEV.RESULTS;
  MATCH=1;
PROC PRINT;
DATA READIN2;
*READ IN COEFFICIENTS AND INTERCEPT VALUE FROM CALIBRATION;
 SET LOCDEV.COEFF;
  MATCH=1;
PROC PRINT;
DATA READIN3;
*READ IN LARGE ZONE DATA FOR CURRENT AND FORECAST PERIOD;
 INFILE SAMPLE2;
 INPUT ZONE SMLAREA $ ZEMPNOW ZEMPFUT ACCNOW ACCFUT;
*
 VARIABLE DEFINITIONS:
 ZONE = LARGE ZONE FROM REGIONAL MODEL
 SMLAREA = SMALL AREA DESIGNATION
 ZEMPNOW=ZONE EMPLOYMENT (CURRENT)
 ZEMPFUT = ZONE EMPLOYMENT (FORECASTED 5 YEARS AHEAD)
 ACCNOW = RELATIVE ACCESS TO ZONE (CURRENT)
 ACCFUT = RELATIVE ACCESS TO ZONE IN (FORECASTED 10 YEARS AHEAD)
CALCULATE THE RATE OF CHANGE IN THE LARGE ZONES SURROUNDING
SMALL AREAS
.
PCHGACC-(ACCFUT/ACCNOW);
PCHGEMP=(ZEMPFUT/ZEMPNOW);
PROC SORT;
 BY SMLAREA;
DATA PREPFCST;
  MERGE READIN1 READIN3;
  BY SMLAREA;
*
COMPUTE FORECASTS FOR INDEPENDENT VARIABLES BY MULTIPLYING THE
BASE-YEAR VALUES BY THE RATE OF CHANGE IN THE SURROUNDING LARGE
ZONES.
;
 EMPLAGF = EMPNOW*PCHGEMP;
 ACCESSF = ACCESS*PCHGACC;
*
COMPUTE FORECASTS FOR VALUE OF COMMERCIAL FLOOR SPACE BY
ASSUMING A UNIFORM INCREASE OF 25 PERCENT FOR ALL SMALL AREAS
;
 VCOMFSF = VCOMFS*1.25;
*CREATE THE BASE YEAR VARIABLE FOR LATER COMPARISON TO THE
FORECASTED VALUE;
 EMPBASE = EMPNOW;
*RETAIN ONLY THOSE VARIABLES NEEDED FOR THE FORECAST STEP;
KEEP MATCH EMPLAGF ACCESSF VCOMFSF RESID EMPBASE;
DATA FORECAST;
*
COMBINE THE INTERCEPT, COEFFICIENTS, AND FORECASTED VALUES OF THE
INDEPENDENT VARIABLES
;
 MERGE READIN2 PREPFCST;
 BY MATCH;
*FORECAST EMPLOYMENT FOR ALL SMALL AREAS;
EMPF = INTERCEP + (EMPLAG*EMPLAGF) + (VCOMFS*VCOMFSF) +
(ACCESS*ACCESSF) + RESID;
*CALCULATE CHANGES AND RATES OF CHANGE FOR EACH AREA;
DEMP=EMPF-EMPBASE;
PEMP=(DEMP/EMPBASE)*100;
IF EMPF = . THEN DELETE;
*PRINT RESULTS;
PROC PRINT;
FORMAT EMPF EMPBASE DEMP PEMP 8.0;
```

Figure 8.8.  **Input Data Set (SAMPLE2)**

| | | | | | |
|---|---|---|---|---|---|
| 1 | . | 1000 | 1200 | .05 | .04 |
| 2 | A | 2000 | 2500 | .13 | .15 |
| 3 | B | 1500 | 1600 | .08 | .07 |
| 4 | C | 600 | 500 | .07 | .07 |
| 5 | D | 2500 | 2800 | .23 | .22 |
| 6 | E | 800 | 850 | .07 | .05 |
| 7 | F | 1500 | −1800 | .13 | .15 |
| 8 | G | 2000 | 2600 | .19 | .20 |
| 9 | . | 2000 | 2200 | .05 | .05 |

Figure 8.9.  **Values for Forecasting Independent Variables**

| OBS | ZONE | SMLAREA | ZEMPNOW | ZEMPFUT | ACCNOW | ACCFUT | PCHGACC | PCHGEMP |
|---|---|---|---|---|---|---|---|---|
| 1 | 1 | | 1000 | 1200 | 0.05 | 0.04 | 0.80000 | 1.20000 |
| 2 | 9 | | 2000 | 2200 | 0.05 | 0.05 | 1.00000 | 1.10000 |
| 3 | 2 | A | 2000 | 2500 | 0.13 | 0.15 | 1.15385 | 1.25000 |
| 4 | 3 | B | 1500 | 1600 | 0.08 | 0.07 | 0.87500 | 1.06667 |
| 5 | 4 | C | 600 | 500 | 0.07 | 0.07 | 1.00000 | 0.83333 |
| 6 | 5 | D | 2500 | 2800 | 0.23 | 0.22 | 0.95652 | 1.12000 |
| 7 | 6 | E | 800 | 850 | 0.07 | 0.05 | 0.71429 | 1.06250 |
| 8 | 7 | F | 1500 | 1800 | 0.13 | 0.15 | 1.15385 | 1.20000 |
| 9 | 8 | G | 2000 | 2600 | 0.19 | 0.20 | 1.05263 | 1.30000 |

Figure 8.10.  **Aggregate Employment: Ten-year Forecast, Base-Year Value, Change, and Percentage Change**

| OBS | EMPF | EMPBASE | DEMP | PEMP |
|---|---|---|---|---|
| 1 | 817 | 600 | 217 | 36 |
| 2 | 522 | 400 | 122 | 30 |
| 3 | 435 | 300 | 135 | 45 |
| 4 | 1183 | 900 | 283 | 31 |
| 5 | 601 | 400 | 201 | 50 |
| 6 | 651 | 500 | 151 | 30 |
| 7 | 854 | 600 | 254 | 42 |

the nine-zone system from a raw data file (see Figure 8.8). The zone forecast values in the latter input data set would, in actual practice, be the product of a regional forecasting model for the nine-zone system. The zonal base and forecast values are combined to calculate their percentage changes over time at the zone level (see Figure 8.9). These percentage changes are then applied to the base-year values of the small areas to produce forecasts for them as well. Notice that this aggregate employment forecast is for only five years for the overall ten-year forecast because the relevant independent variable is aggregate employment lagged five years. The relative accessibility index, on the other hand, must be for the same year as the forecast and so is projected over the full ten-year period.

The program then computes changes and percentage changes in the aggregate employment forecast for the small areas, and prints them out as an output data set (see Figure 8.10).

This step completes the simple forecast example. Notice that this example presents an unconstrained forecast. See part 5 for a discussion of optional constraining mechanisms.

## Part 4: Calculating Relative Accessibility Indices

Relative accessibility captures the influence of several important regional factors on each small area. Its calculation and use in the model are therefore quite important.

### *Data Requirements*

#### *1. Trip Times (Representing All Trip Costs)*

A trip-time table for all pairs of zones in the zonal partition of the urban region is needed. The number of zones in the partition may vary according to local data availability; in any event, the zones will usually be larger than the small areas defined for the LOCDEV estimation. The trip times between two small areas are assumed to be equal to the trip times between the zones containing them. See Figure 8.10 for an example of a four-zone urban region with interzonal trip time indicated graphically and in a trip-time matrix.

#### *2. Median Income*

This is the median income for households residing in each zone.

#### *3. Households*

This is the number of households residing in each zone.

*Procedures for Calculating Relative Accessibility Indices*

Absolute accessibility to local area $k$ is defined as the sum of weighted impedances (trip times) from all zones in the urban region to the one containing local area $k$. The weights are described below. Relative accessibility, which is used in LOCDEV, is computed by dividing each absolute accessibility value by the sum of all absolute accessibilities.

Specifically, the relative accessibility to a particular small area k is:

$$A_{i\,|\,k} = \frac{\sum_{j} Y_j \exp(-\alpha B_{ij})}{\sum_{i}\sum_{j} Y_j \exp(-\alpha B_{ij})},$$

where

$A_{i\,|\,k}$ = Relative accessibility of region to zone $i$ containing small area $k$;
$Y_j$    = activity weight in zone $j$;
$\alpha$    = calibration parameter; and
$B_{ij}$    = travel time from zone $i$ to zone $j$.

The activity weight is median income in the zone of origin in the aggregate employment and commercial floor space equations, and total income in the zone of origin in the retail employment equation. An example of such a calculation for the four-zone urban region follows.

*Sample Calculation of a Relative Accessibility Index*

Consider the four-zone urban region in Figure 8.11. The relative accessibility for zone 1 (which in turn can be associated with small areas within it) is calculated using the above equation, setting $\alpha = 1$. The absolute accessibility for zone 1, the numerator of relative accessibility, is the weight in zone 2 times the trip time between zones 2 and 1, plus the weight in zone 3 times the trip time between zones 3 and 1, plus the weight in zone 4 times the trip time between zones 4 and 1. In actual figures, this is:

$$(20e^{-3} + 30e^{-7} + 30e^{-8}) = 1.033.$$

Figure 8.11 **Hypothetical Four-Zone Urban Region**

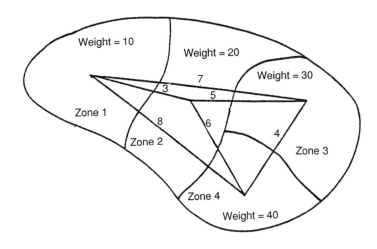

|      | Trip time matrix |   |   |   |   | Activity weights |        |
| Zone | 1 | 2 | 3 | 4 |   | Zone | Weight |
|------|---|---|---|---|---|------|--------|
| 1 | 0 | 3 | 7 | 8 |   | 1 | 10 |
| 2 | 3 | 0 | 5 | 6 |   | 2 | 20 |
| 3 | 7 | 5 | 0 | 4 |   | 3 | 30 |
| 4 | 8 | 6 | 4 | 0 |   | 4 | 40 |

The denominator is derived by summing this and the other absolute accessibility terms:

$$[(20e^{-3} + 30e^{-7} + 30e^{-8}) +$$
$$(10e^{-3} + 30e^{-5} + 30e^{-6}) +$$
$$(10e^{-7} + 20e^{-5} + 30e^{-4}) +$$
$$(10e^{-8} + 20e^{-6} + 30e^{-4})] = 3.103.$$

The relative accessibility index for zone 1 is therefore:

$$1.033/3.103 = 0.333.$$

Repeating this procedure for each zone gives the following list of relative accessibilities:

| Zone | Relative accessibility |
|------|------------------------|
| 1 | 0.333 |
| 2 | 0.240 |
| 3 | 0.223 |
| 4 | 0.194 |

### *Procedure for Determining the Best Value of the Calibration Parameter*

The calibration parameter $\alpha$ cannot be estimated simultaneously with the coefficients of the equation when ordinary least squares regression is used. Its value can be assumed arbitrarily, or based on concrete studies of diversion curves in a particular region. Alternatively, a search technique may be used, for instance by setting twenty values for $\alpha$ and calculating a set of relative accessibility indices for each. The LOCDEV aggregate employment equation would then be estimated twenty times, once for each set of relative accessibility indices based on a specific value of $\alpha$. The $\alpha$ that produces the set of relative accessibility indices leading to the best fit for the aggregate employment equation (as judged by correctness of sign, significance levels of the coefficients, and level of explanation—$R^2$) would then be selected as the correct one for that LOCDEV equation. The same procedure can be repeated for the other two equations.

### Part 5: Constraining Procedures (Optional)

The user may decide that the LOCDEV forecasts produced by the above procedure contain errors that a constraining process could reduce. Constraint procedures require some form of higher-order process that can provide limits, in terms of either levels or signs, to LOCDEV forecasts. The ideal process for creating such limits is a regional model that allocates control totals of aggregate employment, retail employment, and commercial floor space to zones with a substantially larger geographical area than the small areas defined for LOCDEV. The forecast changes at the larger geographical level can serve as the limits for changes in the small area; similarly, the direction of change in the larger geographical area can be used as a binding constraint on the LOCDEV forecast. Determining and implementing such constraints is a study-specific task.

## Conclusion

Although LOCDEV has not yet been tested outside of the Washington, D.C., region, its structure is generalizable and therefore should be estimable in other urban regions. The model must be fine-tuned in each setting; nevertheless, the success of LOCDEV in the Washington region augurs well for its use in indicative forecasting experiments in other urban areas.

# Nine

# Findings and Conclusions

This investigation of the impacts of rapid rail stations on development has led to conclusions about modeling methods for urban regions and small areas within them, and produced findings about the development effects of rapid rail transit stations in the Washington, D.C., region. In this concluding chapter we discuss the possibilities of local development models and the importance of integrating them with regional models in carrying out small-area forecasts, the substantive findings about rail corridors and station areas compared to areas not served by such transportation improvements, the prospective impact of various access and economic variables on station area development, and the future possibilities for station area development in the Washington region based on accessibility and economic considerations.

## Small-Area Modeling and LOCDEV

Unlike regional modeling with its nineteenth-century origin, small-area modeling was virtually nonexistent prior to this project. Small areas have long been thought too idiosyncratic to be amenable to standard modeling techniques; this proved not to be the case.

The Local Development (LOCDEV) model uses a small number of variables in its structural version and even fewer in its forecasting version. It has a high level of statistical quality, belying the fears that random effects in small areas make any cross-sectional or pooled modeling exercise hopelessly suspect. It has potentially very useful implications for policymakers, developers, planners, and citizens' groups because it shows which small areas (in the present study, which rapid-transit station areas) are most hospitable to development according to several important variables. While it does not give point forecasts with narrow confidence bands (after all, only selected economic and accessibility measures figure in its structure and many important factors affecting local development are omitted), LOCDEV does yield important information about where economic pressures are most (and least) intense. Its forecasts can therefore provide important clues about the relative productivity of various levels and kinds of public and/or private policy interventions at individual station sites.

LOCDEV's statistical strength far exceeds that of the few previous models of small areas. Furthermore, LOCDEV models explicit development variables (i.e., employment, commercial floor space, and retail employment levels) at stations (small areas)—a unique effort; previous small-area modeling studies used property values as dependent variables, which tell very little about development potential. Moreover, no statistically based forecasting models have been tried before for small areas, perhaps because the seemingly random fluctuations across small areas appeared too difficult to control. Thus, LOCDEV breaks new ground in three areas of small-area modeling: statistical quality, dependent variables, and forecasting capability. Analysts wishing to study groups of small areas in a region should therefore be encouraged to use LOCDEV-style modeling techniques in their studies and not feel constrained to limit their analyses to particularistic and noncomparative methodologies. Some aspects of the specific form taken by LOCDEV in the study of the Washington region may require modification due to structural variations between regions or differences in data availability, but the model should prove transferable to other regions. The user's guide to LOCDEV (chapter 8) explains how this can be done.

## Contextual Use of the Regional Model ITLUP

A corollary of this project, discussed in detail in Putman (1988), produced important new developments in the widely used regional interactive model ITLUP, most notably mode-split and land consumption modules. The forecasts produced by this improved version of ITLUP, calibrated on a 182-zone system (previous calibrations involved a lower order of magnitude of zones), were used in a novel way: to provide contexts, inputs, and constraints for a small-area model, LOCDEV. This application proved generally successful and led to intuitively reasonable results.

## Washington Region Station Areas as Development Centers

The literature concerning the impact of transit stations on development in their vicinity suggested that, contrary to the conventional wisdom on this subject, little if any development was likely to occur strictly as a result of the opening of rapid rail transit stations. Studies showed some upward influence on property values but apparently this did not generally translate into development. Joint development—i.e., public/private collaboration in development activities in specific sites—seemed to be the way that development emerged at station areas; purely private initiatives seemed not to happen much, or at least to have little effect in most station areas. Even such an apparent exception as Toronto (the aerial view of the city shows great eruptions of development directly over station sites) turns out to be consistent with these findings: Toronto has imposed strict requirements on its developers which have effectively constrained them to build at stations. In this instance, development around station areas is as much due to public planning as to private initiative.

The literature therefore suggests that the public side is extremely important as a general rule in fostering development in station areas. Washington may be a partial exception to this pattern, and to some extent an instance of the old conventional wisdom. Many businesses and developers in station areas there have apparently reaped windfall gains from the increase in value in their properties near stations due to the public investment in Metrorail, which has provoked extensive discussions about "value capture." Even the casual observer cannot miss the local development obviously induced without other public encouragement by many downtown transit stations. Nevertheless, even in this metropolitan region many station areas remain relatively barren.

The statistical examination of development in rail lines and station areas compared to other areas in the region strongly indicated that station areas, and to a lesser extent the corridors in which they are located, are in fact development zones compared to other parts of the region. Employment is generally higher in these rail-transit-impact areas and grows more (and often faster) there than in other parts of the region. These findings are especially true for service and government employment, although basic and retail employment occasionally show the same pattern. The findings are strongest in Montgomery and Arlington Counties.

It is impossible to credit these differentials in development entirely to Metro, if only because many station areas were development centers long before Metro was even aligned; obviously, planners placed some stations so that they would serve existing centers of economic activity. There are a few cases in which levels of development in station areas and nonstation areas were not distinguishable prior to the opening of Metro, but diverged in the wake of the opening of Metro; for these, the development gap may be ascribed to the impact of the station(s). Such examples are limited in extent, so conclusions based on them must be somewhat circumspect.

These caveats having been expressed, a number of things may be said with confidence. First, Metrorail station areas have developed the most when planning activity and economic advantage coincided, as in the cases of Montgomery and Arlington Counties. Second, many station areas have grown substantially and at a rate above that of comparable nonstation areas even in places, like Prince George's County, where planners have not focused their attention on joint development activity at station areas. Third, the massive development in Washington's downtown directly over its stations would have been considerably less without the access advantage of Metro. Fourth, in certain parts of the region, such as non-downtown Washington and Fairfax County, where few if any serious development plans for station areas were made (at least until after the period of this study), station areas by themselves were insufficiently attractive to bring about major development processes. In sum, the interpenetration of three factors— the locations of past activity, conscious planning of Metro to serve existing activity centers, and new development stimulated by Metro— renders a simple definitive conclusion about the independent effect of Metro stations impossible.

### Findings from the Structural Version of LOCDEV

The estimation of the structural version of LOCDEV and the calculation of elasticities (measures of responsiveness of the development variables to the explanatory variables) showed that, over the long run, development responds most positively to improvements in the relative accessibility of each station area. Such improvements can in principle be for any mode of travel. The policy implications of this finding are straightforward: to foster development in a station area over the long run, improve transportation service to it.

New development also responds well to levels of development-in-place in the station area, in a multiplier effect. The apparent tug of development to areas where a large share of land is already used for commercial purposes may well be due not only to positive economic linkages, but also to the relative sparseness of residential land uses in such areas, which automatically mutes organized residential opposition to development. Additional support for this interpretation is provided by the inverse relationship between population in the station area and measures of commercial development there.

Higher real estate values also stimulate high levels of development. This may seem counterintuitive at first blush; businesses, like anyone else, prefer to pay lower rents, other things being equal, and in typical demand models higher input prices drive away firms. But in fact the higher prices mean that if development is to occur at such sites, it must be in densities and uses that allow a relatively high return so that high rental expenses can be met. Thus, high-density, high-rise construction for office use is far more likely to occur than low-rise construction for retail uses in generally desirable locations that have high real estate values. Once in place, of course, the clustering of economic activities itself can stimulate higher prices for real estate in an area.

## Findings from the Forecasting Version of LOCDEV

The forecasting results must be treated cautiously since many important factors are necessarily omitted from this model. Nevertheless, the results indicate areas where accessibility and economic factors are especially favorable (or poor) for development.

LOCDEV forecasts that station areas will remain important centers of development in the region through 1990. (In all likelihood, further iterations of LOCDEV would reveal that these trends will continue further into the future.) The Red Line in Montgomery County and the Orange Line in Arlington will, according to LOCDEV, stand out in this regard, as will the highly developed downtown District station areas. Interestingly, LOCDEV also forecasts that the short Blue Line segment in Prince George's County has economic and accessibility characteristics that should allow development to blossom there; poor station design and relative inattention from county planners (obviously factors that cannot be modeled) may be holding back this potential. Certain other stations appear to have good prospects for development if more attention is focused on them, especially Eisenhower Avenue and Dunn Loring. Many other station areas do not appear to have as high a level of economic/accessibility potential; most of the non-downtown District stations, for instance, would almost certainly need strong government intervention to bring about development, given the low levels of economic attractiveness forecasted for them by LOCDEV. In contrast, certain well-to-do residential station areas in Washington, such as Cleveland Park, are the focus of strong economic pressures for development that should continue to engender vigorous battles over preservation versus redevelopment.

**A Final Word**

Behavioral and statistical modeling have proved to be useful techniques in studying the very complex phenomena of station area development and regional change. The estimates of responsiveness of development to certain variables, and the indicative forecasts, are products of an effort to simplify these complex phenomena and to make this field of study tractable. While not all important phenomena can be captured in a modeling exercise, the present study has demonstrated that the application of modeling techniques to the interactions of urban activity patterns and transportation developments, at both regional and local levels, can provide both the public and the private sectors with substantial amounts of information to help guide their interventions in an ever-more complex urban environment.

# Bibliography

Administration and Management Research Association of New York City, Inc. (AMRA). (1976) *Transit Station Area Joint Development: Strategies for Implementation.* Final Report.

Alexandria. (1980) *Annual Report.* Mark Horowitz, Report Coordinator. Alexandria, VA.

———. (1981) *Annual Report.* George Colyer, Report Coordinator. Alexandria, VA.

———. (1983) *Historic Alexandria's New Development Centers* (Brochure). Alexandria, VA: Department of Planning and Community Development.

Allen, W.G. (1983) "Trip Distribution Using Composite Impedance." Paper presented at the Sixty-Second Annual Meeting of the Transportation Research Board. Washington, D.C., January.

Alonso, William. (1964) *Location and Land Use.* Cambridge, MA: Harvard University Press.

Anas, A. (1975) "The Empirical Calibration and Testing of a Simulation Model of Residential Location." *Environment and Planning A* 7:899–920.

———. (1979a) "The Estimation of Multinomial Logit Models of Joint Location, Housing and Travel Model Choice from Small Area Aggregated Data." Evanston, IL: Department of Civil Engineering, Northwestern University.

———. (1979b) "The Impact of Transit Investment on Housing Values: A Simulation Experiment." *Environment and Planning A* 11:239–55.

———. (1981) "The Estimation of Multinomial Logit Models of Joint Location and Travel Mode Choice from Aggregate Data." *Journal of Regional Science* 21:2.

———. (1982) *Residential Location Markets and Urban Transportation.* New York: Academic Press.

——— (1983) "Discrete Choice Theory, Information Theory and the Multinomial Logit and Gravity Models." *Transportation Research* B 17, 1:8–23.

Arlington. (1980) *Ballston Sector Plan.* Department of Community Affairs, Planning Division, Arlington, VA.

———. (1981) *Courthouse Sector Plan.* Department of Community Affairs, Planning, Housing, and Community Development Division, Planning Section, Arlington, VA.

———. (1982a) *Trends: Hotel Development for the Years 1960 through 1982.* Department of Community Affairs, Planning, Housing, and Community Development Division, Planning Section, Arlington, VA.

———. (1982b) *Trends: Office and Commercial Development.* Department of Community Affairs, Planning, Housing, and Community Development Division, Planning Section, Arlington, VA.

247

————. (1982c) *Trends: Residential Development*. Department of Community Affairs, Planning, Housing, and Community Development Division, Planning Section, Arlington, VA.

———— (1983a) *Data File '83*. Department of Community Affairs, Planning, Housing, and Community Development Division, Planning Section, Arlington, VA.

————. (1983b) *Development in the Metro Corridors: Existing Zoning, Approved General Land Use Plan, Approved Development for the Years 1960 to Present*. Department of Community Affairs, Planning, Housing, and Community Development Division, Planning Section, Arlington, VA.

Artemel, Engin; George Colyer; Allan Baken; Larry Crossman; Raymond Johnson; et al. (1980) *Braddock Road Station Area Plan: A Guide for Action*. Alexandria, VA: Department of Planning and Community Development.

————. (1982) *Braddock Road Station Area Plan*. Alexandria, VA: Department of Planning and Community Development.

Artemel, Engin; George Colyer; Allan Martin; Brooke Miller; and Ralph A. Rosenbaum. (1983) *Office Building Inventory*. Alexandria, VA: Department of Planning and Community Development.

Artemel, Engin; Larry Grossman; Alvin D. Jenkins; Patricia D. Curran; and Mian Rias Ud-Din. (1978) *King Street Station Area: A Guide for Future Action. Part I: Recommended Plan*. Alexandria, VA: Department of Planning and Community Development.

Atherton, Terry J., and Moshe E. Ben-Akiva. (1976) "Transferability and Updating of Disaggregate Travel Demand Models." *Transportation Research Record* 610:12–18.

Baltimore Planning Commission (BPC). (1970) *Baltimore Region Rapid Transit Study*, vol. 1, *Basic Considerations: Influence Area Analysis Model*. Baltimore, MD: BPC.

Batty, Michael. (1967) *Urban Modelling: Algorithms, Calibrations, Predictions*. Cambridge, U.K.: Cambridge University Press.

————. (1972) "Recent Developments in Land Use Modelling: A Review of British Research." *Urban Studies*, 9:151–77.

————. (1976). *Urban Modelling*. London: Cambridge University Press.

————. (1979a) "Paradoxes of Science in Public Policy: The Baffling Case of Land Use Models." *Sistemi Urbani* 1, 1:89–132.

————. (1979b) "Progress, Success, and Failure in Urban Modelling." *Environment and Planning A* 11:863–78.

Batty, Michael, and S. Mackie. (1972) "The Calibration of Gravity, Entropy, and Related Models of Spatial Interaction." *Environment and Planning* 4:205–33.

Batty, Michael, and Lionel March. (1976) *Dynamic Urban Models Based on Information Minimizing*. Geographical Papers no. 48. Reading, U.K.: Department of Geography, University of Reading.

————. (1978) "Dynamic Urban Models Based on Information-Minimizing." In R.L. Martin, N.J. Thrift, and R.J. Bennett, eds. (1978), *Towards the Dynamic Analysis of Spatial Systems*. London: Pion.

Batty, Michael, and P.K. Sikdar. (1982) "Spatial Aggregation in Gravity Models: 4. Generalisations and Large Scale Applications." *Environment and Planning A*, 14:795–822.

Baxter R., and I.N. Williams. (1975) "An Automatically Calibrated Urban Model." *Environment and Planning A* 7:3–20.

Bay Area Transportation Study Commission. (1969) *Bay Area Transportation Report.* Berkeley, CA: BATSC.

Beaumont, J.R., M. Clarke, and A.G. Wilson. (1981) "The Dynamics of Urban Spatial Structure: Some Exploratory Results Using Difference Equations and Bifurcation Theory." *Environment and Planning A* 13:1472–83.

Bederman, Sanford J., and John S. Adams. (1974) "Job Accessibility and Underemployment." *Annals of the Association of American Geographers,* 64 (September), 3:378–86.

Ben-Akiva, Moshe E. (1974) "Alternative Travel Behavior Structures." *Transportation Research Record* 526:26–42.

———. (1977) "Passenger Travel Demand Forecasting: Applications of Disaggregate Models and Directions for Research." In E.J. Visser, ed., *Transportation Decisions in an Age of Uncertainty.* Boston: Martinus Nijhoff.

Ben-Akiva, Moshe E., and M.G. Richards. (1976) "Disaggregate Multimodal Model for Work Trips in the Netherlands." *Transportation Research Record,* 569:107–23.

Bennett, R.J. (1978) "Adaptive Parameter Space-Time Models: An Entropy-Maximizing Application Using the Kalman Filter with Unknown Prior Parameters." In R.L. Martin, N.J. Thrift, and R.J. Bennett, eds., *Towards the Dynamic Analysis of Spatial Systems.* London: Pion.

Berechman, J. (1976) "Interfacing the Land-Use Activity System and the Transportation System." *Journal of Regional Science* 16:183–94.

———. (1980) "A General Framework for the Interaction of a Land-Use Model with a Transportation Model Component." *Journal of Regional Science,* 20 (February):51–69.

Berechman, J., and P. Gordon. (1983) "Linked Models and Land-Use Transport Interactions: A Review." Presented at the International Symposium on New Directions in Urban Modelling, University of Waterloo, Waterloo, Ontario, Canada, July.

Bergsman, Joel, and Howard Wiener, eds. (1975) *Urban Problems and Public Policy Choices.* New York: Praeger.

Black, John. (1981) *Urban Transportation Planning: Theory and Practice.* Baltimore: Johns Hopkins University Press.

Bock, F.C. (1968) *Factors Influencing Modal Trip Assignment.* Report 57. Washington, D.C.: National Cooperative Highway Research Program.

Bovy, P.H.L., and G.R.M. Jansen. (1983) "Network Aggregation Effects upon Equilibrium Assignment Outcomes: An Empirical Investigation." *Transportation Science* 17, 3:248–62.

Boyce, David E.; Bruce Allen; Gene Desfor; and Richard Zuker. (1972) *Impact of Access Distance and Parking Availability on Suburban Rapid Transit Station Choice: Analysis of the Philadelphia-Lindenwold-High-Speed Line.* Contract no. DOT–OS–100044, U.S. Department of Transportation. Washington, D.C.: Office of the Secretary.

Cambridge Systematics Incorporated (CSI). (1981) "Residential Housing and Location Model." In United States Department of Transportation, *Innovative Approaches to Understanding Transportation/Social Interactions.* Washington, D.C.: Department of Transportation.

Callies, David L. (1980) "Value Capture in Metropolis." In *New Urban Rail Transit: How Can Its Development and Growth-Shaping Potential Be Realized?* Hearing before the Subcommittee on the City, of the Committee on Banking, Financing and Urban Affairs, House of Representatives, December 1979. Washington, D.C.: U.S. Government Printing Office.

Cardwell, David B. (1982) *Commercial Development Trends, 1972–1982: Analysis of Nonresidential Construction Activity in the Washington Region Before and After Metrorail.* Washington, D.C.: Metropolitan Washington Council of Governments.

Cater, Joe. (1984) *Employment Changes in Metro Station Areas, 1976–1980.* Washington, D.C.: Metropolitan Washington Council of Governments.

Center for Real Estate and Urban Economics. (1968) *Jobs, People and Land: Bay Area Simulation Study* (BASS). Berkeley, CA: Institute of Urban and Regional Development, University of California.

Cervero, Robert. (1982) *Intergovernmental Responsibilities for Financing Public Transit Services.* Final Report UMTA–CA–11–0023, U.S. Department of Transportation. Washington, D.C.: Urban Mass Transportation Administration.

Chan, Y. (1976) "A Method to Simplify Network Representation in Transportation Planning." *Transportation Research*, 10:179–91.

Charles River Associates (CRA). (1982) *A Disaggregate Behavioral Model of Urban Travel Demand.* Washington, D.C.: U.S. Department of Transportation.

Choukroun, J.M., and B. Harris. (1981) "Modeling Complex Urban Location Systems." In D. Kalm, ed., *Essays in Societal System Dynamics and Transportation.* U.S. Department of Transportation. Washington, D.C.: Research and Special Projects Administration.

Clarke, M., P. Keys, and H.C.W.L. Williams. (1980) "Micro-Analysis and Simulation of Socio-Economic Systems: Progress and Prospects." Working Paper No. 269. Leeds, U.K.: Leeds School of Geography, University of Leeds.

Clay, Phillip L. (1981) "Managing Urban Reinvestment: The Challenge of the 1980's." Paper delivered at the Allied Social Sciences Association Convention, Washington, D.C.

Coelho, J.D., and A.G. Wilson. (1977) "An Equivalence Theorem to Integrate Entropy Maximizing Submodels within Overall Mathematical Programming Frameworks." *Geographical Analysis* 9:160–73.

Cripps, E.L., and D.H.S. Foot. (1969) "The Empirical Development of an Elementary Residential Location Model for Use in Sub-Regional Planning." *Environment and Planning* 1:81–90.

Curran, Christopher, Leonard A. Carlson, and David A. Ford. (1982) "A Theory of Residential Location Decisions of Two-Worker Households." *Journal of Urban Economics* 12, 1 (July):102–14.

Cynecki, M.J., S. Knasnabis, and M.A. Flak. (1982) "Multimodal Logit Travel-Demand Model for Small and Medium Sized Urban Areas." *Transportation Research Record* 848:28–36.

Daly, A. (1982) "Estimating Choice Models Containing Attraction Variables." *Transportation Research* B 16, 1:5–15.

Damm, David; Steven Lerman; Eva Lerner-Lam; and Jeffrey Young. (1980) "Response of Urban Real Estate Values in Anticipation of the Washington, DC Metro." *Journal of Transport Economics and Policy* 14 (September):315–34.

deLeeuw, Frank, and Raymond Struyk. (1975) *The Web of Urban Housing: Analyzing Policy with a Market Simulation Model.* Washington, D.C.: Urban Institute.

Devereux, L.S., M.H. Echenique, and A.D.J. Flowerdew. (1982) "Bilbao Land Use and Transport Model: Result of Policy Tests." Paper presented to the Collaborative Group Meeting, IIASA. Schloss-Laxemburg, Austria, April.

Dewees, Donald. (1973) "The Impact of Urban Transportation Investment on Land Values." University of Toronto—York University Joint Program in Transportation. Research Report 11, Toronto.

————. (1976) "The Effect of a Subway on Residential Property Values in Toronto." *Journal of Urban Economics* 3:357–69.

Dingemans, Dennis. (1975) "Residential Subcentering and Urban Sprawl: The Location of Higher Density Owner-Occupied Housing around the Concord Line BART Stations." Working Paper 275. Davis, CA: Department of Geography, University of California–Davis.

Domencich T., and D. McFadden. (1974) *Urban Travel Demand: A Behavioral Analysis.* Amsterdam: North Holland.

Donnelly, Paget, and Price, Williams and Associates. (1982) *Rail Transit Impact Studies.* Contract no. DOT–1–82–3. Washington, D.C.: Urban Mass Transportation Administration.

Ducca, Frederick W., Jr., and R.H. Wilson. (1976) "A Model of Shopping Center Location." *Environment and Planning A* 8:613–23.

Dueker, Kenneth J., Pete Pendleton, and Peter Luder. (1982) *The Portland Mall Impact Study.* U.S. Department of Transportation, Contract no. DOT–1–83–7. Washington, D.C.: Urban Mass Transportation Administration.

Dunphy, Robert T., and Robert E. Griffiths. (1981) *The First Four Years of Metrorail: Travel Changes.* Washington, D.C.: Office of Planning Assistance, Urban Mass Transportation Administration (September).

Dunphy, Robert T., and Department of Community and Economic Resources. (1982) *Trends before Metrorail.* Contract no. DOT–1–82–3. Washington, D.C.: Office of Planning Assistance, Urban Mass Transportation Administration (March).

Dvett, Michael, et al. (1979) *Land Use and Urban Development Impacts of BART: Final Report.* Contract no. DOT–OS–30176. Washington, D.C.: U.S. Department of Transportation.

Eash, R.; K.S. Chon; Y.J. Lee; and D.E. Boyce. (1983) "Equilibrium Traffic Assignment on an Aggregate Highway Network for Sketch Planning." Mimeo, Transportation Planning Group. Urbana, IL: Department of Civil Engineering, University of Illinois at Urbana-Champaign.

Echenique, M. (1977) "An Integrated Land Use and Transport Model." *Transactions of the Martin Centre,* vol. 2. Cambridge, U.K.: University of Cambridge.

Echenique, M., D. Crowther, and W. Lindsay. (1969) "A Spatial Model of Urban Stock and Activity." *Regional Studies* 3:281–312.

Evans, S.P. (1973) "A Relationship between the Gravity Model for Trip Distribution and the Transportation Model in Linear Programming." *Transportation Research* 7:39–61.

————. (1976) "Derivation and Analysis of Some Models for Combining Trip Distribution and Assignment." *Transportation Research,* 10:37–57.

Eplan, Leone S. (1980) "Transit and Development in Atlanta." In *New Urban Rail Transit: How Can Its Development and Growth-Shaping Potential Be Realized?* Hearings before the Subcommittee on Banking, Finance and Urban Affairs, House of Representatives, December 1979. Washington, D.C.: U.S. Government Printing Office.

Fairfax. (1983) *Standard Reports: Providing a Summary and Analysis of Housing, Construction Activity, Population, Income, and Land Use Data for Fairfax County.* Office of Research and Statistics. Fairfax, VA: Communications Division.

Federal Highway Administration. (1977) *Standard Land Use Coding Manual: A Standard System for Identifying and Coding Land Use Activities.* U.S. Department of Transportation. Washington, D.C.: U.S. Government Printing Office.

Fertal, M., E. Weiner, A. Balek and A. Sevin. (1966) *Modal Split—Documentation of Nine Methods for Estimating Transit Usage.* Washington, D.C.: U.S. Bureau of Public Records.

Fisher, Gordon P., and Arnim H. Meyburg, eds. (1982) *Goods Transportation in Urban Areas: Proceedings of the Engineering Foundation Conference.* Eaton, MD, June 14–19, 1981. U.S. Department of Transportation. Contract no. DTUM60–81–C–71096. Washington, D.C.: Urban Mass Transportation Administration.

Fisk, C.S., D.E. Boyce, and D.G. Brown. (1981) "A Perspective on the Problem of Combining Network Equilibrium with Urban Systems Models." Publication no. 1, Transportation Planning Group. Urbana, IL: Department of Civil Engineering, University of Illinois at Urbana-Champaign (July).

Flick, Ken. (1988) *Employment Changes in the Metropolitan Washington Region, 1980–1985.* Washington, D.C.: Metropolitan Washington Council of Governments.

Florian, M. (1977) "A Traffic Equilibrium Model of Travel by Car and Public Transit Modes." *Transportation Science* 11:166–79.

———. (1978) "A Combined Trip Distribution, Modal Split and Trip Assignment Model." *Transportation Research* 12:241–46.

Florian, M., S. Nyugen, and J. Ferland. (1975) "On the Combined Distribution and Assignment of Traffic." *Transportation Science* 9:43–53.

Foot, David. (1978) *Urban Models 1: A Computer Program for the Garin-Lowry Model.* Reading Geographical Paper no. 65. Reading, U.K.: Department of Geography, University of Reading.

Frank, C. (1978) "The Addition of Modal Choice to the Integrated Land Use and Transportation Package." In S.H. Putman, *Development of an Improved Transportation and Land Use Package.* Washington, D.C.: National Science Foundation.

Goldner, W., S.R. Rosenthal, and J.R. Meredith. (1972) "Projective Land Use Model—PLUM: Theory and Application." Institute of Transportation and Traffic Engineering. Berkeley, CA: University of California.

Gomez-Ibanez, J.A., and G.R. Fauth. (1980) "Using Demand Elasticities from Disaggregate Mode Choice Models." *Transportation* 9 (June), 2:105–24.

Gorham, Williams, and Nathan Glazer. (1976) *The Urban Predicament.* Washington, D.C.: Urban Institute.

Gorove-Slade Associates, Inc. (GSAI). (1983) *Site Access Study for the New Carrollton and Landover Metrorail Station Vicinities.* Upper Marlboro, MD: Maryland-National Capital Park and Planning Commission.

Graebner, Linda S.; Peter B. Giles; Thomas J. Higgins; Ronald S. Jonash; and Emory Curtis. (1979) *The Local Policy Implication for BART Development*. Contract no. DOT–05–30176. Washington, D.C.: U.S. Department of Transportation.

Green, Rodney D., and Arlease Salley. (1983) *Joint Development, Location Theory, Regional Modeling, and Rapid Transit Station Site Development: A Review*. U.S. Department of Transportation Final Report DTRS56–83–C–00003. Washington, D.C.: Office of University Research.

Greenberger, Martin, et al. (1979) *Models in the Policy Process: Public Decision Making in the Computer Era*. New York: Russell Sage Foundation.

Grefe, Richard, and Angus N. McDonald. (1979) *The Economic and Financial Impact of BART*. Washington, D.C.: U.S. Department of Transportation and U.S. Department of Housing and Urban Development (April).

Griffiths, John R., Lester A. Hoel, and J. Demetsky. (1979) *Transit Station Renovation: A Case Study of Planning and Design Procedures*. Final Report DOT–OS–50223. U.S. Department of Transportation. Washington, D.C.: Office of University Research.

Hamer, Andrew. (1972) *Industrial Exodus from Central City: Public Policy and the Comparative Costs of Location*. Lexington, MA: Lexington Books.

Hanushek, Eric A., and Song Byung Nak. (1978) "The Dynamics of Post-War Industrial Location." *Review of Economics and Statistics* 60:515–22.

Harrison, Bennett, and Sandra Kanter. (1978) "The Political Economy of States' Job Creation Business Incentives." *AIP Journal* 44 (October), 4:424–35.

Henderson, J. Vernon. (1985) *Economic Theory and the Cities*, 2d ed. Orlando, FL: Academic Press.

Herr, J. Paul. (1979) "Local Governmental Competition for Business Activity: An Urban Case Study." *Professional Geographer* 31:3.

Hoel, Lester A., and Larry G. Richards, eds. (1981) *Planning and Development of Public Transportation Terminals*. Final Report DOT–OS–50233, U.S. Department of Transportation. Washington, D.C.: Office of University Research.

House, Peter, and John McLeod. (1977) *Large-Scale Models for Policy Evaluation*. New York: John Wiley.

Hutchinson, B.G. (1974) *Principles of Urban Transport Systems Planning*. Washington, D.C.: Scripta.

Ingram, Gregory K. (1979) "Simulation and Econometric Approaches to Modeling Urban Areas." In Peter Mieszkowski and Mahlon Straszheim, eds., *Current Issues in Urban Economics*. Baltimore: Johns Hopkins University Press.

Ingram, Gregory K., ed. (1977) *Residential Location and Urban Housing Markets*, vol. 43, *Studies in Income and Wealth*. Cambridge, MA: Ballinger, for the National Bureau of Economic Research.

Ingram, Gregory K.; John F. Kain; J.R. Ginn; et al. (1972) *The Detroit Prototype of the NBER Urban Simulation Model*. Urban Studies no. 1. New York: National Bureau of Economic Research.

Jewel, W.S. (1967) "Models for Traffic Assignment." *Transportation Research* 1:31–46.

Johnson, Douglas H. (1981) "The Business Investment Decision and Urban Revitalization." Paper delivered at the Allied Social Sciences Association Convention, Washington, D.C.

Kain, John F. (1975) *Essays on Urban Spatial Structure*. Cambridge, MA: Ballinger.

Kain, John F., W.C. Apgar, and J.R. Ginn. (1977) "Simulation of the Market Effects of Housing Allowances, Vol. 1: Description of the NBER Urban Simulation Model." City and Regional Planning Research Report R77–2. Cambridge, MA: Harvard University.

Kain, John F., and Gary R. Fauth. (1977) "Travel Demand Forecasting with Linear Probability Models." Discussion Paper D77–17, Department of City and Regional Planning. Cambridge, MA: School of Urban Planning, Policy Analysis, and Administration, Harvard University.

Kau, James B., Cheng F. Lee, and Rong C. Chen. (1983) "Structural Shifts in Urban Population Density Gradients: An Empirical Investigation." *Journal of Urban Economics* 13 (May) 3:364–77.

Keith, Robert W. (1983) "Incorporation of a Mode Choice Component into the Integrated Transportation and Land Use Package: Preliminary Empirical Results." Unpublished paper. Philadelphia, PA: Urban Simulation Laboratory, University of Pennsylvania.

Knight, Robert L. (1980) "Transit's Land-Use Impacts: Evidence and a Change of Perspective." In *New Urban Rail Transit: How Can Its Development and Growth-Shaping Potential Be Realized?* Hearings before the Subcommittee on the City, of the Committee on Banking, Finance and Urban Affairs, House of Representatives, December 1979. Washington, D.C.: U.S. Government Printing Office.

Knight, Robert, and Lisa Trygg. (1977a) "Evidence of Land Use Impacts of Rapid Transit Systems." *Transportation* 6:231–47.

———. (1977b) *Land Use Impacts of Rapid Transit: Implications of Recent Experience.* Executive Summary. Contract no. DOT-TPI–10–77–31. Washington, D.C.: U.S. Department of Transportation.

Koppleman, E.S. (1977) "Guidelines for Aggregate Travel Prediction Using Disaggregate Choice Models." *Transportation Record* 610:19–24.

Kuner, P. (1973) "Investigation of Traffic Assignment Algorithms." In S.H. Putman, ed. *The Interrelationships of Transportation Development and Land Development.* U.S. Department of Transportation. Washington, D.C.: Federal Highways Administration, Office of Highway Planning.

Leone, Robert A. (1975) "Location of Manufacturing Activity in the New York Metropolitan Area." New York: National Bureau of Economic Research.

Lerman, S.R. (1977) "Location, Housing, Automobile Ownership and Mode to Work: A Joint Choice Model." *Transportation Research Record* 610:6–11.

Lerman, S.R. and M.E. Ben-Akiva. (1975) "Disaggregate Behavioral Model of Automobile Ownership." *Transportation Research Record* 569:34–51.

Levin, Sharon G. (1974) "Suburban Central City Property Tax Differentials and the Location of Industry: Some Evidence." *Land Economics* 50 (November), 4:380–86.

Levinson, H.S. (1978) *Characteristics of Urban Transportation Demand.* Washington, D.C.: U.S. Department of Transportation.

Liou, P.S., G.S. Cohen, and D.T. Hartgen. (1975) "Application of Disaggregate Modal-Choice Models to Travel Demand Forecasting for Urban Transit Systems." *Transportation Research Record* 534:52–62.

Los, M. (1979) "Combined Residential-Location and Transportation Models." *Environment and Planning A* 11:1241–65.

Lovely, Mary E. (1979) "Public Transit and Downtown Development." *Urban Land* (November):14–22.

Lowry, Ira S. (1964) "A Model of Metropolis." Report RM 4125-RC. Santa Monica, CA: Rand Corporation.

———. (1972) *A Model of the Metropolis.* Santa Monica, CA: Rand Corporation.

Lund, Leonard. (1979) *Factors in Corporate Locational Decisions.* The Conference Board Information Bulletin, no. 66. New York: The Conference Board, Inc.

Lund, Leonard, and Linda Winter. (1979) *The Public-Private Partnership in Action.* The Conference Board Information Bulletin, no. 67. New York: The Conference Board, Inc.

Lynch, Allen. (1973) "Environment and Labor Quality Take Top Priority in Site Selection." *Industrial Development* (March/April).

Mackett, R. L. (1979) "A Model of the Relationships Between Transport and Land Use." Working Paper 122, Institute for Transport Studies. Leeds, U.K.: University of Leeds.

———. (1980) "The Mathematical Representation of a Model of the Relationship between Transport and Land Use." Working Paper 123, Institute for Transport Studies. Leeds, U.K.: University of Leeds.

March, L. (1971) "Urban Systems: A Generalized Distribution Function." In A.G. Wilson, ed., *London Papers in Regional Science 2. Urban and Regional Planning.* London: Pion.

Martin, B., and M. Manheim. (1965) "A Research Program for Comparison of Traffic Assignment Techniques." *Highway Research Record* 88:69–84.

Martin, R.L., N.J. Thrift, and R.J. Bennett, eds. (1978) *Towards the Dynamic Analysis of Spatial Systems.* London: Pion.

Maryland–National Capital Park and Planning Commission (MNCPPC). (1975) *Approved and Adopted Sector Plan for the Silver Spring Central Business District and Vicinity, Montgomery County, MD.* Silver Spring, MD: MNCPPC.

———. (1977) *Development Feasibility Study for the Silver Spring Metro Station.* Mimeo. Silver Spring, MD: MNCPPC.

———. (1978a) *Approved and Adopted Sector Plan for the Forest Glen Transit Impact Area and Vicinity, Montgomery County, MD.* Silver Spring, MD: MNCPPC.

———. (1978b) *Approved and Adopted Sector Plan for the Glenmont Transit Impact Area and Vicinity, Montgomery County, MD.* Silver Spring, MD: MNCPPC.

———. (1978c) *Approved and Adopted Sector Plan for the Kensington Sector and Vicinity, Montgomery County, MD.* Silver Spring, MD: MNCPPC.

———. (1978d) *Approved and Adopted Sector Plan for the Wheaton Central Business District and Vicinity, Montgomery County, MD.* Silver Spring, MD: MNCPPC.

———. (1982) *Adopted and Approved City of Takoma Park Master Plan.* Silver Spring, MD: MNCPPC.

———. (MNCPPC-Prince George's County). (1979) *Transit Station Area Development Profile: West Hyattsville and Prince George's Plaza.* Upper Marlboro, MD: MNCPPC.

————. (MNCPPC-Prince George's County). (1981) *Transit Station Area Development Profile: College Park.* Upper Marlboro, MD: MNCPPC.

Masser, I., and P. Brown, eds. (1978) *Spatial Representation and Spatial Interaction.* Leiden/Boston: Martinus Nijhoff.

McFadden, Daniel L. (1973) "Conditional Logit Analysis of Qualitative Choice Behavior." In P. Zarembka, ed., *Frontiers in Econometrics.* New York: Academic Press.

————. (1978a) "Modelling the Choice of Residential Location." In A. Karlquist, L. Lundqvist, F. Snickars, and J. W. Weibull, eds., *Spatial Interaction Theory and Planning Models.* Amsterdam: North-Holland.

————. (1978b) "The Theory and Practice of Disaggregate Demand Forecasting for Various Modes of Urban Transportation." In W.F. Brown, ed., *Emerging Transportation Planning Methods.* Washington, D.C.: U.S. Department of Transportation.

McFadden, Daniel L., and F. Reid. (1975) "Aggregate Travel Demand Forecasting from Disaggregating Behavioral Models." *Transportation Research Record,* 534:24–37.

Metropolitan Transportation Commission. (1979) *BART in the San Francisco Bay Area—The Final Report of the BART Impact Program.* Contract DOT–OS–30176. Washington, D.C.: U.S. Department of Transportation.

Metropolitan Washington Council of Governments, National Capital Region Transportation Planning Board (WASHCOG). (1982) *Trends Before Metrorail: Metrorail Before and After Study.* Washington, D.C.: WASHCOG.

————. (1983) *Travel Findings Report Update: Changes in Travel Behavior. Metrorail Before and After Study.* Washington, D.C.: WASHCOG.

Mills, Edwin S. (1972) *Studies in the Structure of the Urban Economy.* Washington, D.C.: Resources of the Future.

Mills, Edwin S., and James Mackinnon. (1973) "Notes on the New Urban Economics." *The Bell Journal of Economics and Management Science* 4 (Autumn):593–601.

Montgomery County Planning Board of the Maryland–National Capital Park and Planning Commission (MCPB). (1974a) *Approved and Adopted Sector Plan for the Transit Impact Area in Takoma Park, Montgomery County, MD.* Silver Spring, MD: MNCPPC.

————. (1974b) *Sector Plan for the Bethesda Central Business District, Montgomery County, Maryland.* Silver Spring, MD: MNCPPC.

————. (1974c) *Sector Plan for the Central Business District of Friendship Heights, Montgomery County, MD.* Silver Spring, MD: MNCPPC.

————. (1977a) *Approved and Adopted Master Plan for Silver Spring-East, Montgomery County, Maryland.* Silver Spring, MD: MNCPPC.

————. (1977b) *A Sector Plan for the Shady Grove Transit Station Area, Montgomery County, Maryland.* Silver Spring, MD: MNCPPC.

————. (1977c) *Transit Station Impact in Montgomery County, Maryland.* Project Summary Final Report. U.S. Department of Transportation, UMTA–IT–09–0020–13. Washington, D.C.: Urban Mass Transportation Administration.

————. (1978) *Plan for the North Silver Spring Sector, Montgomery County, Maryland.* Silver Spring, MD: MNCPPC.

————. (1980) *Approved and Adopted Olney Master Plan.* Silver Spring, MD: MNCPPC.

————. (1982) *Approved and Adopted Amendment to the Bethesda Central Business District Sector Plan*. Silver Spring, MD: MNCPPC.

Moses, Leone. (1958) "Location and the Theory of Production." *Quarterly Journal of Economics* 72 (May):259–72.

Moses, Leone, and Harold F. Williamson, Jr. (1967) "The Location of Economic Activity in Cities." *American Economic Review* 57 (May), 2:211–22.

Muller, Peter O. (1981) *Contemporary Suburban America*. Englewood Cliffs, N.J.: Prentice-Hall.

Multisystems, Inc. (1982) *Route-level Demand Models: A Review*. DOT–1–82–6, U.S. Department of Transportation. Washington, D.C.: Office of Planning Assistance, Urban Mass Transportation Administration.

Muth, Richard. (1969) *Cities and Housing*. Chicago: University of Chicago Press.

Myers, Phyllis. (1980) "Needed in Joint Development: A Three-sided Partnership to Conserve and Develop Urban Resources." In *New Urban Rail Transit: How Can Its Development and Growth-Shaping Potential Be Realized?* Hearings before the Subcommittee on the City, of the Committee on Banking, Finance and Urban Affairs, House of Representatives, December 1979. Washington, D.C.: U.S. Government Printing Office.

Nakamura, H., Y. Hayashi, and K. Niyamoto. (1983) "Land-Use Transportation Analysis System for a Metropolitan Area." Mimeo. Tokyo: University of Tokyo, Department of Civil Engineering.

Nathanson, J. (1970) "Basic Employment Model: A Model for Intra-Country Location Basic Employment and Land." BATSC Technical Report 222 (preliminary). Berkeley, CA: Bay Area Transportation Study Commission.

Openshaw, S. (1977) "Optimal Zoning Systems for Spatial Interaction Models." *Environment and Planning A* 9,2:169–84.

————. (1978) *Using Models in Planning: A Practical Guide*. Corbridge, U.K.: Retail Planning Associates.

————. (1979) "A Methodology for Using Models for Planning Purposes." *Environment and Planning A* 11:879–96.

Orcutt, G., S. Caldwell, and R. Wertheimer. (1961) *Microanalysis of Socioeconomic Systems: A Simulation Study*. New York: Harper & Row.

Paaswell, R., and J. Berechman. (1981) *An Application of Rapid Transit Investments*. Report NY–11–0022. Washington, D.C.: U.S. Department of Transportation.

Page, Richard S. (1980) "Justifying Rail Transit Investments." In *New Urban Rail Transit: How Can Its Development and Growth-Shaping Potential Be Realized?* Hearings before the Subcommittee on the City, of the Committee on Banking, Finance and Urban Affairs, House of Representatives, December 1979. Washington, D.C.: U.S. Government Printing Office.

Payne-Waxie Consultants and Blayney-Dyett. (1980a) *The Land-Use and Urban Development Impacts of Beltways: Case Studies*. DOT–P–30–80–38. Washington, D.C.: U.S. Department of Transportation, U.S. Department of Housing and Urban Development (June).

————. (1980b) "Urban and Regional Planners." *The Land Use and Urban Development Impacts of Beltways: Guidebook and Final Report*. DOT–P–30–80–38. Washington, D.C.: U.S. Department of Transportation, U.S. Department of Housing and Urban Development (October).

Peat, Marwick, Mitchell, and Company. (1971) "Calibration and Application of an EMPIRIC Activities Allocation Model for the Twin Cities Metropolitan Area." Metropolitan Council, St. Paul, MN. Washington, D.C.: Peat, Marwick, Mitchell, and Co.

———. (1972) *Implementation of the N-Dimensional Logit Model.* U.S. Department of Transportation. San Diego: Comprehensive Planning Organization.

Peskin, R.L., and J.L. Schofer. (1977) *The Impacts of Urban Transportation and Land Use Policies on Transportation Energy Consumption.* Washington, D.C.: U.S. Department of Transportation.

Priest, Donald E. (1980) "Making the Transit/Real Estate Connection." In *New Urban Rail Transit: How Can Its Development and Growth-Shaping Potential Be Realized?* Hearings before the Subcommittee on the City, of the Committee on Banking, Finance and Urban Affairs, House of Representatives, December 1979. Washington, D.C.: U.S. Government Printing Office.

Public Technology, Inc. (1981) Proceedings of the Joint Development Marketplace '80—June 29–July 1, 1980. U.S. Department of Transportation DOT–1–81–4. Washington, D.C.: Urban Mass Transportation Administration.

———. (1982) *Growth Management and Transportation.* An Urban Consortium Information Bulletin. DOT–1–8–82–8. Washington, D.C.: U.S. Department of Transportation.

Putman, Stephen J. (1972) "Intraurban Employment Forecasting Models: A Review and a Suggested New Model Construct." *Journal of the American Institute of Planners* 38:216–30.

———. (1975) "Calibrating a Disaggregated Residential Allocation Model—DRAM." Paper presented at the Eighth Annual Conference of the Regional Science Association, British Section. London.

———. (1976a) *The Interrelationships of Transportation Development and Land Development: Volume 1 (Main Report) and Volume II (Program Documentation).* Washington, D.C.: U.S. Department of Transportation (1st ed., 1973.)

———. (1976b) "Laboratory Testing of Predictive Land-Use Models." DOT–P–5010. Washington, D.C.: U.S. Department of Transportation.

———. (1977a) "Calibrating a Disaggregated Residential Allocation Model—DRAM." In D.B. Massey and P.W.J. Massey, eds., *London Papers in Regional Science 7. Alternative Frameworks for Analysis.* London: Pion.

———. (1977b) "Calibrating a Residential Location Model for Nineteenth-Century Philadelphia." *Environment and Planning A* 9:449–60.

———. (1978) *Development of an Improved Integrated Transportation and Land Use Model Package.* NDF grant APR 73–07840–A02. Philadelphia, PA: Urban Simulation Laboratory, Department of City and Regional Planning, University of Pennsylvania.

———. (1979) *Urban Residential Location Models.* Boston, MA: Martinus Nijhoff.

———. (1980a) "Calibrating Urban Residential Location Models 3: Empirical Results for Non-U.S. Cities." *Environment and Planning A* 12:813–27.

———. (1980b) "Integrated Analysis of Metropolitan Transportation and Location." DOT–P–30–80–32. Washington, D.C.: Office of the Secretary, U.S. Department of Transportation.

———. (1981) "Theory and Practice of Urban Modelling: The Art of Application." Presented at Thirteenth Annual Conference of the Regional Science Association—British Section. Durham, U.K.: University of Durham.

———. (1983) *Integrated Urban Models: Policy Analysis of Transportation and Land Use*. London: Pion.

———. (1984) "Dynamic Properties of Static-Recursive Model Systems of Transportation and Location." *Environment and Planning A* 16:1503–19.

———. (1986a) "Complexity in Urban Systems Modelling: The Effects of Transit on Urban Form." In P. Batey and M. Madden, eds., *Integrated Analysis of Regional Systems, London Papers in Regional Science* 15:54–73. London: Pion.

———. (1986b) "Future Directions for Urban Systems Models: Some Pointers from Empirical Investigations." In B. Hutchinson and M. Batey, eds., *Advances in Urban Systems Modelling*. Amsterdam: North Holland.

———. (1988) "Effects of Transit on Metropolitan Regional Development." Report to the Office of the Secretary of the U.S. Department of Transportation. Washington, D.C.

———. (1991) *Integrated Urban Models 2: New Research and Applications of Optimization and Dynamics*. London: Pion.

Putman, Stephen H., and Frederick W. Ducca. (1978a) "Calibrating Urban Residential Models 1: Procedures and Strategies." *Environment and Planning A*, 10:633–50.

———. (1978b) "Calibrating Urban Residential Models 2: Empirical Results." *Environment and Planning A* 10:1001–14.

Putman, Stephen H., and H.W. Miller, Jr. (1983) "Dynamic Systems of Spatial Interaction Models 1: Simple System Structures." Philadelphia, PA: Urban Simulation Laboratory, Department of City and Regional Planning, University of Pennsylvania (December).

Putman, Stephen H., and Y.S. Kim. (1984) "Calibration of Urban Residential Location Models 4: Effects of Log-Collinearity on Model Calibration and Formulation." *Environment and Planning A* 16: 95–106.

Rassam, P.R., R.E. Ellis, and J.C. Bennett. (1971) "The N-Dimensional Logit Model: Development and Application." *Highway Research Record* 369:135–47.

Rice Center. (1982) *A Guide to Innovative Financing Mechanisms for Mass Transportation*. DOT–1–82–53. Washington, D.C.: Urban Mass Transportation Administration, U.S. Department of Transportation.

Richards, Carol. (1979) *More than a Subway*. Washington, D.C.: Metropolitan Washington Council of Governments.

Richards, Judith W. (National Council for Urban Economic Development). (1982) *Transportation and Urban Economic Development*. DOT–1–82–42. Washington, D.C.: Office of the Secretary of Transportation, U.S. Department of Transportation.

Richardson, Harry W. (1978) *Urban Economics*. Hinsdale, IL: Dryden Press.

Richmond, Donald R. (1980) "Value Capture—The Experience of Metropolitan Toronto." In *New Urban Rail Transit: How Can Its Development and Growth-Shaping Potential Be Realized?* Hearings before the Subcommittee on the City, of the Committee on Banking, Finance and Urban Affairs, House of Representatives, December 1979. Washington, D.C.: U.S. Government Printing Office.

Roberts, P.D. (1978) "Disaggregate Demand Forecasting: Theoretical Tantalizer or Practical Problem Solver?" In W.F. Brown, ed., *Emerging Transportation Planning Methods*. Washington, D.C.: U. S. Department of Transportation.

Robillard P. (1974) "Multipath Traffic Assignment with Dynamic Input Flows." *Transportation Research* 8:567–73.

Ross, Harold M. (1976) *Black Suburbanization: Access to Improved Quality of Life or Maintenance of the Status Quo?* Cambridge, MA: Ballinger.

Ruiter, E.R., and M.E. Ben-Akiva. (1978) "Disaggregate Travel Demand Models for the San Francisco Bay Area: System Structure, Component Models, and Application Procedures." *Transportation Research Record* 673:121–28.

Said, G.M., and B.G. Hutchinson. (1982) Policy-Oriented Urban-Systems Model: Structure and Application." *Transportation Research Record* 848:1–7.

San Diego Association of Governments (SDAG). (1982) *Trends before the San Diego Trolley*. Washington, D.C.: Urban Mass Transportation Administration (July).

San Francisco Department of City Planning (SFDCP). (1971) *Transportation: Conditions, Problems, Issues*. San Francisco: Department of City Planning.

Sarna, A.C., and B.G. Hutchinson. (1979) "A Disaggregated Land Use–Transport Model for Delhi, India." *Transportation*, 8:73–87.

Schaenman, Philip, and Thomas Muller. (1974) *Measuring Impacts of Land Development: An Initial Approach*. Washington, D.C.: Urban Institute.

Schmenner, Roger W. (1975) "City Taxes and Industry Location." Cambridge, MA: Graduate School of Business Administration, Harvard University (December).

———. (1981) "The Rent Gradient for Manufacturing." *Journal of Urban Economics* 9 (January), 1:90–96.

Schneider, J.B., et al. (1980) *Planning and Designing a Transit Center Based Transit System: Guideline and Examples from Case Studies in Twenty-Two Cities*. DOT–WA–11–0007. Washington, D.C.: Urban Mass Transportation Administration. U.S. Department of Transportation.

Schultz, G.W. (1983) "Development of a Travel Model Set for the New Orleans Region." Paper presented at the Sixty-Second Annual Meeting of the Transportation Research Board, Washington, D.C.

Segal, D. (1978) "A Discrete Multivariate Model of Work-Trip Mode Choice." Discussion Paper D78-7. Cambridge, MA: Harvard University, Department of City and Regional Planning.

Senior, M. L. (1973) "Approaches to Residential Location Modelling 1: Urban Ecological and Spatial Interaction Models (A Review)." *Environment and Planning A* 5:165–97.

———. (1974) "Approaches to Residential Location Modelling 2: Urban Economics and Some Recent Developments (A Review)." *Environment and Planning A* 6:369–409.

Senior, M.L., and A.G. Wilson. (1974) "Exploration and Synthesis of Spatial Interaction Models of Residential Location." *Geographical Analysis* 7:209–38.

Southern California Rapid Transit District (SCRTD). (1983) *Joint Development and Value Capture in Los Angeles: Local Policy Formulation*. DOT–1–83–23. Washington, D.C.: Urban Mass Transportation Administration, U.S. Department of Transportation.

Southworth, F. (1975) "A Highly Disaggregated Modal-Split Model." WP–

58. Institute for Transport Studies. Leeds, U.K.: University of Leeds.

Sheftall, Willis B. (1981) "The Residential Rehabilitation Decision." Paper delivered at the Allied Social Sciences Association Meetings, Washington, D.C.

Simpson and Curtin Division, Booz, Allen and Hamilton, Inc. (Simpson and Curtin). (1981) *Bus Route Costing Procedures: A Review.* DOT–1–81–23. Washington, D.C.: Urban Transportation Administration, U.S. Department of Transportation.

Spear, B.D. (1977) *A Study of Individual Choice Models: Application of New Travel Demand Forecasting Techniques to Transportation Planning.* Washington, D.C.: United States Department of Transportation.

Spielberg, F., and S. Andrle (SG Associates, Inc.) and U. Ernst and M. Kemp (Urban Institute). (1981) *Impact of Demographic and Migration Trends on Future Travel in Metropolitan Areas.* DOT–OS–90050. Washington, D.C.: U.S. Department of Transportation, Office of the Assistant Secretary for Policy and International Affairs.

Stokes, B.R. (1980) "Rail Transit Investment and Its Implications for Our Cities." *In New Urban Rail Transit: How Can Its Development and Growth-Shaping Potential Be Realized?* Hearings before the Subcommittee on the City, of the Committee on Banking, Finance and Urban Affairs, House of Representatives, December 1979. Washington, D.C.: U.S. Government Printing Office.

Stone, Donald N. (1974) *Industrial Location in Metropolitan Areas: A General Model Tested for Boston.* New York: Praeger.

Stopher, P.R., and A.H. Meyburg. (1975) *Urban Transportation Modeling and Planning.* Lexington, MA: Lexington Books.

Straszheim, Mahlon. (1975) *An Econometric Analysis of the Urban Housing Market.* Urban and Regional Studies no. 2. New York: National Bureau of Economic Research.

Struyk, Raymond J. (1972) "Evidence on the Locational Activity of Manufacturing Industries in Metropolitan Areas." *Land Economics* 48 (November):377–82.

Struyk, Raymond J., and Franklin J. James. (1975) *Intra-metropolitan Industrial Location.* Lexington, MA: Lexington Books.

Sugimoto, M. (1983) "The Integrated Transportation and Land Use Models: Dortmund, the Federal Republic of Germany." Capstone Project Report. Philadelphia: Urban Simulation Laboratory, Department of City and Regional Planning, University of Pennsylvania.

Talvitie, A., and D. Kirshner. (1978) "Specialization, Transferability and the Effect of Data Outliers in Modeling the Choice of Mode in Urban Travel." *Transportation* 7.

Tiebout, Charles M. (1962) *The Community Economic Base Study.* Supplementary Paper No. 16. New York: Committee for Economic Development.

Train, K.E. (1977) "A Summary of the Results of a Validation Test of Disaggregate Travel Demand Models." *Transportation Research Forum* 18, 1:653–59.

———. (1979) "A Comparison of the Predictive Ability of Mode Choice Models with Various Levels of Complexity." *Transportation Research* 13A (February) 1:11–16.

United States Department of Transportation and United States Department of Housing and Urban Development (U.S. DOT/HUD). (1979) *BART's First Five*

*Years: Transportation and Travel Impacts.* Washington, D.C.: U.S. Department of Transportation.

Van Vilet, D. (1976a) "The Choice of Assignment Techniques for Large Networks." In M.A. Florian, ed., *Traffic Equilibrium Methods.* New York: Springer.

———. (1976b) "Road Assignment II: The GLTS Model." *Transportation Research* 10:145–50.

———. (1976c) "Road Assignment III: Comparative Tests of Stochastic Methods." *Transportation Research,* 10:151–57.

Vaughan, Roger J. (1977) *The Urban Impacts of Federal Policies: vol. 2, Economic Development.* CI–74–114/UA75–53. New York: Charles F. Kettering Foundation (June).

von Thünen, Johann. (1863) *Der Isolierte Staat in Beziehung auf Landwirtschaft und Nationale Ökonomie* (The isolated state). Munich: Pflaum.

Washington Metropolitan Area Transit Authority (WMATA). (1982) Joint Development Materials Package. Washington, D.C.: WMATA.

Watson, P.L., and R.I. Westin. (1973) "Aggregate Predictions from Disaggregate Models of Mode Choice: Some Tests of Transferability." Paper presented at the Intersociety Conference on Transportation, Denver.

Webber, Melvin M. (1980) "The Transportation Problem Is a Problem in Social Equity." In *New Urban Rail Transit: How Can Its Development and Growth-Shaping Potential Be Realized?* Hearings before the Subcommittee on the City, of the Committee on Banking, Finance and Urban Affairs, House of Representatives, December 1979. Washington, D.C.: U.S. Government Printing Office.

Weber, Alfred. (1929) *Theory of the Location of Industry.* Chicago: University of Chicago Press. (Originally *Über den Standort der Industrien,* 1909.)

Wegener, M. (1982) "Modelling Urban Decline: A Multilevel Economic Demographic Model for the Dortmund Region." *International Regional Science Review,* 7, 2:217–41.

Wegener, M., F. Guod, and M. Vannahume. (1983) "The Time Scales of Urban Change." Paper presented at the International Symposium on New Directions in Urban Modelling, University of Waterloo, Waterloo, Ontario, Canada, July.

Weiner, Edward. (1983) *Urban Transportation Planning in the United States: An Historical Overview.* DOT–I–83–43. Washington, D.C.: Technology Sharing Program, Office of the Secretary, U.S. Department of Transportation.

Weisbrod, Glen, and Henry Pollakowski. (1984) "Effects of Downtown Improvement Projects on Retail Activity." *APA Journal* 50 (Spring):148–61.

Wessel, Theodore J. (1982) *Fairfax County Metro Station Area Study: Phase 1.* Fairfax, VA: Office of Comprehensive Planning (December).

Wheaton, Theodore J. (1979a) *Interregional Movements and Regional Growth.* Washington, D.C.: Urban Institute.

———. (1979b) "Monocentric Models of Urban Land Use: Contributions and Criticisms." In Peter Mieszkowski and Mahlon Straszheim, eds., *Current Issues in Urban Economics.* Baltimore: Johns Hopkins University Press.

Williams, H.C.W.L. (1977) "On the Formation of Travel Demand Models and Economic Evaluation of User Benefit." *Environment and Planning A* 9 (March), 3:285–344.

Williams, I.N. (1976) "A Comparison of Some Calibration Techniques for Doubly Constrained Models with an Exponential Cost Function." *Transportation Research* 10:91–104.

Wilson, A. G. (1970a) "Disaggregated Elementary Residential Location Models." *Regional Science Association Papers.*

———. (1970b) *Entropy in Urban and Regional Modelling.* London: Pion.

———. (1974) *Urban and Regional Models in Geography and Planning.* New York: John Wiley.

———. (1981) *Catastrophe Theory and Bifurcation.* London: Croom-Helm.

Wilson, A.G.; J.D. Coelho; S.M. Macgill; and H.C.W.L. Williams. (1981) *Optimization in Location and Transport Analysis.* New York: John Wiley.

Wilson, A.G.; A.G. Hawkins; G.J. Hill; and D.J. Wagon. (1969) "Calibration and Testing of the SELNEC Transport Model." *Regional Studies* 3 (December), 3:337–50.

Wilson, A.G., P.H. Rees, and C.M. Leigh, eds. (1978) *Models of Cities and Regions: Theoretical and Empirical Developments.* New York: John Wiley.

Wingo, L. (1961) *Transportation and Urban Land.* Baltimore: Johns Hopkins University Press.

Wolf, Marianne M. (1979) "Public Investment in Transportation, Expected Transportation Costs, and the Urban Housing Market." Ph.D. diss. Johns Hopkins University.

Woodward, Lynn. (1977) "The Scientific Way to Locate an Office." *Real Estate Today* (October).

Yinger, John. (1977) "The Capitalization of Transportation Costs, Neighborhood Amenities, and Local Fiscal Variables." Discussion Paper D77–16. Cambridge, MA: Urban Planning, Policy Analysis and Administration, Department of City and Regional Planning, Harvard University.

Zumwalt, Barbara A. (1978) *Land Use Impacts of Fixed Guide Transit Systems: Implications for Downtown People Mover Projects.* DOT–UT–50016. Washington, D.C.: U.S. Department of Transportation.

Zupan, Jeffrey M. (1980) "Public Transit in Urban America." In *New Urban Rail Transit: How Can Its Development and Growth-Shaping Potential Be Realized?* Hearings before the Subcommittee on the City, of the Committee on Banking, Finance and Urban Affairs, House of Representatives, December, 1979. Washington, D.C.: U.S. Government Printing Office.

# Index

Tables are indicated in *italic* type
Figures are indicated in **bold** type

## A

Alexandria, Virginia, 52–53
  comparison or employment
    rates and changes, *43*
  basic, *103*
  government, *104*
  retail, *105*
  service-sector, *104*
  total, *103*
  development variables, *168*
  forecasting station area
    development, 209
Arlington County, 51–52
  comparison of employment
    rates and changes, *43*
  basic, *101*
  government, *101*
  retail, *102*
  service-sector, *102*
  total, *100*
  development variables, *168,*
    *169*
  forecasting station area
    development, 207–209
Atlanta, Georgia
  MARTA system, 16

## B

Ballston plan, 29
BART Impact Program (BIP), 13
  conclusions, 15
  land-use pattern deelopment, 14
  recommendations, 15–16
BART study. *See* Bay Area
    Rapid Transit Syatem
Bay Area Rapid Transit System
    (BART study), 5 12, 13
BIP. *See* BART Impact Program
Business location decision and
    transit, 22–24

## C

CBD. *See* Washington central
    business district
Chamber of Commerce, 20
Community Redevelopment
    Agency, 20
Comprehensive Plan, 19
Coordinated Preservation and
    Development District,
    28–29
Corridors
  station and nonstation areas
    within, statistical ananysis,
    62–72
  statistical analysis, 55–62

**Rodney D. Green** (Ph.D., American University) is Professor of Economics at Howard University, where he is Director of the Collaborative Core Unit in Labor, Race, and Political Economy. He has published extensively in scholarly journals in the fields of urban economics, political economy, economic history, and energy economics. He is the author of *Forecasting with Computer Models* (1985).

**David M. James** earned his doctorate in mathematics from the University of Chicago. He is Associate Professor of Mathematics at Howard University. His major research field is algebraic topology, in which he has held National Science Foundation fellowships.